THE BEAST I LOVED

A Battered Woman's Desperate Struggle to Survive

Robert Davidson

WILDBLUE
PRESS

WildBluePress.com

THE BEAST I LOVED published by:
WILDBLUE PRESS
P.O. Box 102440
Denver, Colorado 80250

ISBN 978-1-947290-59-4   Trade Paperback
ISBN 978-1-947290-58-7   eBook

Originally published in the United States by The Ballantine Publishing Group, a division of Random House, Inc., New York, and simultaneously in Canada by Random House of Canada, Limited, Toronto, in 2000, under the title, **Fighting Back***. This revised edition published in the United States by WildBlue Press, 2018.*

PRAISE

"A superbly written, riveting—often horrifying—story urgently needed for our time. Davidson—with a reporter's eye for detail—delivers a powerhouse page-turner about the limits of what a human being can endure…and still come out victorious. With mesmerizing suspense and the heart-stopping twists and turns of a fast-paced crime novel, here is an important book that ensnares the reader from the first page, and should be read, then read again."

—Susan Page, bestselling author of *If I'm So Wonderful, Why Am I Still Single* and Executive Director of the acclaimed San Miguel Writers' Conference

*****

"As gripping as *The Burning Bed*"

—John Saul, *New York Times* bestselling author of *Suffer the Children*

*****

"Horrific and inspiring all wrapped into one book as relevant today as it was when it was first published."

—Steve Jackson, *New York Times* bestselling author of *No Stone Unturned*

*****

"The book is gripping; it reads like the best of mystery novels and the reader cannot wait to find out what happens in the next section or chapter. It is an excellent supplemental reading source for the upper-level undergraduate and graduate courses I teach on Family Violence. The author does a superior job of getting the reader into the mindset of a woman experiencing both the battered woman syndrome and learned helplessness... The outcome is totally unpredictable and a reader would be well-advised to avoid the temptation to turn to the end in order to learn the final outcome."

—Raymond Teske, Jr., Ph.D., Professor, Criminal Justice Center, Sam Houston State University

*****

"As a counselor, I have provided counseling to hundreds of victims, both women and men, in the area of domestic violence. The case of June Briand is one of the most devastating accounts of spousal abuse ever documented, and hits the reader with the same gripping force as one other true life story, *Life With Billy*. Even with all my years of training and experience behind me, a story such as this one still touches me to the core..."

—Sandra D. Peters, Counselor
(Prince Edward Island, Canada)

*****

THE BEAST I LOVED

Table of Contents

PREFACE

On New Year's Eve, December 31, 2017, a huge electronic billboard in New York City's Time Square lit up with the faces of five women who, along with countless others, had endured sexual harassment and other disturbing sexual behavior from men, and were being called by *TIME* magazine "The Silence Breakers." The rallying cry became *Time's Up!* — and indeed it is. With the torrent of women's stories emerging night after night, day after day, on radio and television shows and social media, the abuse of women is finally getting the attention it deserves — attention that has been woefully lacking given the dominance and control of men in powerful positions that has stymied the growth, freedom, and dignity of women for way too long.

There is, however, another more insidious scourge affecting even more women that has not received anywhere near the attention that the Times Square billboard did, though its victims suffer far deeper, more painful and often tragic consequences. While the current stories making news are certainly past due, the one told in this book is that of another "silence breaker" who also had the courage to step forward and speak out, to tell her harrowing story in the hopes that it would help other women break the cycle of violence from which most see no escape, and no way to vocalize their plight — lest they endure even more severe punishment by their tormentors.

This is a true story of an abused wife who took her husband's life and was subsequently sentenced to fifteen years to life for her crime. Many of the names and identifying characteristics have been changed to protect privacy. The events, however, are factual and if anything, understated, because no matter how it is written, much of what happened to June Briand cannot be described in words.

Ordinary cases of domestic violence don't make national news. This one did, but then, it was anything but ordinary — it was *extraordinary*. Extraordinary that after finally putting an end to seven torturous years of horrendous physical and emotional atrocities, administered by the cruelest of men, June Briand was punished still further — this time by a confused and compassionless legal system that was incapable of distinguishing self-defense from criminal intent, child of circumstances from cold-blooded killer, and indeed, right from wrong.

After ABC's Peter Jennings reported the story on the evening news on December 4, 1996, New Hampshire's channel 9 WMUR anchorman Tom Griffith followed, saying, "The Briand case is one of the most controversial murder cases the state has ever seen." A *Concord Monitor* editorial read: "The June Briand murder case has attracted attention because of the sensational nature of her crime ... Talk shows and dinner tables have been abuzz with talk of the case."

That buzz continued the next morning on NBC's *Today Show* when Maria Shriver interviewed Pat Moss, the tenacious lawyer who took June's case pro bono and turned it into a *cause célèbre* unlike anything New England had ever seen.

This is not another grimly, amusing true crime story about sadistic sex and homicide, though it includes both. Nor is it a study on Battered Woman Syndrome or domestic violence. This is a story about fear and control — and the insanity that stems from them. It chronicles unthinkable acts of cruelty June suffered at the hands of her brutal husband, a man described by his young daughter in a psychologist's report as "a big, black, hairy monster, too ugly to look at, with scabs and bruises, that pops your eyes out." And it describes, as it must, the abject sexual depravity June endured for seven long years.

Perhaps most important, this book offers readers a clear understanding of the debilitating, heartbreaking state of "learned helplessness" that results from chronic abuse, and definitively answers once and for all the question of why women cannot simply pack up and leave their abusers. It makes the case that it is way past time to stop blaming the woman, to stop victimizing the victim. *If anything is to change, the public must first understand the issue.* If ever there were a purpose for this book, this is it. If ever there were a time to shine a spotlight on this growing cancer that our society has failed to curtail, this is it.

The Justice Department says there are nearly a million acts of domestic violence reported every year — a gross underestimate of the actual number, which, according to the FBI, is closer to *four* million or "an assault on a woman every fifteen seconds." The National Coalition Against Domestic Violence reports the incredible statistic that *one in three* women have been the victims of physical violence by an intimate partner within their lifetime. So pervasive is such violence that Congress recently passed funding to study what the Surgeon General called "a public health crisis."

But it is more than that: it is an epidemic, a sickness permeating all strata of society — from unskilled laborers to doctors and CEOs — which will continue to spread if it is not brought to the forefront and exposed for all to see. Exactly what abusers fear most. And exactly what June's story does with painful clarity.

Now the public can see in vivid detail what goes on inside the walls of homes where men punish women for igniting their insecurities, where their cowardice directs them to beat their women in the back, the legs, the stomach — anywhere the bruises will not be discovered. This story is intended to tear down those protective walls men hide behind so everyone can witness for themselves the horrors that go on everywhere, every day.

The *Today Show* continued with Pat Dawson saying, "June Briand has spent ten years waiting for a chance at freedom ... she carried the hopes of a legion of battered women across the country to whom her story of abuse may have sounded all too familiar."

PART I: A BIZARRE & BRUTAL CHILDHOOD

No one went down to the cellar in the old farmhouse. For one thing, water rats the size of skunks lived there. And for another, "it was haunted." The damp, foreboding house, covered with weathered, brownish-black shingles, sat alone atop a knoll in a quiet old community in a remote part of Merrimack, New Hampshire, where neighbors were distant — both geographically and socially. Not one of them had come by to welcome the Jacksons to the neighborhood the day they moved into their new residence, and no one was there when they moved out three weeks later.

The neighborhood, located near the western bank of the Merrimack River in southern New Hampshire, was nothing like the town of Hudson, some ten miles further south, from which the Jacksons had moved near the end of 1968. There, the modest home they had occupied on B Street was located in an unremarkable middle-class neighborhood full of dogs, cats, and giddy children who played hopscotch on the sidewalk, and often stopped by the Jacksons to play pinball on one of the brightly-lit machines June's grandfather, Harold, had renovated and set up in the garage.

Merrimack, on the other hand, had anything but the carnival atmosphere of B Street. Though June wasn't sure of the "creepy sounds" coming from under the old pine floor boards each night, she knew the rats were real when one morning, while standing in the kitchen before going off to her kindergarten class, her grandmother suddenly gasped, turned even more ashen than she already was, and let loose with a primal scream emanating from deep in her tortured soul.

June's grandmother, Mary Jackson, was a fearful, deeply religious woman who seldom spoke, and when she did, often quoted scripture or other doomsday proclamations while thumping on her well-beaten Bible. Fifty-four and already completely grey-haired, Mary had shrunk into a four-foot-ten "plump butterball," but looked taller because of her erect posture and equally rigid demeanor.

Normally it took a great deal to shake the stoic woman, but she weakened when it came to such things as insects, snakes, rodents, and the like. Rats, after all, were "of the devil," the type of "signs" he would have sent to those whose thoughts were less than pure. And whose might fit such a category? Surely not Mary's. Nor June's nor her sister Diane. Perhaps Harold was thinking impure thoughts? He did spend an inordinate amount of time poking around in the musty netherworld of rats and whatever else dwelled in that godforsaken pit under the house. Pestilence, disease, famine — all of it, according to Mary Jackson, came directly from Satan himself.

Apparently heeding his call, water rats regularly made their way up the banks of the Merrimack and into the warm cellars of the older homes in the area. Having no contact with her neighbors, Mary Jackson had no way of knowing that it was not just she who suffered from such a plague — a plague made frightfully evident that morning when a duo of stealthy black varmints found their way up the cellar stairs and somehow squeezed their fat, wet bodies under the kitchen door.

Standing at the kitchen sink, Mary saw movement out of the corner of her eye, and instinctively turned to see, not three yards from her slippered feet, the devil's messengers scurry across the floor and disappear into the dark space behind the old Franklin stove. Mary Jackson had witnessed it all, and screamed to All Mighty God above for help. But the help came from a soft voice below.

"Grammy, do you want me to stay home with you?" asked five-year-old June, looking up at her anguished grandmother. Rather than acknowledge her granddaughter's offer of consolation (she rarely acknowledged that the child even existed), Mary turned on her heel and bolted for the living room where, as he did every morning, Harold Jackson sat reading the morning paper and watching the news on a television that was switched on at dawn and off at midnight most evenings.

Harold was a gaunt, serious man who looked well in excess of his sixty years. Other than his horn-rimmed glasses and salt-and-pepper mustache, his most noticeable features were his meshtopped fisherman's hat — which he rarely removed — and the cheap briar pipe he perpetually clamped between his brown-stained teeth. He occasionally puffed on a Sherlock Holmesstyle calabash pipe, and sometimes switched to his dime store corncob. But mostly he favored his cheap Dr. Grabow pipe, in which he smoked a sickeningly sweet mixture of Turkish tobacco and cherry syrup.

The fisherman's hat, however, was more wishful thinking than anything else. The one and only time he took his granddaughters fishing, he proved that he was, in fact, a fraud.

"He was scared out of his wits when we started rocking the boat. A dragonfly buzzed around us in the row boat and when we swiped at it, the boat rocked. When we got back to shore, Grandpa was shaking like a leaf. He told us later that he was scared to death because he couldn't swim. Then we found out that the big trout he used to bring home for supper were really from the hatchery where his friend worked. He let Grandpa net the breeders, but we always thought he caught them and that he was a great fisherman."

Like his wife, Harold had little to say to the grandchildren. This morning, however, he muttered a few words to June, who wasn't sure whether she should leave for school or stay home and somehow help her distressed grandmother.

"Run along, June," said Harold as he hobbled into the kitchen, still hunched over as if molded permanently by his beloved La-ZBoy recliner. He clutched his crumpled paper in one hand, and his black glasses rested crooked just above the swollen bulb of his veiny red nose. June knew not to question him, and on second thought, decided it was best to get out of the house before the hysterics began.

As for the other unexplained sounds coming from somewhere below the living quarters of the hundredyearold farmhouse, at least some of them had to be the handiwork of Bloody Bones and his partner Soap Sally. According to "weird Uncle Bill," they lived down in the dank cellar and would grab you the moment you reached the bottom of the cellar stairs. Uncle Bill related the story to then five-year-old June and eleven-year-old Diane one night as the rain relentlessly beat against the building's weathered shingles.

He explained that Bloody Bones would dismember you one limb at a time "so you got to see yourself gettin' ripped apart;" then he'd toss you over to Soap Sally who would grind you down and make soap out of you, and sell the bars off the back of her soap wagon to neighbors who would ask, "Pardon me, miss, but have you seen the little girls who live in that old farmhouse down the way? They seem to be missing."

"Yep, I seen 'em not too long ago," she'd say. "Think it was down in their cellar. Why not go down and take a look for yourself, heh, heh, heh?" And so, by this clever ruse, Soap Sally would keep herself and Bloody Bones in business forever and ever.

The teller of this tale was Bill Parker, a distant uncle whose roots were never determined, and who visited now and then from Alabama. As a house gift, he always brought with him a supply of his homemade, 150-proof moonshine, bottled and labeled in mason jars he stored in the trunk of his car.

During one visit, he had just walked around to the trunk and was twisting off the lid of one of the jars, about to give June and Diane a taste, when Mary caught sight of him and bellowed from the front porch, "Don't you *dare* give those girls that poison of yours, Bill Parker! Why, of all the crazy things I have ever seen!"

Mary was not, however, adverse to accepting a few jars for her own "rainy day," and settled down the moment Uncle Bill carried into the house a half dozen jars of the clear firewater he was so proud of.

Besides being a brew master, Uncle Bill was an avowed and openly proud member of the Birmingham chapter of the Ku Klux Klan, and often talked about the Klan meetings he attended. On one visit to the Jacksons, he told another story, this one true and bloodcurdling, and verified with photos from the homicide book he liked to carry around and show off, or just leaf through while sipping lemonade on the back porch.

A policeman for the city of Birmingham, Uncle Bill was not above boasting about how, a few months earlier, he and his "boys" burned out the Birmingham headquarters of the Black Panthers. This was the late 1960's, when the Black Panthers were at the height of their power and prestige, and with leaders such as articulate, rebellious young men like Huey Newton, Eldridge Cleaver, and Bobby Seale. Uncle Bill had no affection whatsoever for "that element," and went on to tell how, just before the burning, a lynching had occurred.

A young black man had been accused of some sort of indiscretion with a white woman — perhaps looking at her for a little too long — and for it was summarily hung by his neck from an old oak tree situated high on a hill that could be clearly seen from the town where he had lived. "They used that tree in particular," said Uncle Bill, "to teach the rest of them bloods a lesson."

While telling the story, Uncle Bill flipped through the homicide book, which contained photographs of numerous infamous killings. "Want to see what happens to uppity niggers?" he asked the girls. Not waiting for a response, he found the page he was looking for and thrust the book into June's lap, pointing contemptuously to the photo of the unfortunate young man hanging from the tree.

"It was terrible. The man had been hanging there for days and his neck had stretched out about three feet. It was so ugly to look at. I can't believe Uncle Bill showed it to us little kids. He said he was mad, and that blacks ... well, niggers was the word he used ... he said they were taking too many liberties with our white girls. He said, 'I wanted the bastard's head to come off but it just wouldn't. Damn, he was a stubborn nigger!'"

A week after the rat incident, a torrential storm raised the Merrimack River to within a foot of its banks and sent rats by the thousands scrambling for high ground — and warm cellars. Another rat incident — this time in the middle of dinner — along with a house full of pots and buckets filled to their brims with malodorous water from a badly-leaking roof, was enough to drive the Jacksons out of their new abode and into another house back in Hudson, New Hampshire.

Though they returned to their old town, the Jacksons selected a different area and now lived on Pinedale Avenue in a quiet neighborhood occupied mostly by older people without children. Their colorless ranch house at the end of a dead-end street rested atop a steep fifty-foot cliff, which fell off precipitously into a tributary of the Merrimack River.

Because of the treacherous dropoff, virtually no children lived at this end of the street. But Mary Jackson was delighted to be here, certain that the fifty vertical feet between her and the water would alleviate any further rodent problems. And Harold was content to settle into the nicest house he had ever rented.

In the past, Harold Jackson had made enough money to get by working as a security guard. Then he found work as a laborer in a paper factory where he doubled his income and was able to put away small amounts of money for his retirement. Now, at sixty, he was enjoying the "golden years," and spent the better part of his day plopped in his threadbare, green and orange plaid recliner. His wife had a similar model, but it was upholstered in "antique brown Naugahyde," which she adored.

Sitting side by side, Mary held her own, keeping up Harold's regimen of watching virtually every soap opera, game show, and news story available from dawn till dusk. This was 1968, before television remote controls were widely used, so for the most part, the Jacksons simply selected a channel, sat back, and took in all that it had to offer for hours on end.

It was, in part, because of these two beloved vices— the television and the recliners—that the Jacksons paid so little attention to their adopted granddaughters. One had to consider the fatigue factor as well: Having raised eight children of their own, the Jacksons had little interest in raising their daughter's castoffs.

June had been dumped at the front door of her grandparents' home the day she was born, as had her sister six years earlier. Their mother, Ann Jackson, was neither capable nor interested in raising children — she only enjoyed making them. Diane was sired by one man, June by another, and Dan, who came along three years later, by yet another unnamed and unknown father whom Ann had met and bedded after one of her nightly drinking bouts in an equally undistinguished local bar.

Diane was the product of a tryst between Ann and a married man who lived in a house behind the Jacksons'. Likewise, June was the result of another affair, only this time Ann knew her suitor much longer. She had been having sexual relations with the man for several months until his wife died in a freak accident one sunny Saturday afternoon in Hudson, New Hampshire. While watching a stock car race, a car suddenly spun out of control and careened off the retaining wall. It flipped and sent a tire flying into the crowd, hitting the young woman and killing her instantly. Ann continued her affair with the man and eventually became pregnant with his child. In a bizarre display of deference for the dead woman, Ann named the baby after her—the woman's name was June.

"A complete absence of love" was how June characterized her childhood. "And quiet. It was too quiet in our house. My grandparents never spoke. They just didn't care about us, couldn't be bothered. There was no interaction between us: no input, no punishment when we misbehaved, nothing. We never went anywhere or did anything: no beach, amusement park, picnics — none of the normal things families did. We even made our own breakfast when we were little.

"I remember climbing up on the stool in the morning to get the cereal down from the cupboard. And when I took a bath, I took it alone. I didn't have rubber duckies or anything like that to play with. My grandmother would leave me and come back thirty minutes later to see me shivering in the cold water."

Apparently, the mothering flaw was genetic, for on the rare occasions that Ann Jackson took the time to come visit her daughters at her mother's house, she treated them exactly as their grandmother did. When she'd drive up in one of her boyfriend's cars, the girls were ecstatic, at least at first. By the end of the visits, June was always in tears.

June's routine was always the same: kneel by her mother's chair and tug at her sleeve trying to get her attention, saying over and over, "Mama, Mama, I'm so glad you're here, I have so much to tell you." But Mama was never interested in her younger daughter, and always turned her attention to Diane.

"I think I spent most of my childhood trying to get my mother's attention. And I never quit. Any normal kid would have given up at some point, but considering the source, I wasn't what you would call normal. I kept hoping against hope that my mother — or my grandmother or grandfather or *somebody* — would love me. They never did."

No one knew where Ann Jackson lived or what she did, but one thing they knew was that she was an alcoholic. And she was not an attractive woman. Perhaps the two issues were related. "She didn't have a very pretty face. And she was uneducated. I don't know if she went to school or for how long. I remember hearing something about reform school or a juvenile detention center."

But she compensated. Ann attracted men by wearing cheap perfume and outlandish clothes: big hoop earrings, bright red lipstick, tight pants. She was only five-foot-four, but made herself taller with spiked heels and a beehive hairdo. And it worked. She always had boyfriends (all heavy drinkers like her), but none of them stayed around very long.

"There was always someone new in Mom's life, and she was always complaining about them and her relationships. When we were a little older, all she'd do was complain about how terrible things were for her, and never ask how we were doing."

It's not that Ann Jackson didn't pay attention to her children. She did. But she had to be sufficiently inebriated to accomplish the task. "I made Mom a little troll doll out of plaster of Paris once. It was the ugliest thing you ever saw, but I couldn't wait until she came over so I could give it to her. I had painted it all different colors, and they all ran together; it was so bad!

"When she finally came by, she had been drinking, as usual. I handed her the doll and she looked at it and said, 'Oh, honey, it's beautiful. It's the most beautiful thing in the whole world.' And then she started to cry. She cried and cried and cried."

On another occasion, Ann Jackson came to see her daughters and again she was drunk. "This time she came to take us away, take us back. She had been drinking and she got all sentimental. She always got emotional when she drank. Sometimes she got mean too. She did that day.

"Mom seemed all right when she came in, but then she got into a big fight with my Aunt Margaret, who lived across the street and had come over when she saw my mother pull up. Mom was pounding on the walls and ranting about wanting her baby — me — back. She was running around the house like a madman trying to find me. Diane grabbed me and put me in the clothes hamper and told me not to make a sound. It was a wicker hamper and I could sort of see through it. I remember seeing this crazy lady running right towards me and then past me, not realizing I was watching the whole thing."

Three years prior, Ann Jackson had been successful in absconding with the children. She had taken them for the afternoon, saying she would buy them lunch and take them to the park. It sounded odd to Mary because her daughter never took the girls *anywhere*, let alone the park. When she did not return by five o'clock, Mary knew exactly what had happened: Ann took off with the children and drove day and night to Tennessee, where she had been living with her current boyfriend in a filthy apartment, but one well-stocked with whiskey and cigarettes.

The abduction, however, was not motivated by sentiment, it was driven by *money*. Ann discovered that she would be eligible for state aid if she was an out-of-work mother with children to support. Such was the case for Harold and Mary Jackson as well, who had been collecting a nice stipend from the state of New Hampshire — and were not about to give it up easily.

So, at five the following morning, Harold and Mary got in their Chevrolet station wagon and drove the thousand miles up and over the Appalachian Mountains to the address in Mary's address book, from which she had sent Christmas cards the previous season. The next afternoon, they knocked on the door of what turned out to be a dilapidated tenement on the outskirts of town rather than the "nice little apartment in Memphis" their daughter had described.

On entering, the Jacksons could barely believe what they saw: Crumpled newspapers and crushed beer cans littered every corner of the apartment. Ashtrays overflowed onto the floor, and cigarette butts lay where they were ground into the carpet. Paper plates with encrusted food were piled on a kitchen card table, and another pile of plates towered in the kitchen sink. The smell of stale beer and cigarette smoke permeated the air, as did an overpowering stench of dog urine and cat feces which, combined, had turned the lime green shag carpet into a blotchy mass of matted, dung-colored hair.

June and Diane, then two and eight, were naked and unwashed, and their stringy hair had osmotically taken on the look of the soiled carpet on which they played. Due to finances, their mother had never purchased disposable diapers and instead used cloth diapers, all of which Mary Jackson discovered stinking in the broken-down washing machine in the rear of the apartment.

When the elder Jacksons had entered the apartment, Ann was putting June into a highchair to give her a lunch of Wonder Bread and grape jelly. As usual, the woman was drunk, and now became highly agitated because of the unannounced visit by her parents. Having just locked June into the chair, she turned to face her parents.

"Oh no, you don't!" she barked, knowing full well why her parents had come.

As her mother made a move toward June, Ann grabbed the child and tried to pull her out of the highchair. But she forgot that she had locked her in, and so she struggled without success. Screaming from the pressure on her tiny thighs, June further incensed her inebriated mother, who began wildly screeching at her parents, Diane, and her boyfriend, who lay stretched out on the couch, drunk and oblivious to the ruckus going on around him.

The Jacksons collected the foul-smelling diapers in a green garbage bag, stuffed the rest of the girls' belongings into another bag, and headed back to New Hampshire, stopping at the first filling station to wash the girls the best they could and buy them sodas and cookies.

June and Diane did not see their mother until a year later when she pulled up to the house directly across the street from theirs on Pinedale Avenue. Ann got out of her car carrying a bundle wrapped in a blue blanket and slipped inside the house belonging to Ann's sister, Margaret.

Margaret was in her early thirties, a few years younger than Ann, and had been desperately trying to have a child, but without success. Just as she was giving up hope that she would ever have a child of her own (she had determined that she was sterile), Ann had her third child, Dan, in Tennessee. Though she would have received a few dollars a month from the state, Ann decided it wasn't worth the effort it would take to raise a child and gladly turned him over to her delighted sister.

There was, however, one condition that Margaret insisted on, and she made her sister swear on the Bible to uphold it: Dan could never know who his real mother was. He was never to be told where he came from, and as far as he was concerned, his mother was Margaret and his aunt was Ann — not the other way around.

Dan could never know that the little girls directly across the street were his sisters, nor were they supposed to know he was their brother. But a foul up had occurred: Ann had absentmindedly failed to call ahead to her mother, as planned, to remind her to keep the children away from the window when she drove up with the baby. And that's exactly where they were when she dumped off her third unwanted child. Now they had to be in on the lie, and they, too, had to swear on Mary Jackson's old Bible that they would never reveal to their playmate who he actually was.

"This was the beginning of a life of lies. When Mom would occasionally come to visit us, Dan would ask, 'Who is that lady going into your house?' We'd have to lie and say it was a friend of Grandma's. His own mother! And no one could tell him.

"The significant thing for me was that I learned at an early age that even though things seemed wrong or somehow out of place, it would all be okay if we kept it a secret, if nobody knew. Keep things hidden, pretend they weren't happening. It was the perfect training for what happened to me after I married my abusive husband."

As luck would have it, Aunt Margaret was not sterile after all, and went on to have three more children of her own. This was a boon for June and her sister, because without the four kids across the street to play with, the neighborhood would have been very quiet indeed. Few children lived on the block, and Mary Jackson couldn't be bothered interacting with her grandchildren. But she made an exception on Sunday mornings when she took them to her "fire and brimstone" church in downtown Hudson.

"It was the only time Grandma paid any attention to us. She made us get dressed in our Easter dresses and patent leather shoes, and we had to be ready to walk out the door by seventhirty sharp. It was a fourhour ordeal, starting at eight and not ending until noon. We hated it. Everyone was yelling and moaning, singing hymns praising Jesus with their hands waving in the air. It was right out of the movies."

Harold Jackson paid even less attention to his grandchildren than his wife did, living mostly in his own television world or tinkering mindlessly with contraptions he'd assembled and disassembled in the garage. But at least he provided some comic relief when he let his dog, Mort, sit at the dinner table after supper.

Mort was a mediumsized poodle with large patches of hair gnawed off his rump. He was allergic to fleas, and was constantly biting at the itchy skin or licking his private parts for hours on end, which kept them inflamed and bleeding.

After supper, Harold would interrupt Mort's maintenance rituals and call him to his place at the table where he sat like one of the family and joyfully lapped up the last drops of Harold's creamed tea. It was the only time the old man showed any emotion, happy that his poor brute was enjoying a respite from the itching that tormented it so and which kept the animal endlessly dragging its hind end across the carpet, trying for relief that never came.

"On top of everything else, Mort was an epileptic. He fit in perfectly with our dysfunctional family. He'd have a seizure and Grandma would go running for the Bible saying the demons were killing the dog. Then Grandpa would push her out of the way and try to hold Mort still while he was convulsing. And we two little kids were watching all this craziness around us."

But Grandma wasn't watching the kids. Though June was only five, she often found her way down the treacherous fiftyfoot cliff abutting the back of the Pinedale property, and was allowed by her oblivious grandparents to play along the riverbank and in the storm drainpipe that jutted from the side of the cliff.

One day, while sailing leaves down the drain, June looked up to see that a group of boys had followed her down to the river. They waited until she made her way into the twenty-foot-long pipe, then quickly boarded up the ends with scrap lumber they were going to use to make a fort. Only June's high-pitched wailing resounding off the cement pipe walls convinced the boys that their fort-building days would be over for good if they did not let the little girl go.

With her face muddy from tears and dirt, June clawed her way back up the cliff and reported the incident to her grandparents. But the timing wasn't right. All Mary Jackson could do was hush the child up, telling her, "Not now, our show is on! Get in the bathroom and clean yourself up, you're a mess!"

An epileptic dog that drank tea; playmates who were really brother and sister but didn't know it; a grandmother who rarely spoke, and when she did, preached hell and damnation with the same fervor as the finest pulpit preachers; a mother who gave away kids like they were unwanted dolls so she could continue bar and bed-hopping. "The only thing missing was a complete nut case, and he came along after we'd been at Pinedale about a year."

Uncle Charley was the Jackson's thirty-five-year-old son, and had been clinically diagnosed as a full-blown paranoid schizophrenic, suffering from delusional episodes that lasted anywhere from a week to several months. Charley lived on and off at the Pinedale Avenue house, and had had chronic bouts of depression, mania, and obsessive compulsive disorders ever since his young son was stabbed to death by a drug-crazed amphetamine addict.

Subsequently, Charley's wife divorced him and he started roaming the streets of small southern New Hampshire towns, dropping in at his parents' when necessary, then meandering off again to destinations unknown but in hopes of "striking it rich."

Money was such an obsession with Uncle Charley that once, when he seemed to be coping quite well and was acting, for the most part, normal, he walked into June's room with a cardboard box sealed with what looked like an entire roll of packing tape. "Money," he whispered to her with wild eyes as he held the box in front of him. "Millions of dollars from God," he said, looking to June then back to the box, then back to June.

June was young enough to believe him, and was thrilled to think of all the toys she could buy with the money. Then Charley slit open the box with his pocket knife and lifted up handful after handful of shredded newspaper, crushing the girl's dreams of presents and riches.

At times, Charley was so delusional that he would run down the street pulling strips of ripped paper from a suitcase and throwing them into the air like confetti, declaring once again that it was "money from God" and that he was "richer than Rockefeller." He would often stand on street corners declaring that he *was* God, or a prophet sent by God to save the world from eternal damnation.

"Here we go again," June would say to herself, knowing her uncle was entering one of his manic periods. It was incidents like this that caught the attention of local police, who knew Charley well and knew well where to take him: New Hampshire Hospital, the state mental hospital.

Heavy mesh wire covered the white-washed windows of the red brick building. The front door opened onto a long cream-colored tiled hallway that had on both sides locked rooms with small windows cut into the heavy doors. This was the "lock down" ward. Inside the rooms were patients who generally were quiet and peaceful — until someone walked by. Then they came alive, flinging themselves at the doors and pressing their faces against the windows, distorting them into grotesque, fleshy shapes. They'd start yelling then, and banging on their doors with their fists, feet, and heads.

Charley was no stranger here. When admitted, the attendants assigned him to his usual room — Room 7 — which he insisted on because "seven is God's number." The less violent patients and those like Charley, who responded well to the psychotropic drugs that kept them calm, were allowed to assemble in the common area.

"We hated going to visit Uncle Charley. Every Sunday after church we had to go see him. It was just like *One Flew Over the Cuckoo's Nest*. People walked around like zombies. Half of them had no idea where they were or *who* they were. The common area was so noisy: TVs and radios were blasting; people were chattering away — half the time to no one in particular, just gabbing to themselves.

"And the place smelled awful. People had messed themselves and no one had cleaned them up. Some people sat in their plastic chairs and you could see urine and brown fluid running down their legs. Others walked around with their hospital gowns open in the back leaving them exposed, but they didn't know it, and they wouldn't have cared anyway. It was a sad place."

Most of the time Charley was fairly coherent, spending most of his time in the smoking area with other patients who were well enough to survive in the general hospital community without constant supervision. He was unshaven and his fingers were yellow from chain-smoking unfiltered cigarettes down to the very end. The one thing Charley looked forward to was not so much the Sunday visit from his parents and nieces, but the carton of cigarettes they invariably brought as a gift.

Uncle Charley usually stayed in the institution for three months at a time, then came home for another three months or so before getting picked up by the police again. It was during his last stay that Charley met and fell in love with Gertrude, another patient who stayed mostly in the smoking area and who also suffered from delusional behavior.

Gertrude was the same age as Charley, thirty-five, and scaled in at one hundred and ninety pounds — extremely portly for her five-foot-five frame. Her balding red hair was forever unbrushed, and shot off her oversized head in an electrified explosion befitting Albert Einstein. She was quite a contrast to her skinny beau, who towered over her at six feet two inches, and wore his hair in a no-nonsense crew cut.

Gertrude had pasty, translucent skin, while Charley's ever-present dark circles under his eyes told the story of his protracted battle with internal enemies only he could understand. But now with Gertrude, he hoped his life would turn around for the better. It didn't.

"Gertrude didn't like baths. She fought them like they were acid baths, like they were going to kill her. Maybe she thought they would. When she came home with Uncle Charley to live with us, we could hear them in the bathroom fighting about her taking a bath. And she needed them — she stunk."

But Gertrude didn't think so. Neither did she think she was overweight. In fact, she thought the human body was beautiful — hers in particular — and tried to prove it one morning while June was sitting at the kitchen table waiting to go to school.

"Aunt Gertrude, as we called her, walked into the kitchen and right past me. Then she stopped, pulled her nightie over her head, and let it drop to the floor. Before anyone could do anything, she was running out the door and down the sidewalk stark naked and with a fist full of BandAids, tossing them into the air just like Charley did with his paper strips. I don't know if he told her about his money from God, but she did the exact same thing with the BandAids and was showering the neighbors with gifts from the Lord.

"All the kids in the neighborhood heard about the incident and I begged my grandmother to let me stay home from school, but she wouldn't. They already thought my family was weird; now I knew they'd hate me all the more. I cried all day and hid in the cloak room at lunch time. Then I ran the whole two miles home from school without stopping. I was so humiliated."

Alcoholism, insanity, religious fanaticism, paranoia, lies, secrets, deceit, embarrassment. Everywhere young June Briand looked she saw bizarre behavior and was told to accept it. When her Uncle Charley ranted at the dinner table, claiming he was possessed by evil spirits, Mary Jackson told her granddaughters to ignore him and finish eating their meals as if nothing unusual was happening.

"What I learned most from those days was to stuff my emotions; to pretend everything was all right when everything was crazy. I didn't know what normal was or what other kids' houses were like, but I knew that my mother was an alcoholic, my uncle was insane, and my grandparents were completely out of touch.

"And they were much older than other kids' parents. That's why the other kids didn't like me: my parents were old and my uncle was crazy. It was like my whole family had cooties. The worst of it was, I had to keep all this to myself and not let on that anything was wrong. And I know now that by accepting everything — the alcoholism, the madness, the violent behavior — I was being groomed to be a victim, only I didn't know it until it was too late."

By the time Diane was twelve and June was six, Diane had garnered enough youthful independence to make an unprecedented announcement to her grandmother: "I'm not going to church anymore," she stated confidently one Sunday morning as her grandmother poked her head into the girls' room inquiring why they were not up and dressed for church. "I'm sick of that crazy minister and I'm not going anymore. Neither is June."

With that, Mary Jackson bolted to her bedroom, grabbed her Bible, and started raving. "Jesus will never forgive you for this!" she screamed as she paced back and forth in front of the girls' room, waving the Bible in the air. "*This* what you need! *Scripture!* The word of *God!*" She thrust the Bible through the door, shaking it violently at each of the girls, then stomped down to the end of the hall, reversed direction and stomped back to rave some more. This was where Mary's passions lay. God, heaven, hell, sin, damnation. She lived by and for the scriptures, and when she saw they were being threatened, she burst forth like a dormant volcano come to life.

Harold came to see what the commotion was all about. He told his wife enough was enough, that she should go into the living room and cool off, which she did. But within five minutes she was heading back. This time she was reciting scripture. When she reached the girls' room, Diane threw another punch: "And we don't believe in God either."

That was all Mary needed. "Get out! Pack your bags! There will be no demons living in this house! I will not permit it! Get out! Get out! *Get out!*"

Mary ranted and raved some more, but the girls held firm, and Mary Jackson stomped off to church by herself, as she did every Sunday from then on.

Harold wandered off, shaking his head and trying to light his pipe. It was the first time anyone could remember Mary having much to say about anything.

The lack of structure and discipline in June's life was mitigated by that which she received from her one and only love in life: gymnastics. From age five to twelve, gym and dance were the lonely girl's passions. Friendless, parentless, young June threw herself into an activity that demanded discipline, responsibility, and devotion — all the things that were lacking in her life and which helped her maintain her sanity when those around her were losing theirs.

"If I hadn't had gymnastics, I don't know what I would have done. Maybe I'd have become a religious fanatic like my grandmother. Or I would have gone nuts like everybody else."

Three times a week June took instruction from Mrs. Thomas, a rigid woman who, in her prime, had been a prima ballerina with the San Francisco Ballet. She had since turned the basement of her split-level home into a windowless twelve-by-sixteen-foot gymnastics and dance studio, and charged a nominal fee of four dollars per lesson to those students who were willing to bear the pain.

On lesson day, Mrs. Thomas would enter the basement studio at precisely four o'clock. She was a tall, slender woman of forty-two, and wore a black unitard "cat suit" at every lesson. Her flame-red hair was pulled back in a tight bun. Students were required to be "at the bar" by 3:59, and if they weren't, they need not bother to attend that day's class — or even attempt it.

One such unfortunate girl tried to slink in the side door at the same moment Mrs. Thomas entered the main door. Without a word, Mrs. Thomas bore her black eyes into the girl, lifted a hand elegantly, and pointed to the door through which the girl had just come. With the girl in retreat, Mrs. Thomas brought the class to order with the loud *BANG!* of her regiment stick.

"She carried a five-foot hickory staff that had an ornate silver head and brass tip. Mrs. Thomas used it to keep us erect while holding positions, some of which lasted far longer than necessary. She was stern and she was cruel. Sometimes she put us in a position, then left the room. We had to hold the pose even if our legs cramped up or our toes bled (which the girls noticed after removing the wool from the tips of their ballet shoes).

"If you started to sway your back or lower your chin, *BANG!* came the stick right behind you. Still, I loved going. I loved the discipline, and I'm sure it was because I had none anywhere else in my life. And it was also because, as mean as she was, Mrs. Thomas cared about me."

But no one else did. Neither Harold nor Mary were ever inclined to attend June's gymnastics events. Though she excelled in the parallel bars and was exceptional in the difficult vault, bringing home ribbon after ribbon, no one came to see her perform — except Mrs. Thomas. Unlike her teammates, who proudly displayed their ribbons on their bedroom walls, June stuffed hers in her dresser drawer.

Over the years, June rose to the top ranks in her competitions. By the time she reached seventh grade, her coach was convinced she was Olympic material. He had taken the team to New York for the state Junior Championship meet, at which June took first place overall. It was then that he decided to send her to pre-Olympic training camp in California, and it was then that her gymnastics career came to an end.

The cost of sending June to camp was four hundred dollars, far in excess of what Harold could afford. But knowing young June's heart was set on going, he asked his son, Gerald, then a successful businessman, if he would lend him the money. Gerald refused, arguing that the two adopted girls had already been a burden on his elderly parents, and enough was enough. With the demise of the one thing in the world June truly loved and desperately needed, her world began to crumble.

The first of a long series of ominous events occurred about the time June quit her beloved gymnastics. Perhaps it was an omen of things to come; perhaps it was willed by an angry, God-fearing grandmother who never got over the girls' rejection of the church. Whatever precipitated it, the attack on June was as vicious as any she would later suffer at the hands of her brutal husband. But unlike those attacks, this one was completely unexpected. And it happened at the home of one of the few friends June had made while in gymnastics.

Gymnastics may have seemed a likely place for June to meet and interact with other kids her age, but it was not. Mrs. Thomas discouraged socializing, and it was just as well. June was so focused on her rigorous routine that it left her little time to make friends. And having lived in the dysfunctional family she did, June lacked any social skills and developed an inferiority complex that stayed with her most of her life. It was her self-image of herself as a flawed misfit that later caused her to seek out people who would not treat her as she deserved.

Nevertheless, June did manage to make a couple of friends at school, one of whom invited her over after school one day for a rare visit. June was a little nervous and not certain how to act in such social situations, but welcomed the invitation by her friend, Lisa Emerson, and after school skipped the whole three blocks to Lisa's house. When she arrived, Lisa invited June into her room. She never made it.

"All I remember is walking into the living room, when suddenly Lisa's Dalmatian jumped out from behind the couch and went right for my face. I didn't feel anything. I just heard a growl and saw a flash of black and white in my face. Lisa turned around and screamed, 'Oh June! Your face!' I didn't know what she was screaming about. Then Mrs. Emerson ran in and saw me. Luckily she was a nurse. She stayed calm and grabbed a washrag and held it on my face.

"I wanted to see what happened, but Mrs. Emerson wouldn't let me. I felt her pressing the washrag hard against my face and knew something was terribly wrong. I struggled to break free and run to the bathroom and look in the mirror, but she held me tight saying, 'No, no. You can't look!'"

What Mrs. Emerson didn't want June to see was not just a bite, but a deep hole where a piece of flesh the size of a walnut had been ripped off her lower right cheek and subsequently eaten by the dog. With his one vicious bite, the animal had severed a number of the facial muscles around June's mouth, and from then on, the right side of her face drooped slightly, especially when she smiled — which she rarely did now.

Mrs. Emerson immediately called June's grandmother and told her what had happened, asking, "Do you want me to pick you up or just meet you at the hospital?" To the woman's astonishment, Mary didn't select either option and simply said, "Oh, it's all right. Bring June home."

"Oh, no, Mrs. Jackson," replied Mrs. Emerson. "You don't understand. This girl has a severe wound. It's very deep and will have to be cleaned and disinfected. I'm sure she'll need several stitches, antibiotics, maybe a tetanus sh..."

"Just bring her home," interrupted Mary. "She'll be all right."

If Mary wasn't worrying about what God was thinking of her, she was worrying about money, and how little of it she had. The Jacksons didn't have any kind of health insurance, and Mary knew hospitals were expensive. Thus, the directive to have June delivered to her living room instead of the emergency room.

Reluctantly, Mrs. Emerson dropped June off at her grandparents' home. June got out of the car holding the bloody washrag to her ravaged face. "Are you sure someone's home?" she asked, concerned that no one was waiting to greet June at the curb. Yes, June was sure. Her grandmother was home — she was *always* home, sitting in front of the television with Harold.

That's just where she was when June walked over to her and removed the washrag. Mary squinted and scrunched up her nose and inspected the wound from her recliner, then put down her knitting with an impatient sigh and said, "Harold, pull the car around. We've got to go to the hospital after all."

Upsetting as it was, Mary was going to have to part with some money. She could see that this was not a wound she could seal with a Band-Aid and Bactine as she had hoped. Not only did the gash continue to ooze a thick yellowish fluid, it was much deeper than she had anticipated. And, as the ER nurse explained later, it was possible that June may have contracted rabies.

Rather than go through a series of expensive rabies shots, the Jacksons opted to have the dog kept under quarantine, after which it was determined that the animal was healthy. But due to its unprovoked attack — during which the dog displayed a taste for human flesh — officials decided it would be best if the animal were destroyed. In the process, June destroyed any hopes of retaining her friendship with Lisa, and immediately became an outcast among Lisa's friends and the neighborhood children. Thereafter, whenever they saw June, the first thing they did was yell, "You killed Spotty!" It didn't help build June's already shaky self-esteem.

Harold Jackson, however, saw a potential bonanza in the incident, and promptly filed a lawsuit against the Emersons. He saw a once-in-a-lifetime opportunity to make the kind of money he had heretofore only dreamt of. One lawyer told Harold he could win a judgment "in the hundreds of thousands, maybe even a million." Harold bit the carrot but only ended up with a paltry nine thousand dollars, three of which went to the attorneys, leaving him a grand total of six thousand dollars. Seeing that this kind of money wouldn't do much to change his life style, he put the money in trust for June, to be held there until she turned eighteen or got married, whichever came first. It would be the latter — and way earlier than the birthday.

June's face did not heal well. The deep bite left the right side of her face slightly crooked and with a noticeable scar that did not heal smoothly. Whether it was her belief that she was no longer pretty, or the fact that she had now lost her best friend as well as her best activity — gymnastics — or a combination of the three, June's life plummeted to its lowest point yet. And then it dropped further.

The second of the series of unfortunate events caused June to feel an even greater sense of inferiority, hopelessness, and shame — the dominant psychological traits that, over the years, would continue to build to the point of desperation. This time, late one summer evening shortly after her thirteenth birthday, a pale, shaking June crept silently into her grandparents' home choking back sobs and holding her torn blouse together with one hand and her crotch with the other.

It was eleven o'clock, and though she was worried she might be in trouble, June secretly hoped her grandmother would still be up. Up waiting for her, sitting in her recliner as she did most evenings, only this time concerned that something had happened to her granddaughter, that perhaps she needed help, care, love. Such emotions, though, did not exist in the Jackson household. Whatever love and care might have been available was long ago exhausted on the Jacksons' own children, who now rarely even visited their prosaic, fanatically religious parents.

Shutting the front door quietly behind her, June quickly dismissed her fantasy. She now had another concern: Who might have seen her dashing across the lawn in only her underpants and torn blouse? She didn't have time to consider the implications. Instead, she shook out the balled-up pants under her arm, slipped them on, and tried the best she could to smooth out the wrinkles. It *was* possible Grandma would be up, and if she was, there would be a lot of explaining to do. Or would there?

Creeping quietly down the central hallway holding her shoes in her hand, June looked down and stepped gingerly around the squeaky board on the left. When she looked back up, fear and relief collided as she caught the frozen glare of her grandmother's eyes at the far end of the hallway. Grandma was up after all. She was there for June, there to help. Scold maybe, and then help as any grandmother would.

"Do you know what time it is?" asked Mary placidly.

"Yes," replied June softly, looking at the floor and waiting for her grandmother's response. But there was none. There was nothing more to come. No "I'd like to talk to you about this." No "Come here, dear, and tell Grandma what happened." Not even "Is everything all right?" Mary Jackson simply took one long look at the distraught, disheveled girl, turned away, and went back to bed.

Such was the emotional void in which June Briand grew up. The one, perhaps, that led her to accept a ride that summer evening from a man who had pulled to the side of the road as she walked home from the convenience store. June had wanted soda, and though it was nine o'clock in the evening, it was still light out and the store was less than a mile from home. Mary approved the request.

"Hi, need a lift?" the man asked in an affable tone. He drove an old, dented car speckled with putty and primer, but June saw nothing wrong with accepting a ride from the friendly stranger. Grateful that someone was nice enough to offer, she didn't hesitate. "Okay," she said, jumping in the car. Minutes later, she knew it was a mistake.

Instead of turning right at the stop sign as June had indicated, the driver went straight, saying he knew the way and was taking a short cut. A block later, he fell silent and pulled off the main street onto an unfamiliar dirt road. June stole a quick glance at the stranger, but he was too intent on his driving to notice. He was in a hurry, driving fast down the rough road, jerking the wheel right and left to avoid the bumps and gullies. He was on a mission and she knew it.

A wave of nausea suddenly washed over the thirteen-year-old and she felt sick to her stomach. Her cheeks flushed and her temples began to throb. She sensed danger, sensed this was the wrong place to be and the wrong person to be here with. Her senses had not deceived her.

When they came to Robinson Pond, the driver turned off and headed down another road to a wooded area near the water. From there, the car could not be seen from the road. He pulled over, cut the engine, and turned monstrous. Without a word, he turned his black, dilated eyes on his bewildered victim, paused for a moment, then grabbed her by the hair and dragged her out of the car and threw her in the back seat where he pounced on her.

With grunts more animal than human, he clawed wildly at her chest, tearing open the white cotton blouse June had so carefully ironed that morning. It was one she was particularly proud of because she had just bought it — and with her own money. Now, buttons were popping in all directions as her attacker groped for the tiny, half-formed breasts inside. With the other hand, he worked the zipper of her white and yellow polka dot pants.

"I don't remember much after that. It's like I was in a fog, like it wasn't real. I couldn't believe what was happening to me."

The one thing June could remember — and vividly — was the oppressive weight on her. This was a large, heavy man, and she was a ninety-pound child. All she could think about was getting air. "I couldn't breathe. It was as if I was choking, but I couldn't say anything or do anything. There was just this heavy weight on me."

Breathing. Staying alive. Somehow she was managing. But her attacker wasn't. He couldn't achieve an erection. He couldn't pierce the prey he had trapped beneath him. And he became frustrated, then enraged at his impotence. Here was a woman-child he had intended to control, to teach a lesson about who was powerful and who was boss. And he was failing miserably. No one had any business wresting his power from him, least of all a defenseless little girl. So he took revenge.

Suddenly and without warning, June felt a white-hot jolt of pain between her legs, then warm fluid flowing down her thigh. "I felt something sticky. I didn't know what it was. Then I looked at my fingers and saw the blood." The emasculated predator had regained the control he so desperately needed. He had won back his manhood by ripping virginity from a child with the end of a broken beer bottle.

June lay on the back seat, too afraid to say or do anything. Her attacker, who had been drinking all afternoon and evening, exited the back seat and took the driver's seat, where he fell asleep, snoring deeply. June thought about running from the car, but she was afraid that opening the door would wake her attacker, and she would be punished further, maybe even killed. So she stayed curled up on the back seat, waiting, waiting.

June, too, fell into a hazy half-sleep, and when she awoke, it was dark and the car was moving. The bumpy road again, then smooth pavement. They were moving from a remote area to a populated one, and June was relieved. After driving for a few minutes, the car slowed for a red light. June had been lying on the back seat, and now mustered the courage to look up over the seat to see familiar territory: Just across the intersection was the bowling alley near her house. "Stop here," she commanded, surprised by the authority in her voice. Miraculously, the driver obeyed.

June clutched her shoes and pants to her chest, opened the back door, and sprinted for the bowling alley. She darted across the parking lot and disappeared around the side of the building. It was dark there and June felt afraid. She hesitated for a moment, but realized she had no choice, no other escape route. She entered the darkness.

Halfway up a dirt path that ran alongside the building June heard someone behind her yell, "Wait!" Her attacker had spoken very little during her ordeal, so she wasn't sure of the voice. She shot a glance over her shoulder to see that it was, indeed, the rapist, and he was gaining on her. At that point, the half-naked youth ran for her life.

As the glow from the parking lot lights faded and the path turned black, June increased her speed. She wanted to make the field that lay between the bowling alley and her house. It was more open, safer. She needed to be there — and fast. But her desire to flee interrupted her thinking and her coordination, and she tripped.

She dropped her pants in the dark and began groping wildly for them. She couldn't go home in just her underwear! She *needed* those pants! Glancing over her shoulder, she could make out a dark figure fifty yards away coming up the path. She turned back to her search, clawing in the darkness until she felt one leg of the pants, and scooped them up. She sprang to her feet and bolted for the field only twenty yards away.

She was right. It was safe there. Open, too open. A moment later, her pursuer stopped at the edge of the building, still cloaked in darkness and unwilling to venture further. "You're a lucky girl!" he yelled, panting. "Damn lucky!" Then he turned and disappeared into the night.

June never saw him again. Never filed a complaint with the police. Never told anyone. She just locked herself in her grandmother's bathroom, sank down on the tile floor, and picked glass fragments from her bleeding vagina as she cried quietly to herself that lonely summer night.

The effects of the rape lingered the rest of the summer. Had June been able to talk to someone about it and share her grief and anger and shame, she might have been better prepared to face a new school year, especially now that she was entering high school. But the odds were against her: She no longer fit in anywhere. She had always relied heavily on gymnastics to keep her life on course, and now that support system was gone. So was her only friend, Lisa, who hated her. And the violent summer attack left June feeling dirty and used. "I thought I was a dirty girl, a bad, bad girl after that."

With her declining self-image came a concurrent decline in June's school performance. Only a few months before, she had proudly packed away her junior high school graduation dress in a cedar chest in the attic, vowing to "save it forever" to remind herself of how well she had done in school. Once as good a student as she was gymnast, June's grades fell precipitously when she entered her first year of high school. What where mostly As and a few Bs in junior high, rapidly plummeted to Ds and Fs. An ambitious, competent youngster quickly deteriorated into a depressed, despondent, and — for the first time — rebellious teenager.

There was little keeping June afloat. So when an acquaintance from school called her with a wild idea, June was immediately intrigued — and more than willing to participate.

Deborah was a troubled young girl the same age as June. But while June was a slight, ninety-pound youngster with a cute adolescent appeal, Deborah was an obese child, weighing nearly two hundred pounds by age ten — and carrying an equal amount of emotional baggage with her. Her pimply face was a constant source of embarrassment for her, but she could not resist picking at her acne, which was forever raw and bleeding. Her long, stringy hair went unwashed for days at a time.

Deborah had met June at school only a few weeks after the school year began. It had been a lonely and violent summer, and her self-image was in such tatters and her interest in school was so low, that she willingly accepted Deborah's invitation to run away from home.

Deborah had conceived the idea after being suspended from school for smoking pot one morning rather than attending class. When the bell had rung for class, she started toward the building but then broke ranks and ran off to the baseball diamond where she hunkered down in one of the dugouts. Had she thought to look out and survey the landscape before lighting a marijuana cigarette, she would have seen the teacher heading her way to inquire why she had detoured to the ball field. Upon his arrival, the teacher no longer cared what her reasons were; she was going to the Dean of Women, and she was going to be suspended from school.

Unable to bear the shame of suspension, Deborah called June and explained a plan to run away to Boston. The idea immediately appealed to June. "It fit perfectly with my view of myself. Runaway? Why not. No one cared about me. And I didn't care about school anymore. Going to Boston sounded like a great idea. I remember thinking it would be like a day at the zoo. And except for the weekend when we went to New York for gymnastics, I had never been out of New Hampshire. I was ready."

But Deborah wasn't. She had conceived of the plan, but she was frightened. She had, however, picked the right traveling companion. While on the bus to Boston, June consoled her weeping friend, telling her, "Don't worry, we'll get jobs. We love McDonald's — we can work there! We'll have a wonderful time. We can pool our money and get an apartment. It'll be great!"

This cheered up the dejected girl, who wiped away her tears and caught June's enthusiasm. She then joined in the planning as if they were going to be gone forever. "Yeah, we'll get jobs," said Deborah. "And we can eat candy for dinner if we want. No more rules, no more school!"

Earlier that morning, the girls had raided their respective financial resources in order to buy Trailways bus tickets to Boston. Deborah had stolen the money from her mother's petty cash coffee can, and June had taken the entire twenty dollars and change she had saved in her koala bear bank. She kissed the bear goodbye, and made her way to the bus station.

The girls didn't plan their trip very well, though: They took no luggage; no change of clothes; no money for a return ticket; and for June, no sanitary napkins — not that she would have known what to do with them. Such items and their function were well beyond the realm of acceptable subjects for Mary Jackson. June knew nothing about sex — other than the dismal lesson she had learned at Robinson Pond — and so, when she got her first menstrual period on the Trailways bus, she was ill prepared to deal with it.

"Deborah was crying on and off the whole trip to Boston. But she came out of it when I told her I was bleeding. I bled right through my pants onto the bus seat and didn't know what was going on or what to do. Finally Deborah did something besides cry. She said, 'Go in the bathroom and use toilet paper.' 'What am I supposed to do with the toilet paper?' I said. 'Make a pad,' she said. 'You're supposed to have a pad but you don't so go make one. Go on.'"

June just finished rinsing out her pants when the bus pulled into the Boston Commons Station. The girls got off the bus wearing T-shirts, jeans, and sneakers. June tied a sweat shirt around her waist to hide the wet spot on the back of her pants. Deborah had two dollars in her pocket, and June had five. They couldn't have been happier.

The girls' worldly education began immediately. "We were just starting to walk across the Commons, taking in everything like kids at a carnival, when I saw my first black person. Living in New Hampshire, you don't see many blacks — or Hispanics or Asians, for that matter. She was a prostitute. She wore big platform shoes and a halter top and had her hair teased way up high. It was sort of bleached blonde but it didn't bleach very well and ended up orange instead. I didn't know she was a prostitute until I heard some boys pointing and talking about hookers and money. I didn't know what it all meant, but I was starting to get the idea that sex seemed to be involved in everything."

The two wide-eyed girls wandered aimlessly around downtown Boston until they found their way to an entrance ramp to the Mass Pike. Since they had no predetermined destination, and no money for transportation to get there, they decided to hitchhike and see what happened.

Wisely, June pushed her chubby girlfriend to the rear and stuck out her thumb. At the same time, she glanced up the ramp and saw a policeman looking at her. But he didn't do anything. He just watched her, not seeming to care that a little, obviously underage girl was alone on a freeway ready and willing to accept whatever came her way. That was nothing unusual for June. No one ever cared before. Why should they start now?

If the officer was inclined to take action — which he didn't appear to be — he didn't have time. The first car entering the ramp stopped. It was Jake the Snake. June and Deborah jumped in the old, rusting Toyota hatchback, Deborah in the back seat, June in the front. Jake was a twenty-five-year-old hippie-type, with long hair parted in the middle and a drooping moustache. Because he was holding up traffic at the busy on-ramp, Jake caught the attention of the policeman, who now began walking toward the car. But it was too late. Jake reached across in front of June, slammed the door, and zoomed right by the policeman, who attempted without success to flag the driver over to the side of the road.

Jake pulled out onto the freeway headed for Brighton, Massachusetts, with a car full of booty. He knew it was his lucky day when he spotted the two unescorted females, but he was ecstatic when he discovered that they didn't know — or care — where they were going. They were *runaways*, and they were looking for a good time! Jake the Snake was more than willing to oblige.

"Where ya headed?" he asked after he passed the policeman.

"We don't know," was the answer he was tickled to hear. The girls explained how they happened to be in Boston, why they ran away, and how they planned to stay there and get jobs and make a new life for themselves.

"How old are you?" asked Jake.

"Thirteen."

"*Thirteen?* That's it? Thirteen? Are you sure it's all right to stay here? I mean, what about your parents?"

June was quick to respond. "Oh, they don't care," she said, not realizing how true her statement was.

Jake was dressed in pale green hospital scrubs, which prompted June to ask if he was a doctor. "Of sorts," he replied with a snicker. June didn't understand his answer, and Deborah in the back seat was too afraid to partake of the conversation anyway, wondering now if coming to Boston was such a good idea after all. Her doubts increased when Jake expounded on his name. "I'm Jake, but people call me Jake the Snake."

"How come?" June asked innocently. But rather than answer the questions, he explained that he lived at home with his parents, so he couldn't take the girls there. He decided to take his trophies across town to his friend, Juan, whom he knew would appreciate them.

Juan was an unemployed prep cook who spent most of his days lying around his apartment smoking marijuana and watching daytime television and reading *Hustler* magazine. The fleshy pictorial was the first subject of discussion after cursory introductions by Jake, who was beaming with pride for the catch he had brought in.

Juan told the girls to sit down on the couch, and promptly positioned himself between them. He reached under it and pulled out the magazine, excitedly flipping through the pages until he found the photo he was looking for. He held the magazine at arm's length and said, "There. What do you think of *that*, girls?"

Juan had opened the magazine to a page showing the rear view of a naked woman kneeling and looking back at the camera with her hand between her legs and her middle finger fondling her genitalia. Deborah looked away immediately, but June lingered for a moment trying to make sense of the image; then she, too, looked away, embarrassed. But the damage was done. Juan sensed — incorrectly — that the photo had interested June, possibly aroused her as it had him. Now he turned his full attention to her.

"Well," he said. "Aren't you going to answer my question? What do you think of the picture?"

"Umm, I don't know," said the modest teenager, who had never seen a photo like this before.

"Did you like it?"

"It's okay," said June, not knowing how to respond — and making exactly the *wrong* response to a pervert in heat. To Juan, "okay" meant "I'm interested in pornography and want to have sex." So he took June by the hand and started leading her to the bedroom.

Seeing the frightened look on June's face, Jake did something most uncharacteristic. He stepped forward and said, "Hey, Juan, we just came by to say hello, man. No time for that stuff right now. I've got to get back to my house and drop off a package, but we'll come by later tonight. We'll see you later."

"This won't take long," Juan replied, ignoring his friend and continuing toward the bedroom.

"No!" exclaimed Deborah, jumping to her feet. "We have to go! Jake's right. Let's go June, we have to go — right now!"

Seeing he was outnumbered, Juan relented, telling Jake he had better come back that night, and that they could smoke pot and drink Southern Comfort. "That's girls' booze," he said. "You'll dig it. We're gonna rage tonight!"

Promising he'd return, Jake shepherded the girls back to the car and drove directly to his parents' house. But rather than stop, he drove past the house, checking to see if his parents were home. They were. He decided to wait until dark before sneaking the girls in, and drove to a local bar in a strip mall a few blocks from the house.

"Hey, Snake man," said the bar tender as the trio walked into the dimly-lit bar. "Whatcha got there, jail bait?" Everyone laughed and turned to look at the girls.

"No, just a couple of thirsty little birds that flew away from home. How about a few beers?"

"Why not? How about a few lines, too?" said the bartender, pulling out a tiny silver spoon that was hanging on a gold chain around his neck. He came out from behind the bar and sat down at a table with Jake and the girls. Deborah, as usual, was petrified of everything, looking around the bar as if her mother was going to walk in any moment.

June watched the bar tender, who removed from his pocket a small plastic bag containing white powder. "How about a snort for the little ladies?" he said, ignoring Deborah and fixing his gaze on June. She didn't say anything, and had no idea what he was talking about anyway.

"I'm talking to *you*, sweetheart," he said, taking June's chin in his hand and turning her face toward him. "Want to try some good blow?"

"Don't think they're into it," Jake cut in. "But *I'll* take a hit." His friend looked annoyed, but dipped his spoon into the bag and brought forth a little mound of cocaine which he held under Jake's left nostril. Jake leaned into it, pinched off his right nostril and inhaled forcefully, instantly vacuuming up the magic mountain. He repeated the ritual on the other nostril, then looked at June contentedly.

"Want to try some?" he asked.

"What is it?" replied June.

"Coke. Good coke."

"Uh, I don't think so," she responded, not knowing what he meant by "coke" and not willing to find out.

"Makes you feel good," said the bartender, now looking June up and down with interest. She caught his glaze and began to feel uncomfortable.

"That's okay. We're kinda tired and..."

"Well, how about a beer then?" he interrupted, getting more annoyed. "Ya gotta have *something.*"

"No, that's okay," she said again, feeling more uncomfortable and thinking about Juan, an hour before, and the Robinson Pond incident, a month before. "I think we better go."

Jake saw how nervous both girls were and thanked his friend for the hospitality and left. He drove back past his parents' home but they were still there. He decided it was best if he parted company with his young friends, and asked if they wanted a ride back to the bus station. Both said emphatically that they did not, so he drove them to Boston's North End and dropped them off. He pulled from the rear of his car an old woolen blanket covered with dog hair, and told them to keep it. Then he said, "Good luck" and drove away.

"I don't know how we managed on so little money, but we did. We stayed in Boston for almost a week—in the same clothes, with no jackets, just wandering around with the old blanket Jake had given us. It was September and warm, so we fared pretty well living on the streets. We tried to get jobs at McDonald's by saying we were eighteen, but the manager just laughed at us. The same thing happened at Burger King.

"We slept in doorways most of the time. Deborah was scared to death all night long. She'd say, 'Someone's going to rape us. They're going to kill us.' And I'd tell her that I'd stay awake all night so no one could get us. I'd always be sitting up and Deborah would have her head in my lap shaking like a puppy. I tried to stay awake, but by three or four in the morning, I'd conk out too. Then we'd get woken up at five or six by the garbage men or cats fighting. It was exhausting."

The girls' adventures in Boston ended one morning while they were standing on a street corner trying unsuccessfully to comb the knots out of their hopelessly tangled hair. June was in particularly bad condition, and smelled from having not been able to wash herself or her underwear, which was blood-stained from days of relying on makeshift toilet paper sanitary pads.

Though they refused to admit it, they were both ready to come home, and breathed a collective sigh of relief when Jake's rusty hatchback unexpectedly rounded the corner and stopped in front of them.

"Get in," was all he said at first. The girls obeyed. "Here," he said, handing June a twenty dollar bill. "I'm taking you to the bus station. Buy tickets and go home. This is no place for you kids." By now the girls were inclined to agree. Even though they knew they would soon face an inquisition unlike anything they'd ever experienced, they were too tired, hungry, and filthy to argue.

Deborah expected her mother to be livid when she picked her up at the bus station, and she was not disappointed. The first thing the woman did was slap her daughter hard across the face the moment she was within reach. June watched "almost with envy" as Deborah's mother berated and continued to hit her daughter for running away. It was something June had never experienced from her grandparents, and though humiliating, it was the type of concern she had always longed for but never received.

For June, however, this day would be no different from any other. She thought that with the severity of the infraction, there might be *some* discipline or restrictions by her grandparents. But she was wrong. Being away so long, June forgot where she had come from: She was the Jacksons' granddaughter. These people had less concern for her after thirteen years than Jake the Snake had after six days.

There were no slaps, no questions; in fact, no words whatsoever when Harold picked up June. He simply leaned over and opened the passenger door to let June in the car, then proceeded to drive home in silence with a thirteen-year-old who had been missing for nearly a week. Neither he nor his wife had thought to call the police and file a missing person's report. But June's sister had. And she now called the police again to let them know June was on her way home.

"I walked in the house and my grandfather went directly to his recliner. I was so hungry that I opened a can of spinach and was eating it out of the can when the phone rang. My grandmother got it and I could hear her say to the person on the other end, 'I'll tell her but I don't think she's going to go with you.' It was the police department, and they were sending a car over to pick me up.

"I had to go down to the station, and I was mad. I was tired, hungry, and now I was mad. They put me in a room and a rookie policeman came in to interrogate me. When he came in, he said, 'Why are you here?' I guess I thought I was a big shot having been to Boston and all, so I gave him a smart aleck answer: 'First degree murder, what's it to ya?' It was the same room they brought me to ten years later after I killed my husband."

After a reprimand and lecture from the police, June returned to school the next day, but had no interest in her classes anymore. She needed something else to give her life meaning now, and found it a few weeks later on Main Street in downtown Hudson. She had been shopping on a Saturday afternoon and had just left a discount variety store when someone tapped her on the shoulder. June turned to see a tall, good-looking man, perhaps six-foot-two, with brown curly hair. He appeared to be in his late twenties, and by the looks of his huge biceps and lean, V-shaped torso, was obviously a body-builder. More than anything, June noticed his "nice smile."

"Hi, I'm Ron. Ron Jensen. I saw you in the store," he said. "Find anything good?" June was taken aback. She had just turned fourteen and wasn't adept at conversing with handsome young men, particularly those with devastating smiles. She was flattered by the attention though, and blushed without saying anything.

"What's the matter, lose your tongue?" he teased.

"No, I have a tongue," she replied, warming slightly. She may have been fourteen, but her feminine instincts were beginning to bud. She turned demurely and started walking down the street, testing his interest. He passed.

Ron followed June, making small talk as she walked down the street to the bus stop. June did mostly listening, and when the bus came and she was about to board, Ron asked, "Can I could call you sometime?" June quickly gave him her phone number, and was embarrassed on the ride home, realizing she had blurted out the number almost before he finished asking the question.

At about two o'clock the next afternoon, the phone rang. June skipped across the kitchen floor, cutting off her grandmother and catching the phone on the fly before the second ring. Sure enough, it was Ron asking if he could come by and take her for a ride. Unfortunately, Mary Jackson had already made plans for June (Diane had moved out by then), so she had to decline. He said he was disappointed, that he "really liked" June and wanted to see her again soon. He asked if he could meet her after school the next day.

"I was so excited he called that it was hard to contain myself. I tried to act calm and said, 'Well, I suppose so,' but I was bursting with joy inside. No one had really paid much attention to me before, and I had never had a boyfriend, so I was flattered by Ron's interest."

June suggested they meet at three-thirty by the front entrance to the school, but Ron didn't like the idea. He suggested the baseball diamond, at the path leading off into the woods. When June asked how he knew about the path, he lied, saying he had gone to the same high school. In fact, he *had* gone into the woods there — many times — but never while in high school, which he attended years earlier in another state.

Unable to concentrate on any subject except Ron, June watched the clock all day Monday. She was nervous but exhilarated at the prospect of a date with the "cute guy." At lunch time, she couldn't eat a thing, and was content to sit at the school picnic table and sip her milk while gazing off toward the baseball diamond. She was still daydreaming when the three o'clock school bell startled her. She had been staring out the window thinking about all the things that had happened to her lately, and hadn't realized the time slipping by so fast. She got a hold of herself, grabbed her backpack and jacket, and hurried to her school locker. She threw everything in, ran to the bathroom, and primped in the mirror for twenty minutes.

When she felt she was ready, June put her comb in her pocket, painted on some lipstick a classmate had loaned her (she didn't wear makeup), and headed for the diamond. When she arrived, her heart sank: no one was there. She looked around, thinking maybe there was another path and that she was at the wrong one. But she couldn't see any other path. This *had* to be the one Ron was referring to; kids often took it as a short cut to the road on the other side of the school property.

As she stood there trying to figure out what to do, she heard someone call from the woods, "Hey cutie, up here." It was Ron. June tried to contain her glee. It took all the will power she had to keep herself from running to his voice. She walked up the path a few feet and then called back, "Where are you?" He responded by jumping out from behind a tree twenty yards up the trail.

"What are you doing in there?" June asked.

"Waiting to surprise you."

"Well, I didn't think you were even here."

"I said three-thirty, didn't I?"

Ron was aware that he was much older and far bigger than the high school kids, and knew he would have looked conspicuous loitering by the baseball field. June was beyond such reasoning, and was thrilled to be back with the man she hadn't stopped thinking about since Saturday afternoon.

The afternoon was chilly, but June decided to leave her jacket in her locker along with her books. She wanted Ron to notice her nice blouse and hoped to make the best impression on him that she could. The jacket, however, was the first thing he mentioned. "Where's your jacket?" he asked like a father.

"In my locker," said June matter-of-factly.

"That's no place for a jacket on a day like this. You've got to take better care of yourself. When it's cold, you wear a jacket. I bet you don't even wear a hat when it snows."

"How'd you know?"

"Because you're not wearing a jacket now, so I put two and two together."

"I'll be okay," said June, very aware that the handsome man next to her had gotten closer. Then he put his arm around her shoulders.

"Come here, I'll keep you warm. But from now on, take your jacket with you when it's cold, okay?"

"Yes, Daddy," said June.

As they walked, Ron asked how June was doing in school and why she didn't have any books with her. She answered that she used to do well in school, but ever since quitting gymnastics, she wasn't very interested. He told her that her attitude had to change. "Got to keep your grades up," he said. "They're important."

When they crested the top of the hill and started heading down the other side toward the road, Ron led June off the path onto another, less trodden trail that went deeper into the woods. "We need some privacy," he said. "There's a nice spot down this path. I'll show you."

June didn't object. Rather, she obliged by putting her arm around her suitor's waist. It was a bold move for her, but she felt somehow confident that Ron really did find her attractive and she was willing to take some chances. As her arm wrapped around his waist, she felt his warmth and his muscles and curiously, was not afraid. Though she had undergone a brutal rape only months before, she knew there was no danger here. This was the way it was supposed to be: You meet someone; he calls; you go for a date. Everything's fine. This is what she wanted.

Fifty yards into the woods, Ron stopped. He leaned against a tree, pulled June close and kissed her. His tongue immediately went deep into her mouth and she didn't know what to do. So she submitted, and opened her mouth further, letting him probe every crevice; she had no idea kissing was like this. "I thought you put your lips on the other person's lips and sort of pressed. Ron explored my entire mouth: the roof, under my tongue, all along my teeth. He was slobbering all over me, but do you think I cared? I was already in love. He could do anything he wanted to me."

Ron asked June if he could meet her the next day at the same place. She, of course, agreed, and again met him at "our tree." This time he had a blanket with him. She eyed it without suspicion, and again walked with her arm around his waist to the trysting spot. There he spread the blanket, laid down, and asked June to lie on top of him. She carefully removed her shoes before stepping onto the blanket, then crawled on top of the big man.

The first thing she noticed was a prominent hardness below Ron's waist as her thigh came to rest on it. She squirmed a bit, trying to adjust herself away from it, and in the process, signaled to Ron that she had discovered his erection. He responded by raising his hips off the ground slightly, driving the firmness into her thigh. Again they started to kiss.

June thought it would please Ron if she tried to demonstrate what she had learned the day before. Keeping her eyes shut tightly, she stuck her tongue directly into the crease between his lower lip and chin but quickly adjusted her aim and inserted her tongue into his mouth.

Yes, he was pleased. And he knew then that he had a willing participant. Without hesitation, he took June's hand and led it to his bulge. She did not withdraw. Then he asked June in a whisper to unzip his pants. She complied. And she didn't hesitate when he asked her to take off her shirt.

As June lifted her knit shirt over her head, Ron worked at her jeans zipper, and a minute later she was lying on her back naked with Ron looking down at her. His eyes slowly scanned up and down the length of her supple white body as he rested on one elbow and stroked her belly. She looked up at him, ready to please him in whatever way she could. "He was so gentle, so loving. He told me I was beautiful. I never heard that before."

Keeping his shirt on, Ron removed his sneakers and stripped off his pants. June watched as he removed his briefs. Then she became alarmed. "His penis was massive. I know now that it was twice the size of a normal man's. I had no experience back then but I knew I was only fourteen years old and ninety pounds, and there was no way this man was going to fit inside me. And he didn't; he couldn't even begin to get it in."

But he tried. Other than the bottle incident at the pond, June never had sex before. She had not even inserted a tampon. Ron understood this, and backed away. He would have plenty of time to "break in" his lover, and made a date for the following afternoon as they walked back to his truck.

Ron was a carpenter, and had a built-in tool box behind the cab of his truck. He folded the blanket and put it in the box, and gave June a ride home. On the way, he pulled out a package from under the front seat. It was the first of many "little girl" gifts he would shower on his new lover. This time it was a doll lamp.

"I thought it was so cute. The lamp shade was her hat. I loved it. A few days later he gave me a rainbow comforter for my bed, and then he bought me a pair of pajamas—the ones with the feet in them like little kids wear."

The two kept up their clandestine meetings every day after school at three-thirty, and at each love session Ron worked himself into his tiny lover a little more and a little more until she could accommodate almost half of his bulk.

"It hurt, but I didn't care. And it was over quick — in about ten minutes. I'd get undressed, and a few minutes later, I'd get dressed again. I think I saw Ron as kind of a father *and* a boyfriend. I was being loved and nurtured for the first time in my life. He kept telling me how important school was, how I had to do better in class, how smart I was. No one ever told me those things before. He kept encouraging me, and my grades started going back up."

One afternoon the following week, Mary Jackson looked out her window and saw June getting out of Ron's truck; she also noticed a goodbye kiss between the two. "Well, who was *that*?" she asked when June entered the kitchen.

"A friend."

"Looks like more than a friend to me," said Mary without looking up from her stew pot.

"Well, maybe a *little* more than a friend. Maybe a *boyfriend*," June said a bit snidely, knowing her grandmother would disapprove. But she was wrong.

"Bring him in sometime," came the unexpected retort from Mary Jackson. June stopped short and looked in amazement at her grandmother.

"You want to *meet* him?" she asked incredulously.

"Of course I want to meet him. It's about time you had a boyfriend. You're getting older now, you know."

June walked to her room, closed the door, and did a handspring onto her bed. She couldn't believe that her grandmother was in favor of Ron. "I knew I'd have some explaining to do when they finally met, seeing as how Ron was older than me. I didn't know how much older because he wouldn't tell me. Not yet, at least. But the fact that Grandma wanted to meet him was something I never expected."

The next day June met Ron at their designated spot. He was already lying on the blanket and seemed more intense than usual. June couldn't wait to tell him the news that her grandmother wanted to meet him, but when she started to explain, Ron interrupted her.

"I want you to shave," he said flatly. June wasn't sure she heard him right. She looked at him, waiting for a further explanation. "I want you to shave," he repeated. "I like the little girl look." It was then that June caught his meaning.

"You mean ... down ... down *there*?" she asked.

"Yeah, down there. You don't mind, do you?"

"Well ... uh ... no, I guess not," said June, still not comprehending but, as always, willing to comply. She would later learn that it was not just the "little girl look" Ron liked — he was a sexual deviant of the first order. June would also discover that he was not twenty-two, as he had told her and Mary when they met the next Saturday; he was *thirty-eight*, a drifter, and had an uncanny ability to charm the ladies — especially grandmothers.

After their introduction, Mary told June that Ron was "a fine boy, a very good boy," and she approved of the relationship. Whether she meant it, or she really saw Ron as a means of sweeping the last bird out of the nest, is debatable. Nevertheless, she encouraged the courtship and repeatedly invited Ron over for coffee and pies, which she baked special for him.

It worked. Two weeks later, in late September of 1977, Ron Jensen would marry June in the living room of the Jackson home. Since June was only fourteen, the law required her to obtain her grandparents' permission to marry. The day after Ron proposed — and a week before the wedding was to take place — June approached her grandfather while he watched television in his recliner. She had not yet told anybody about Ron's proposal, but on one occasion had let slip to her grandmother how wonderful it would be to get married and raise kids — Ron's kids.

Now June kneeled by her grandfather's chair and said, "Sorry to interrupt you, Grandpa, but could you please come into the kitchen. Grandma's in there and I need to talk to you both — it's important." Harold didn't budge. "Grandpa," June repeated. "Did you hear what I said? I need to talk to you." Finally Harold turned and looked at his granddaughter. There were tears in his eyes; he knew what she wanted to talk about.

For the stoic man that he was, Harold Jackson still had emotions. He may not have shown them much over the years, but he *had* raised June from birth and couldn't help but be attached to her. He rose from his recliner looking more feeble than he should have for his sixty-nine years, and hobbled slowly into the kitchen. June waited until he was seated at the dinette table. She looked at him, then at her grandmother, then back to him. Finally, she came right to the point: "You know Ron? We want to get married."

There was a long silence. Tears welled up in June's eyes. Her grandmother looked at the floor, and Harold pulled a hanky out of his hip pocket and blew his nose. He stuffed it back in and looked at June. "He only wants your trust fund," Harold said, referring to the six thousand dollars from the dog bite settlement. She objected immediately.

"He does not! He loves me! He'd never do that!"

June had told Ron about the lawsuit money and how they could use it to get a "good start in life." Ron agreed wholeheartedly, saying it would "come in handy." Though he was careful not to show it, he was extremely interested in the trust fund, and questioned June extensively about how and when the money was to be released. She explained that she would have access to it when she turned eighteen or got married, whichever came first.

June looked at her grandfather. Now she was mad. "You have to sign papers." she said. But he didn't respond. He was not at all convinced that the marriage was the right thing for June.

"I don't know," was all Harold could say, but it was enough to throw June into a tantrum.

"I'll run away again!" June cried. "I'll leave and you'll never see me again! You *have* to sign the papers! When someone's underage, the parents have to give permission. You have to go to city hall and sign papers." Turning to her grandmother, June asked, "What do *you* think?"

All Mary could say was, "Can't I sign them here?" Except for four hours of church every Sunday morning, Mary rarely left the house, even to go shopping, which Harold did alone on Saturday mornings. "And it's so hot in those public buildings," she complained, worrying more about the heat than the fact that June was about to marry a man old enough to be her father. But she acquiesced, and the next day drove with Harold to city hall to sign papers.

The ceremony took place at one o'clock the following Saturday afternoon. Ron showed up at a quarter to one in an ill-fitting tuxedo he had rented for the occasion. He had with him no friends, no family, no present, no flowers, and a thirty-dollar ring he had picked up on sale at K-Mart.

Harold was conspicuously absent, saying later that though he "couldn't put his finger on it," he knew something was "not right about the union." June's mother came bursting through the door a moment after Ron, smoking a cigarette and reeking of whiskey. Ann's sister, Aunt Margaret, had come across the street an hour before, and was in June's bedroom adorning the bride's hair with a tiara of white gardenias, and helping her put on the gown she was to wear for her ceremony: her junior high graduation dress.

"I was so glad I kept that dress in the cedar chest. And of course it fit perfectly because I had just graduated junior high a few months earlier. Plus, there was no way we or Ron could have afforded a wedding gown. But our finances didn't bother me. I was thrilled to be getting married, and for the first time I felt like a grownup instead of a child."

Also attending the ceremony were Mary Jackson, June's brother, Dan, from across the street (who still didn't know he was her brother), Dan's sister, Carmen, their brother, Gil, and a friend of Dan's who acted as witness to the proceedings. Earlier in the week, Aunt Margaret had helped June select a Justice of the Peace from the yellow pages, and by one-fifteen, the ceremony was over and June and Ron were man and wife.

Someone popped a bottle of champagne — which Mary forbade June to touch — and everyone had a piece of yellow sheet cake with white frosting, served on paper plates. Whoever ordered the cake had forgotten to include a decorative inscription wishing the couple well, so with a match stick, someone carved in the frosting, "Good Luck June & Ron."

Twenty minutes later, the newlyweds ran from the house into a pouring rain and jumped in Ron's beat-up car. It was raining so hard that June's graduation dress was soaked through by the time Ron got in his side of the car and reached over to let his soggy bride in the passenger door. The dress, it turns out, got drenched again three years later. "I wore it for my second wedding when I was seventeen. It rained that day too."

As the wedding party stood in the doorway waving goodbye, Ron threw his jacket in the back seat, loosened his tie, and took off, headed for a two-day honeymoon at a cheap Salisbury Beach motel. He had not even reached the end of the block when he turned to June and said, "You know this is only a temporary thing, don't you?"

She had not, of course, thought of her marriage as a "temporary thing," and was thrilled with the idea of matrimony. "I was thinking about how wonderful it was to be grown up and out of my grandparents' house — and to be *married*! I didn't know what to think when he said that, but I wasn't about to let on that only two minutes after getting married I was heartbroken.

"I wanted to look adult, and I didn't want to seem stupid because Ron always said I was so smart. So I played along and said, 'Oh, I know.' Being loved was such a big deal to me that I didn't realize it wasn't love at all — even after our exhausting honeymoon at the beach, which was basically an around-the-clock sex fest."

It was usually about an hour drive to the beach traveling east along Route 101 through the southern part of New Hampshire. This day it took longer because of the torrential downpour that impeded the newlyweds' progress. That was fine with June. She was content just to be sitting next to her new husband — "a dream come true" — while her husband wouldn't be content until he got his new bride stripped naked in the Sun 'n Surf motel where he had reserved a room for the occasion.

After reaching Coastal Route 1 in Salisbury Beach, Ron turned left and headed north looking for the motel. He passed numerous beach bungalows and cottages intermixed with old motels that were in urgent need of refurbishing, but could not locate the Sun 'n Surf. He drove back and forth in the area where he thought it should be, and finally stopped at another motel that had hanging on a post a vacancy sign; below it was another sign reading: "2 for $25."

Ron got out, dashed through the rain, and popped into the office. No one was there. He stood there dripping, then noticed a silver bell on the counter. He banged it impatiently several times, and finally an elderly woman in a ragged housecoat shuffled through the door in the rear of the office.

"One tap's enough, young man," she said.

"I'll take one of the twenty-five-dollar rooms," he said hurriedly.

"We only take cash — in advance."

"Okay, okay," he said. "Here's the cash. Just give me the key, it's my *honeymoon*!"

The woman looked at Ron, suddenly understanding his eagerness. An almost imperceptible smile broke from one side of her wrinkled mouth, but she quickly regained control.

Ron signed the register, they exchanged money and keys, and he was back in the car headed for room 202. When he pulled up to the room, he backed the car in to the parking spot and unlocked the trunk. In it was June's suitcase, his duffel bag, and another case June did not recognize. He handed the key to June so she could unlock the door, lifted all three cases from the trunk, and followed her into the room.

"The first thing Ron did was turn on the television to a porno movie. Then he opened up the case. I was shocked. I had never seen sex toys before — marital aids, he called them. And he sure hadn't told me he was bringing them along. What an assortment! He had all kinds of contraptions and things like vibrators and rubber male appendages he wanted to use on me.

"He also brought along a little bikini bathing suit he had purchased for the honeymoon. It had a tiny lace crotch and no back at all—just a string. The top was thin, see-through nylon like hosiery material. He made me model all around the motel room, turning this way and that. Then we started with the sex.

"It was the most draining weekend of my life. We didn't do anything but have sex — hours of it nonstop. Once I passed out from pure exhaustion. But Ron didn't care. He'd go on and on and on. We'd sleep for a while, then he'd wake up and want sex again. It was hard for him to get satisfied. Even after he was, he'd only rest thirty minutes or so and then start up all over again."

While Ron hurt June sexually — on their honeymoon and in the months ahead — he got away with it because "he was a charmer." As the marriage progressed, Ron continued to play sex games with his wife. A favorite one was to sneak up on June by crawling on his stomach into the bedroom, then jump on her and rip her panties off. "He wouldn't *take* them off, he had to *rip* them off. A lot of times the elastic wouldn't rip and it would cut into me. Then he'd pin my arms behind me and say, 'Fight me!' but I didn't want to fight."

During particularly painful sessions with vibrators and other sex toys, Ron would put his hand over his young bride's mouth and turn her head away so he wouldn't have to look at her anguished face. "Ron knew he was hurting me but he didn't care. And he wouldn't stop, even when I asked him to. It's not that he *liked* hurting me, it's that the things he did to get excited were painful. He also was obsessed with reflections.

"He had three full length mirrors, and he would position them around the room so he could watch himself having sex. He got excited by the reflection, the image in the mirror. That's why he never wanted me on top, because he couldn't see himself if he was on his back.

"He'd pull me by the legs and put me in position so my crotch would always be facing the mirror. Then he'd insert one of his toys in me, and they were huge—bigger than him. Or he'd make me stand naked in front of a mirror while he sat in a chair and directed me to touch my nipples or my crotch. I tried not to be part of it, to put it out of my mind."

Ron Jensen was also an exhibitionist. One night he pulled June onto the kitchen table to have sex. He enjoyed making his wife submit to unusual practices, but it was not just the kitchen table that excited him; it was the window next to it that he focused on. As always, Ron had the lights on. When he had penetrated June and had her immobilized, he reached over and flipped up the window shade.

"Anyone walking by could look in and see us. I said no, pull the shade down, but he wouldn't. I tried to reach over and pull it down myself but I couldn't reach it; that turned him on too—seeing me struggle. All I could do was turn my head away from the window and daydream about something else, usually gymnastics. The more painful or humiliating he was, the more specific my thoughts were. I wouldn't just think about gym, I'd concentrate on specifics like how I'd take off on my vaults or the landings.

"The other thing about Ron was, he never kissed me. That was strange because at first he was so passionate. But other than those first dates behind the school, he never kissed me; he just had sex with me all the time."

On the way home from the beach after their honeymoon, the couple had stopped off at Vic's Diner, a local eatery two miles from Hudson. Vic's was not known for its food or its decor, which, rather than following the motif of a true chrome-and-neon diner, was more like a small, 50's Formica countered cafeteria one would find in a Woolworth's department store of that era.

Since Vic's Diner was the only place in town, the locals patronized it, including firemen, policemen, and local judges who knew Vic well because he was the principal bail bondsman in the town. He, his wife, and their emotionally unstable son, Alfred, operated the establishment. Vic was a huge, perpetually-sweating man of three hundred pounds, whose massive belly spilled over his black-and-white checkered chef's pants like a great wave of slow-falling dough.

When Ron and June had stopped in for lunch, Alfred was yelling at one of the waitresses. His job was dishwasher, and, having a foul temper, was known to throw dishes or slam whole trays of glasses against the wall when things weren't going his way — which they never were.

After the couple finished their lunch and Ron paid at the register, he asked Vic if there was any work available at the restaurant. "Sorry," Vic said, wiping his hands on his filthy apron. "Don't have anything for you."

"It's not for *me*," said Ron. "It's for my *wife*." He gestured toward June, who was stunned by the news that she was now applying for a job at a restaurant, something she had no experience in whatsoever. Vic's attitude changed abruptly. He slowly looked over the lithe fourteen-year-old, starting from her feet, pausing on her exposed midriff, and coming to rest on her youthful face. "How old is she?" he asked, like everyone else.

"Fourteen, but we just got married so she's legal. She's got plenty of restaurant experience though, and she's a helluva worker, you can bet on that."

Vic looked at June lecherously. She looked away from the plum-faced man only to catch an even more lustful stare from his son, who had stopped washing dishes and was fixated on June's naked stomach — or perhaps a few inches below it.

"Have her here tomorrow morning, five-thirty," said Vic. "And get her a smock. I don't care what kind, just something that she can wait tables in."

And so, without one day's experience at *any* job, let alone waitressing, June walked into Vic's diner the following morning to add another new dimension to her life. Without any discussion at all, Ron had decided that June's schooling was no longer a priority and put her to work two days after she was married. "You've got to earn your share, ya know," he said. "This is a real break! Waitresses make big bucks on tips. We're gonna clean up!"

The next day at five-fifteen, Ron and his bride walked through the door of Vic's diner. Two men in dark business suits were having an animated debate in one booth. A truck driver was wolfing down ham and eggs in another. Ron took a seat at the counter while June reported to Vic. A few minutes later, she was across the counter from Ron, wearing an apron and hairnet and a scared smile. "Hi there, honey," he teased. "How about a cup of coffee?"

June looked as if the request had been made in a foreign language. She stared at her husband, rubbed her hands together, then quickly turned around, looking desperately for coffee and a cup to put it in. Somehow she managed to find the necessary accoutrements to fill her first order, but moments later Ron beckoned her over again. "Uh, waitress, you might want to check the cup," said Ron, pushing his coffee cup toward his wife.

"Oh my God!" June gasped.

"He's doing a pretty good backstroke, don't you think?" said Ron, referring to a large cockroach that was lying on its back, legs flailing wildly as it tried to survive in the hot brew. Its body extended nearly the entire diameter of the cup.

Ron looked at his wife who was now totally incapacitated. He could see that she needed a pep talk, and reminded her that she was smart, had a good memory, and that she would catch on fast. "Don't worry, this will be a breeze, he said." Nothing could have been further from the truth.

June got her first order wrong. The second one turned out wrong too: "Hey, girl, can't you hear? I said eggs over *easy* and crispy bacon. You gave me scrambled and *no* bacon. Jesus!" By six-thirty, June was in tears and vowed never return to the place. She had to be shown how to make coffee, how to write an order the cook could understand, how to refill cups without being asked. But by noon she was coping fairly well — except for the proximity to Vic's contemptuous son, who was either staring at June's rear end or screaming at the other waitresses.

Alfred washed the dishes wearing thick, black, rubber gloves. The steam from the scalding water enveloped him so that most of the day, one could see only the outline of a man within in a hot, steamy cloud. Apparently the work took its toll on his nerves.

"Around lunch time, when it started getting busy, one of the waitresses did something wrong and he yelled out so the whole restaurant could hear, 'You stupid bitch!' He was always grumbling, but that one was loud, and it was too much for Vic. He grabbed Alfred and shoved him against the wall. He said something I couldn't hear, and afterwards Alfred calmed down for a while."

By the end of her first week of work, June was doing so well that she was opening the restaurant. And she was making money for the first time in her life—more, in fact, than her thirty-eight-year-old husband who had found work as a finish carpenter at a tract housing development. But their combined incomes were not enough for him. He decided that June was young and energetic enough that after finishing her shift at two o'clock, she could come help him stain doors and install molding. She was smart. She could learn. And with her helping, he'd be able to take on more work and make more money. She was coming in *very* handy.

Draining as the routine was for June, she did not complain, and the two started to amass a respectable amount of money. With both of them working, they had been able to rent a comfortable one-bedroom apartment shortly after they got married. The odd appearance of a very young girl with a considerably older man had made it difficult to find an apartment to rent, but they eventually succeeded.

When they first got married, Ron had been living in a dingy, one bedroom apartment in Derry, a blue collar working town about twenty minutes north of Hudson. He slept on a bare mattress on the floor in his sleeping bag; the paint was chipping off the walls; there were no curtains on the windows; and he took showers in an old, stained claw-foot tub—the type with the shower curtain hanging from a ring around the top of the tub.

"I told him there was no way I was going to live in that place. So we started looking for an apartment as soon as we got back from the beach. No one would rent to us, though. We'd go up to the manager and he'd say something like, 'We really don't allow that here,' or 'We don't allow kids!' Ron would yell, 'This is my wife!' No one believed us. Finally someone agreed to rent to us, but it took a lot of doing."

After more than a year of working two jobs, getting little sleep, and putting up with late night sex sessions that often left her with no sleep at all, June finally called her sister, Diane, who had moved to California. She asked if it would be all right if she Ron and came out to the West Coast for a little vacation, "just to put my toe in the Pacific Ocean."

Diane said that would be fine, and two weeks later June quit the diner and the two headed out to California in Ron's new vehicle: a 1969 Chevy Malibu. "It was brown, and it was rusty like the other car, but it ran good. We almost crashed it the first day because Ron wanted oral sex while we were driving. When he climaxed, he lost control of the wheel; we never did that again.

"We camped the whole way. When we went through the southwest, I saw things I had never seen before: cactus, American Indians, Mexicans. We took in all the kooky sights, too, like buffalo farms, alligator wrestling, the world's biggest ball of yarn. It was all fascinating to me."

After passing through the Grand Canyon National Park, the couple made their way through the desert to Las Vegas. Ron had been talking about Vegas the entire trip, hoping to "strike it rich" on the craps tables. He had wanted to play roulette too, but read in a tourist brochure that roulette provided the worst odds of any game, and decided to focus all his attention on the craps tables.

Before making their way to the casinos, Ron and June stopped at another establishment Ron had seen advertised in the tourist pamphlet. "PASSPORT PHOTOS & IDs" read the heading. After a quick photo session, the proprietor sealed June's new identification in a laminating machine. June was suddenly twenty-one, and now able to gamble legally. Ron paid him twenty dollars, and they were off to the strip.

The Desert Inn was packed wall-to-wall with gamblers of every description, most of whom puffed frantically on cigarettes as if this was their last smoking day before quitting. A platinum-blonde woman of sixty in lime green Lycra tights overflowed a stool at the slots, playing three machines at once while smoking long, slim cigarettes and jabbering to the woman next to her, who was coiffed in the exact same hairdo.

A middle-aged black man with a paper bucket full of quarters sat bleary-eyed at "The Pirate Chest"—a highly addictive game that required the hooked gambler to continually drop in quarter after quarter in hopes of knocking over a tantalizing pile of quarters that had built up from previous gamblers, all of whom ran out of money before realizing the booty.

June entered the casino wearing an outfit Ron had bought for her on the outskirts of town: a blue crushed-velvet micro-mini dress that just covered her buttocks, and snake skin stiletto heels she could barely walk in. And that was all. "Underwear," he said, "adds unnecessary bulk."

He also insisted on thick eyeliner, heavy mascara, and blue eye shadow to match the dress. Other than her age and the fact that she did not have an expensive chinchilla stole draped over her shoulders, June looked no different from the hookers who slunk around the cocktail lounge and the baccarat table hoping to snag a rich gambler whose wife was home tending the kids.

"Ron planted me at the slots and left for the tables. It wasn't just that old men came leering around looking at my legs, it was that I was in the middle of hundreds of people and had no idea where my husband was. Then, as luck would have it, I hit a jackpot! Bells started ringing; lights were going off; I was having a ball! People were coming over to see what all the fuss was — and one of them was a security guard. The first thing he asked for was my ID. He knew right away it was fake, and said, 'Let's go talk to your husband.'

"When we finally found Ron, I said, 'This guard doesn't believe you're my husband.' Ron tried to be funny and said, 'I'm not. Who are you, anyway?' The guard didn't think it was funny. He said, 'You need to get her out of here.' Ron didn't argue. Plus, we had just won a hundred-dollar jackpot and he was ecstatic."

Ron and June got in the Chevy and decided that since it was still early, they would try for Diane's house. Diane lived in Monrovia, California, on the edge of the Angeles National Forest near the San Gabriel mountains. Within an hour they were in the middle of the Mohave Desert zooming west along Interstate 15. They stopped for a hamburger and shake in Barstow, and were just about to pull back on the interstate when Ron diverted and headed down an old two-lane highway that used to be the main thoroughfare before the freeway was constructed. The road still had some traffic, but at this hour it was light.

It was ten in the evening but the desert was still warm. Ron pulled to the side of the road and got out of the car. He bent down and felt the pavement. The black road had absorbed the sun's rays all day and it, too, was still warm to the touch. He returned to the car and looked at June with a big smile and said, "Let's do it. Take off your clothes."

"Yeah, right," said June sarcastically, thinking her husband wanted to take her into the woods but ready to give him several arguments against it, one being their promise to be at Diane's home by midnight.

"Ron came around to my side of the car and pulled my dress up to my waist. He was serious—he wanted it off. I sat there for a moment, but I knew it was no use: He wanted sex, and when Ron wanted sex, there was no stopping him. Seeing as how I wasn't wearing much, it didn't take long to get undressed.

"I looked around, thankful there weren't any cars driving by, and figured that if we had to do it, it would be pretty private in the woods. Only *getting* there from the car was going to be tricky. Then, when I'm all naked, he pulls me in front of the car. Not toward the woods, towards the center of the road! And he left the lights on, of course. It was the same Ron as always. He liked the lights on when he had sex, only now they were *high beams.*

"Ron was over six feet and built like a rock, so I never tried to resist when he wanted to do weird things with me; it was no use. But this time I tried to get away. He did lots of kinky things in the past, but this was going too far. A car could come any minute, which, it turns out, is just what he wanted.

"He turned on all his charm and said, 'Oh, come on, it'll be fun. Let's do it on the yellow line!' Oh my God, I thought to myself. He's crazy! I'm saying no, he's saying yes, and he's pulling me toward the middle of the road. Then a car comes by and slows down. I try to hide behind him but he jumps out of the way so I'm left standing completely naked in the middle of the road. I was so embarrassed. The strange thing is, here's a little nude girl struggling with a big, older guy, and no one even stops!

"Finally I give in, hoping no one else will come by and we can get it over with quickly. We don't though. Ron's all excited and loving it. Cars come by, slow down, some turn around and come by again. But no one stops. Meanwhile my back is getting all scraped up. There's pebbles and gravel in the road, and Ron's on top of me having sex. Finally he saw I was in a lot of pain and stopped."

When the pair got back in the car, Ron tried unsuccessfully to cheer June up. "See, no one cared," he said. But his wife did. And her back was bleeding and dirty. Pebbles had gouged her skin, and several spots on her buttocks and back were rubbed raw. Ron knew he had to do something, and drove to a motel where he tried to make amends. He called Diane to say they wouldn't be coming until morning, and then drew a bath for June.

"He was the nicest I had ever seen him. He knew I was hurt and embarrassed, so he turned on the charm—he was good at that. He went out to the car and got a board game I liked called Stratego, and we played it and he let me win. It was the kind of thing he would do when he went too far, and this was definitely too far."

Ron had taken notice of the prostitutes in Las Vegas. In fact, when he first left June to play the slots and headed for the crap tables, he caught the glance of two glamorous women in their early twenties sitting at the bar sipping daiquiris. He detoured toward them and ordered a beer. He seemed to be unable to find any spot to place his order other than between the two women, and took advantage of his close proximity to start up a conversation.

During his chat he learned that, as he suspected, they were "working girls." They offered him "a date" which he said he regretted he could not accept because he had recently gotten married. With that, they rolled their eyes and giggled and went back to their drinks.

But he was still intrigued by the pair, especially with their business and how much money they made. He discovered that not only did they make substantial sums, there was great competition among the prostitutes. One said she was mad at a prostitute named Joy because she had just bought a brand new champagne-colored Lincoln Continental, and hers was a two-year-old Cadillac Seville. When Ron delved further, he found that on a good night the women could "easily make a thousand bucks, maybe two if the guys aren't cheapskates." It was that money Ron now thought about as he sat on the motel bed playing Stratego with his pouting wife.

The following morning June refused to have sex for the first time in her marriage. Ron knew better than to push this time, and packed up the car for the trip to Monrovia. He had seen his wife step out of the motel shower with red abrasions all up and down her backside, and knew it was not going to be a pleasant ride to Diane's house. He was right. June was still angry about the escapade the night before and said nothing as she sat brooding and looking out the window.

When they pulled into Diane's driveway, she came running out to welcome the couple. It was 1978, and having been in California for some time now, Diane had been introduced to a wide array of drugs. Since her little sister was coming to visit, Diane thought it appropriate to celebrate by taking LSD first thing in the morning so she would be "tripping" by the time company arrived. Her "trip" was manifest mostly through uncontrollable laughter and endless hugging and crying.

Arm in arm, the two women walked back to the house chattering away like anxious squirrels. Diane gave June a tour of the modest tract home she was renting while Ron unloaded the car. After carrying the last load from car to house, Ron went back to the car and reached into the glove compartment to withdraw a small wooden box. Before buying the Chevy Malibu, he kept the box in the glove compartment of his work truck. For the drive to California, he moved it to this car. It was something he was never without, and that night after dinner he brought it out for entertainment.

"I knew Ron was weird about sex, but I never knew how *overall* weird he was until that night. At that point I still had only known him a little over a year, and didn't know all his peculiar traits. The night before I had learned about one of them, but this was something no one could have guessed in a million years.

"We were all sitting around the living room drinking and having a good time. Diane was coming down from her all-day acid trip but was still in a party mood. She was talking about drugs—cocaine, pot, speed; she became a real junkie after moving to California.

"Then Ron opens his box. Inside was a velvet bag, and inside that bag was another plastic bag with grey powder in it. 'Try it,' he says to Diane, knowing she would think it was some new drug. Immediately she wet her finger and stuck it in the powder and tasted it. Then Ron says, 'It's my brother' and starts to laugh. We had no idea what he was talking about. 'It's my brother's ashes. I keep 'em with me,' he said.

"Knowing how strange Ron was, I believed him right away. And it turned out to be true. He told us the story of how his brother, Jeff, was beaten to death by lobster fishermen in Maine when he was caught stealing their traps. That's one thing you don't do — mess with lobstermen's traps. He said the family had Jeff cremated and gave all the members some of the ashes to keep. And he got Diane to *taste* them! Now I was mad all over again."

After visiting for a few days, Ron started getting anxious. He had come out to California to go to the beach, and all he was seeing was desert and cacti. He wanted to head towards the Pacific—about an hour's drive across Los Angeles if the traffic was good. Ron repacked the car and everyone said their goodbyes. He then pulled the Chevy Malibu onto Interstate 605, picked up Interstate 10 in El Monte heading west, then turned south onto Interstate 710 near east Los Angeles, en route for Long Beach.

When he got to the coast, he pulled into the beach parking lot, eager to view the expansive blue Pacific. Instead, the first view he had was of a young woman with long, silky blonde hair to her waist whizzing by on roller blades. She was wearing two clam shells strung together for a top, and a thong bikini that exposed her entire firm, bronzed buttocks. June looked at her husband and said, "I suppose you want me to do that too. Well sorry, I can't skate."

"You can learn," he said with a smile, opening the car door and stretching.

June took off her shoes and walked with Ron along the wide, cement boardwalk. It was Saturday, and the area was jammed with skaters, bicyclists, joggers, mothers with baby strollers, old men sitting on benches drooling over the scantily clad body worshipers. June jumped off the walkway down to the sand and ran for the water; Ron followed. When they reached the waves, June did what she promised to do:

stick her toe in the water. Then her foot. Then she rolled up her pants and waded in to her knees.

Standing there looking out at the water, she noticed something odd: islands. Beautiful little tropical islands with waterfalls and mirror-glazed buildings that looked like luxury apartments of some kind. She turned to show Ron, but he was already gazing at the extravagant complexes. When a passerby came near, Ron stopped him and asked if he knew how to rent one of the apartments, but the man just smiled and continued on down the beach.

June and Ron sat down on the sand and started fantasizing about how, if they could find work and make enough money, they'd be able to move to California and rent one of the luxury apartments and "live life to the hilt." June could help her husband with his carpentry and they could work as they had in New Hampshire — as a team. They agreed to start looking for work that afternoon.

On the way from the beach to the car, they stopped another beachcomber and again asked about the island apartments. This time they got an answer — one they weren't looking for: the "apartments" were actually oil rigs camouflaged to look like buildings. A group of disgruntled home owners had brought a lawsuit against the city, claiming the unsightly derricks diminished the value of their beachfront property. As a result, the oil companies agreed to hide the machinery by putting up facades, replete with cascading waterfalls and palm trees.

Even though the glass walls and foliage were as much a fantasy as Ron's dream of becoming rich, the couple was not deterred. Ron loved the Southern California climate, and wanted to live there. June had her sister nearby and nothing calling her back to New Hampshire. Within two days Ron secured work at a large housing project. He would have June as a helper again, and figured that with two of them working ten-hour days, they'd make out fine.

With job secured, Ron flew back to New Hampshire, packed up the apartment in a rented U-Haul truck, and a week later he and June were in a new apartment in Long Beach, a few miles from the worksite. The first day on the job, dark clouds split open and released a thunderous downpour that turned the worksite into a massive mud field. It was warm and June thought it best to put on her overall shorts since the mud was knee high in spots and she would be wading through it, carrying five-gallon buckets of tools and supplies to wherever Ron needed them.

Being the only female on a site filled with hundreds of men, fourteen-year-old June attracted some attention. She unwittingly brought on more attention when, to avoid getting mud all over clothes, she rolled up her shorts as far as they would go, and tromped through the mud wearing big, black rubber boots five sizes too big for her. The workers took notice.

"With fifty houses under construction, the developer needed a large crew, and employed a high percentage of illegal aliens from Mexico. When I'd walk by a group of them, they'd cat-call or whistle and sometimes throw money down and laugh. Once I went to a house to deliver some tools to Ron and he wasn't there. When I turned around, two guys were behind me, blocking the door. And they weren't smiling, they were serious. One came over to me and starting touching my hair. I pulled away and right then Ron walked in. They left in a hurry, but the incident had given Ron ideas."

On a Friday night after working at the development, Ron and June cleaned up and went to dinner at their favorite restaurant, Jack in the Box. Because June couldn't cook and the fast-food restaurant was only two blocks away, they dined there several times a week. After eating, they went to a local bar frequented by other members of the development crew as well as truckers heading up the coast to San Francisco. June had been there once before with Ron but had formed no real opinion of the place other than it contained mostly men and very few women. Ron had noticed this too.

"Ron said he couldn't stop thinking about the prostitutes in Las Vegas and how rich they were. He said we could make a ton of money if I'd 'sleep with a few guys.' I had wondered why he made me put on a mini skirt and tube top and lots of makeup before we left, and now I knew. I also knew why he used to make me stand naked in the mirror and touch myself: he was trying to desensitize me and get me over my shyness so he could move me toward prostitution. It had always been his long-term plan.

"In the bar he would point out some guy and tell me to go over and ask him if he wanted a date. At this point in our relationship, nothing Ron did shocked me anymore. I told him I didn't want to do it, and he said, 'Just go try it.' So I'd go over and fake it. I'd say something about the bar or pretend that I felt sick, and wouldn't ask them if they wanted date. Then I'd go back to Ron and say they weren't interested and he'd be all disappointed. He made me do it all night and I kept faking it until he finally gave up."

It didn't take long for the couple to tire of their daily routine: labor ten or more hours a day; return to their apartment to clean up; go for dinner at Jack in the Box; then go to the bars and try to make money playing pool until one in the morning. They adopted a stray dog that added a bit of joy to their lives, but after eighteen months of living under these conditions, the marriage started to flag. They were not getting rich as Ron had expected, and June was not about to prostitute herself to reverse the trend. Consequently, Ron became more and more frustrated, and finally decided California was not the paradise he thought it would be.

The couple had been married less than three years when June called her grandmother, saying they were coming back home. They packed up the car, and returned to New Hampshire. On the way there, June discovered she was pregnant. Upon arriving back in Hudson, June and Ron moved in with the Jacksons, but said nothing about the pregnancy.

Harold was not happy about the arrangement, but Mary— though not saying much about it—secretly was delighted to have Ron back in the house. He was a charmer, and she had fallen for his feigned affection for her the first time she met him. Now she had an opportunity to bake more pies — one of her few joys in life.

The same day they returned, June got a job at Scotties shoe factory down the street, gluing insoles into baby shoes; her job would start the following week. Ron was equally fortunate that day, securing part-time work with a local contractor; his employment would begin the next day at noon.

In the morning, before starting work, Ron took June to an abortion clinic they had called from the road while traveling. Ron sat in the waiting room while June underwent the procedure, after which he drove her home, and then left for work. That evening while June was recuperating from the operation, Ron insisted on having sex with his still-bleeding wife. June was shocked by the idea, and said, "No, Ron, we can't do anything like that yet; not until the doctor says it's okay."

But Ron could not be stopped. He climbed into bed and forced himself into June—an act which, five days later, resulted in a massive pelvic infection that sent her back to the clinic from which she had just come, this time burning up with fever. After the physicians irrigated June's uterus with a saline solution and injected her with double doses of antibiotics, Ron drove his pale and weakened wife back to the Jacksons home and put her to bed. It was only a week after they had returned from California, and now, after tucking June into bed, he handed her one of her stuffed bears, took a step back, and announced, "We need to get a divorce."

"I wasn't sure I heard him right. I know we hadn't been having much of a marriage for some time, but he never made any indication that he wanted to end it. I had no idea; it came out of the blue."

With that, Ron went downstairs to the basement and started sorting out their belongings. He was not upset or bitter, and to the contrary, was quite nice to June, telling her she could come downstairs when she felt up to it and see if he had separated things correctly. Only he didn't give her the chance to act on the offer: After spending nearly three hours in the basement, June heard his car start up and pull away. She got out of bed and went downstairs to an empty basement.

"Everything was gone. He took my clothes, my dolls, my books. Everything. He even took the dog. The next day I called the bank and found that my six thousand dollar life savings was gone too. It turns out Grandpa was right. That's really what Ron was after the whole time. He used me for sex; he used me for labor—and *child* labor, at that; then he used me for my money. In the end, I finally understood what he meant when he said on our wedding day, 'You know this is only a temporary thing.'"

To make himself look better in Mary Jackson's eyes, and provide an excuse for abandoning his wife, Ron told June's grandmother about the abortion, knowing what her reaction would be. He said that he was the one who had saved June; who "got her off the streets" and "gave her a decent life." But the abortion. Well, that was the reason he had to leave. He didn't *approve* of such things. He said June insisted on it and that he tried to dissuade her from going through with it, but she just wouldn't listen.

Ron Jensen was a con man, and his strategy worked: Mary was not angry with him for leaving, and bought his story completely. But June caught her wrath. Mary immediately laced into her when she came up from the basement. She was already stunned by what had just happened, and now had to face her grandmother, who paid no heed to June's physical or mental condition.

She started in: "You'll never be forgiven for this! You're *marked* now! You're going to *hell* for what you did! God doesn't forgive people who *kill babies!*"

June retreated to her room and slammed the door. She threw herself face down on the bed and buried her head in her pillow. "'Now what do I do?' I thought to myself. 'Go back to school? Go out and get a job? Which rules do I follow? Adult rules? Kids' rules?' I had no idea."

After contemplating and crying for an hour, June got up, walked to the kitchen, and picked up the phone to call someone she hadn't talked to in a long time. It was the one person in the world she desperately needed at that moment: her mother.

"When I called my mother, she said she was just on her way out, that she was going to the Canadian Club for a drink—a real low-life bar in the toughest section of Nashua. If I wanted to go, she'd come by and pick me up and we could talk. I was surprised she had invited me, and even though I wasn't feeling very well, I immediately said yes.

"I watched anxiously out the front window until she pulled up. I remember her stepping out of a beat-up old Thunderbird one of her boyfriends had given her. She was wearing her tight leopard pants, ruby red lipstick, and these awful, fake eyelashes. When we got to the Canadian Club, she introduced me around and bought me drinks and we talked — mostly about her problems. That's the way it always was. Nothing had changed. We'd talk about me for a few minutes, and things would quickly turn to how lonely she was and what a terrible life she was leading; that sort of thing.

"After a while, I noticed this huge biker guy standing in the corner drinking a beer. It was dark in there, and all I could see was this figure in the background. He was big, about five-foot-ten and two-hundred-sixty-five pounds. He had long hair that he wore tucked into a black bandanna. I found out later that he was the town tough guy, and was known for punching you out if you looked at him wrong or happened to bump into him by accident. His name was Jimmy Briand."

PART II: THE ABUSIVE MARRIAGE

June fell from her sexually abusive first husband directly into the arms of the pathologically violent man who would become her second husband. On the very day Ron Jensen left her, June's courtship with Jimmy Briand began.

It was July 1980. June was now seventeen and Jimmy was twenty-four. Taking a long pull on his beer, Jimmy wiped his mouth with the back of his hand and stepped out of the shadows to take a closer look at the youthful newcomer with the long dark hair, sitting peaceably with a woman he had seen many times but never paid much attention to. It was usually older women who sat nursing their gin and tonics alone in the dark, pretending they weren't interested in socializing but secretly praying a man would come talk to them.

Though teenagers could easily slip into the seedy bar without being questioned, the Canadian Club wasn't the kind of place youngsters would elect to frequent. It was located in the midst of a shabby residential district, where rusting car parts and garbage littered front yards and sidewalks. The area was zoned "mixed use," which allowed commercial buildings to be peppered in with the low-income duplexes.

One such building housed the bar, which was located in the basement of a small factory of some kind. Once downstairs, the long bank of windows near the ceiling were at street level, and afforded bar patrons a first-rate view of the lower half of people's legs, car tires, and the faces of curious dogs that came sniffing around them. Drinks here were a dollar, and generic draught beers were seventy-five cents. Jimmy Briand had just started on his fourth beer when he noticed the attractive young lady sitting with her mother.

Other men had noticed the twosome as well, but they also noticed Jimmy's interest in them, and knew it was best to see where it led before making a move toward the women's table. The regulars had seen many displays of Jimmy's wrath, which he often unleashed onto whomever was unlucky enough to be nearby. Once such incident had occurred at the bar only two weeks earlier.

The patron made the mistake of sitting next to Jimmy who, having been drinking for two days straight, was in a worse mood than usual. The hapless man had tipped his beer high, quaffing down the last few drops, then slammed the mug down on the countertop with a loud smack that resounded along the varnished pine slab. Jimmy was in no mood for loud noises, and instantly wheeled around and grabbed the startled man by the throat. Without a word, he squeezed relentlessly with his two powerful hands until the man turned blue, went limp, and dropped to the floor.

Today, however, Jimmy was in a better mood — made better yet by his proximity to the juvenile before him. Downing the rest of his beer in three huge gulps, Jimmy approached Ann and asked for an introduction. An hour later, he was thoroughly inebriated, celebrating his success at procuring June's phone number — with her mother's blessing. After Jimmy scribbled down the number and went back to the bar, Ann Jackson complained, "Well, that's the kind of guy *I'd* like to meet but never do. You sure got lucky."

"Oh, cheer up, Mother," June said. "You'll meet somebody too. Just wait." And June was right. When she and her mother left the bar, they were no longer a duo: Ann had a drunken construction worker in tow, and bid a hasty farewell to her daughter at the bus stop, saying she had to "get the poor fellow home and put to bed" and "would it be too much trouble if you took the bus this time, sweetie?"

Having just had an abortion and losing her husband, June smiled and said that would be fine.

Jimmy Briand's stepmother would later say that "when Jimmy was young, yes, he did get into some scrapes like a lot of teenagers do, but he grew out of it." Nothing could have been further from the truth. Not only were the "scrapes" severe enough to land him in jail numerous time, he never "grew out of it" and instead, got more rebellious as the years went on.

Jimmy Briand was known in the community as an incorrigible, uneducated brute who was constantly in trouble with the law. Court records outline a history of violence that went way beyond his regular Friday night barroom brawls: When he was eighteen, Jimmy was charged with disorderly conduct and felony theft. He had a penchant for stealing car parts — and whenever possible, the car itself. At nineteen, he was charged with criminal mischief, disorderly conduct, public intoxication, resisting arrest, and a litany of other misdemeanors and complaints, totaling seventeen in all. Two years later, on one September day in 1977, Jimmy outdid himself. Being in a particularly foul mood that day, he racked up a dozen charges in less than three hours, ranging from criminal mischief to assault to criminal threat against a police officer.

During the threat incident, one of Jimmy's intoxicated cousins had flipped his middle finger at a policeman who happened to be driving by. The officer stopped and eventually arrested the belligerent man. Court records show that when Officer Sal Bernstein was restraining the subject, Jimmy arrived on the scene and pulled a Buck knife from his boot and screamed at the officer, "Release my fucking cousin or I'll knife you, you cocksucker." When backup officers arrived, they ordered Jimmy to drop the knife but instead, he waved the weapon and challenged an officer who had drawn his gun and leveled it at Jimmy's chest. "Shoot, you fucker," said Jimmy, "because I'll kill you too."

Then the standoff began. Jimmy and the officer stood with their weapons poised at each other for over two hours. Finally, when Jimmy was distracted, one of the policemen overpowered him and took him into custody. While in the courthouse awaiting the hearing, police handcuffed the incensed Briand to the steel cell crossbars, and gladly responded to Jimmy's taunts by tightening the cuffs a notch every time they went by. When he finally appeared before the judge, his hands were so black from lack of circulation that the judge halted the proceeding and sent him to the hospital. Upon his return to court, Jimmy was sentenced to several months in the New Hampshire State Prison.

When he arrived at the prison, officers brought Jimmy into R&D (Receiving and Discipline). While in his cell awaiting processing, he put his face up to the bars to take a look at his new surroundings. Another inmate — and member of the dominant prison gang, Satan's Sons — spotted Jimmy, whom he knew to be a member of a rival motorcycle gang. The inmate had recently broken his arm, and without warning, slammed his cast against the bars, splitting Jimmy's nose open. Jimmy would not forget the incident, and a month later retaliated by fracturing the perpetrator's skull with a twenty-pound free weight while he was working out. Such was the life of Jimmy Briand.

Jimmy was known to police, neighbors, family, and co-workers as a violent man with an unpredictable temper. He was also known as a madman who liked to speed around town, drunk out of his mind on his Triumph motorcycle — so drunk that one afternoon shortly after his release from prison, when he was feeling particularly invincible, he zoomed down a dead end street at eighty miles per hour, then ran out of street. In a failed attempt to avoid crashing into the house at the end of the cul-de-sac, he jammed on the brakes, flipped the bike three times end over end, and put the steel foot peg through his right cheek. After the accident, he grew a beard to hide the long, jagged scar, but he continued to ride totally intoxicated as often as possible.

Jimmy was well on his way to becoming the alcoholic he was by age twelve. He developed his drinking habit at family cookouts, which were held every weekend throughout the summer. By thirteen, he quit school and left home, partly because he hated his stepmother, Leslie, and partly because he feared his stepfather, Randolph Norton.

Once, when ten-year-old Jimmy got into a fight with his cousin, Randolph walked over and grabbed the two boys by the scruff of their necks — not to stop the fight, but to *continue* it. He said to Jimmy, "You better keep fightin', and you better *win*, cause whoever loses is gonna have to fight *me!*" After forty-five minutes of the boys beating each other bloody, Randolph finally stepped in to stop it.

As Jimmy grew up, he was verbally and physically abused by his hard-drinking stepfather but still had a deep, abiding love for the man and desperately needed his approval. As for his stepmother, Leslie, he felt she was responsible for ruining his childhood because she was the one who broke up the family. (Jimmy's biological father, Wayne Briand, left when Jimmy was an infant, and his mother, Carol, remarried Randolph Norton. She would eventually be replaced by Leslie.)

Jimmy knew Leslie was the culprit because of what he witnessed one summer day shortly after the fight with his cousin. He had ridden his bicycle to Robinson Pond (where June's sexual attack would later occur), and was peddling along a dirt access road when he was delighted to see his stepfather's car parked off to the side of the road.

He peddled over and jumped from his bike and put his face to the windshield, but it was steamed up and hard to see through. He then went around to the rear door window and caught sight of two figures lying naked on the back seat of the car. He wasn't sure if one was his stepfather until the window rolled down a crack and a man covering himself with his trousers sheepishly said hello. It was, indeed, Randolph, and he had beneath him a woman who was not his wife.

It was around this time that Randolph and Carol grew further apart. She began drinking heavily — apparently because she had learned that her husband was cheating on her — and what were once cantankerous verbal battles gave way to protracted physical contests that found Carol clawing her husband's face in a rage, and him responding by pinning her to the ground in headlocks until she calmed down.

Randolph eventually divorced Carol and married his backseat mistress, Leslie, but their tryst at Robinson Pond had taken its toll on young Jimmy. From then on he would say that "women can't be trusted" and "they're no damn good." If anyone ever questioned his wisdom, he simply related the Robinson Pond story, saying "a whore" had kicked his mother out of the house.

Two years later, he dropped out of eighth grade and left home, still embittered by the fact that his stepfather had "left Mom for a slut." Thereafter, Jimmy blamed women for all the ills of the world, and every problem he personally encountered in life. He would, for years to come, vent his rage on anyone and anything that caused him to remember his painful childhood.

After leaving home, Jimmy wandered from cousin to cousin, friend to friend, sometimes living on the streets, sometimes returning home for a long weekend, especially when one of his beloved cookouts was planned — cookouts that really were excuses to get together, get drunk, and beat one another.

When Leslie married Randolph, the Norton extended family grew to a huge mix of aunts, uncles, nieces, and nephews who brought the entire clan to some thirty-plus relatives ranging in age from ten to sixty, most of whom were just as dysfunctional and alcoholic as Randolph. Jimmy often proved that point by rolling up his pant legs to display the spot on his ankle where a bullet from his cousin's .22 rifle still lay lodged.

Early Saturday morning the phone rang. It was the day after June had met Jimmy at the Canadian Club, and he was hungover from the previous night's drinking binge. But he hadn't lost her phone number, and insisted he was well enough to come over and take June for a ride to the beach.

"I jumped at the chance to go out with him. Yes, I was upset about Ron leaving, but I was also excited by Jimmy. He was big and strong and I knew he was the kind of guy who would protect me. I felt safe with him, and I was flattered by his interest in me."

Jimmy arrived at the Jackson house about ten-thirty in the morning with bloodshot eyes and breath reeking of stale beer. June had been waiting by the window for him, and to avoid laboring through a long explanation to her grandmother, bolted from the house as soon as he pulled up. She jumped in the car and slid across the seat next to her date. He asked her which beach she wanted to go to, and she immediately said, "Hampton Beach — where I had my honeymoon."

"By the time we got to the beach, we were already holding hands and kissing; we fell for each other right away. Jimmy said I was the best thing that happened to him in a long time. I loved hearing that. Ron never said anything like that.

"When we passed the motel where Ron and I had stayed, I pointed it out to Jimmy. He immediately did a U-turn and pulled into the parking lot. We got a room and made love. He was nothing like Ron. He was slow and gentle with me. And he kissed me, which Ron never did. I tried to impress him with sex because I wanted him to like me. And he did. He said I was wonderful and that I pleased him so much."

From that day on, June and Jimmy were rarely apart. They saw each other nearly every day. Jimmy was living in his aunt's house in Nashua, and he would sneak June into his room without her knowing it. She was often lying on the couch asleep or half-watching a television show when Jimmy snuck his new girlfriend up to his room.

"There'd be boxes and debris everywhere in the old house. I'd be laughing and holding my hand over my mouth to keep from making noise as we climbed the stairs trying not to trip over everything and wake her up."

Equally oblivious to the couple's courtship were the Jacksons, who seemed not to notice their granddaughter run in to take a shower every morning after staying all night with Jimmy, then run out to get to work on time at the shoe factory. When June ended her shift at four o'clock, Jimmy would be waiting in his car at the front gate. Then they would drive over to the Canadian Club to drink beer, eat peanuts, and play pool all night.

On one occasion Jimmy asked June if she'd like to "take a trip," and offered her a dose of LSD. Knowing that her sister never seemed to have any ill effects from the drug, June thought nothing of it and swallowed the tiny white pill with a swig of beer. An hour later she was laughing hysterically and having difficulty making pool shots. "The table kept getting smaller, then larger. It would bow out in the middle, then get skinny like an hour glass. I couldn't hit the ball at all. I thought it was so funny.

"Later on I started hallucinating at everything. The bartender, who was bald, looked like a Martian; Jimmy looked like a gorilla with his beard and long hair. And the noise — it sounded like thousands of people were in a stadium yelling and screaming. I was having the time of my life."

The trip was such fun that the following week June went to work with two more "magic pills" supplied by Jimmy, who suggested she take them "to make the day go by faster." They did, and they also cost June her job. "My co-worker and I took the pills after lunch and pretty soon we were laughing like crazy. We laughed at nothing all day, and when the manager came over he said, 'I don't know what's wrong with you two, but when you leave today, don't come back.'"

Jimmy did not take kindly to the news that his girlfriend had been fired. For past two months, June had been giving him her paychecks "so he'd like me," and now that she was unemployed, his source of additional income dried up. Now, he was forced to rely on his own meager income, which he earned from his new job at Triangle Pacific where he stacked wooden pallets and butted heads with anyone who got in his way. He had been working as a cabinet maker previously, but was fired after assaulting a co-worker.

Shortly after he started working for Triangle Pacific, Jimmy walked down the street during a lunch break one day and inquired at the Teledyne Company about work for June. The personnel manager said they had an opening, but only for someone experienced in microscopic wire soldering. Jimmy said he could produce such a person, and the next day led June to the manager's office, whereupon she lied herself into the highly technical position.

Fortunately, June was bright enough to learn the skills she needed while on the job, and soon became adept at soldering tiny electrical wires through a high-powered microscope. It was tedious, eye-straining work done sitting on a tall stool all day, but June was grateful for the job and liked the responsibility that came with it.

With both Jimmy and June now working, and their three-month affair becoming more serious, the couple decided to move in together. In October of 1980, they pooled their money to rent a tiny apartment on Kinsley Street in Nashua. At first the manager balked, as others had when Ron tried to rent apartments with his fourteen-year-old bride. Now, at seventeen, June still looked too young to be living with anyone but her parents, but after verifying the couple's employment, the landlord rented them the apartment.

For the second time, and with a heart full of hope, June moved out of her grandparents' house and into another relationship. Though Harold Jackson again had reservations, the idea that this relationship would also end in failure never entered June's mind. The notion that it would be not just a failure, but an unmitigated disaster with the most tragic of consequences, was something no one could have anticipated.

The dilapidated Victorian on Kinsley Street had one vacancy: a small, three-room apartment consisting of a kitchen, bathroom, and an eight-by-eight living room, which was located in the turret portion of the home. The living room was so small that the second-hand sleeper sofa Jimmy bought spanned the diameter of the round room, leaving just enough space in front for a television, and space behind for a coat rack and a few storage boxes. But it was a home of their own, and June was once again happy to be involved with a man — this time one "who truly loved me."

Two weeks after the couple moved into the apartment, Jimmy received a phone call from a woman named Cheryl, with whom he had been living for the past three years. Eight months before meeting June, Jimmy and Cheryl had split, with Jimmy retreating to his aunt's house and Cheryl retaining the apartment with their daughter, Jana, who was now eighteen months old.

June answered the phone. Instead of saying hello, the woman on the line said only, "I want to talk to Jimmy." June handed him the receiver. He listened without responding for twenty or thirty seconds, then said, "Okay" and hung up. He told June he had somewhere to go right away, and that he would be back as soon as he could.

After their split, Jimmy called Cheryl asking to see his daughter, but she would not allow it. Subsequently, the couple became distant, with no contact whatsoever between them. Now, for no apparent reason, Cheryl had called offering Jimmy a chance to visit with Jana. The meeting was to take place in the parking lot of a nearby A&W Root beer restaurant. Cheryl said she would be there in thirty minutes; Jimmy arrived in twenty. Nervously puffing on a cigarette, he waited at the assigned spot, watching his rear view mirror for signs of his former girlfriend. She didn't appear. Thirty minutes came and went. Forty minutes. Fifty minutes. Then a car pulled up next to him; it was Cheryl.

Without looking over at Jimmy, Cheryl opened her door and walked around the rear of her car to the back door. She opened it, unbuckled Jana and pulled her from her car seat. Holding the girl, she reached back into the car and produced a diaper bag and a grocery bag stuffed with the baby's clothing. She sat the girl on the ground, threw the bags down beside her, turned to Jimmy and said, "You want her, you take her," and drove off.

Apparently the woman had grown weary of raising her child, so when she heard that Jimmy now had a live-in girlfriend, she saw the perfect opportunity to rid herself of her burden.

Not knowing what else to do, Jimmy scooped up the girl and her belongings and brought her home to June. "When Jimmy walked through the door, all I could see was this little bundle wrapped up in an raccoon coat. I ran over and parted the fur to see a baby. A baby! I couldn't believe it. It was like the greatest present in the world. Where did she come from? Whose was she? I had no idea, but I grabbed her and held her. By the second day, I was in love with her. By the fourth day, she was calling me Mama."

Adding Jana to the equation brought June everything she had always wanted. Finally she was becoming part of a family, a real family with a man who, unlike her first husband, loved and genuinely cared for her. And on top of that, a baby! It didn't matter that she and Jimmy were not married. She was happier now than she had ever been. She had a job, a mate, an apartment — and now a child she could raise as her own. Things were looking up after all. And she was falling more and more in love with a man who seemed like a dream come true.

Then everything changed. June witnessed the first exhibition of Jimmy's hair-trigger temper late one night after everyone had gone to bed. Jana was thumping the side of her crib with her foot and cooing softly to herself. The prior week she had been mumbling to herself a great deal, and June surmised it was because Cheryl often left the child alone for long periods of time. She also had a hard time falling asleep before midnight because Cheryl kept late hours and kept the child up with her.

"All of a sudden, about one in the morning, Jimmy jumps out of bed and grabs Jana out of her crib. It startled her and she started to cry. That made Jimmy really mad and he started screaming, 'Make her stop crying! Make her stop, goddamn it!' But she wouldn't stop, and he started going crazy, yelling and screaming more. That made her cry even worse. Then he opened the window and hung her out of our second-story window by her ankles.

"He kept screaming, 'Make her stop or I'll drop her! I mean it! She better fucking stop, goddamn it!' I jumped out of bed and tried to wedge myself in between him and the window, but I couldn't get to her because he was in the way. He kept screaming like a madman and threatening to drop her, but somehow I got in between him and the window and pulled her inside."

June took the wailing infant back to bed and tried to soothe her by talking and rocking her back and forth. Jimmy got dressed and left, and didn't return for three days. It was then that June had her first thoughts of leaving what appeared to be a completely insane lunatic. But several problems immediately came to mind: "Where would I go and what would I do with a child who was not mine? How would I care for her? If I left her with Jimmy, what would happen to her the next time he had a fit and I wasn't there to intervene?"

June pondered her options briefly, then fell back on her earlier training. "My grandparents taught me to ignore problems and accept craziness, pretend everything was okay. Uncle Charley could rant and rave at the dinner table, and we were told to go on eating our dinner like nothing was happening. Here was another Uncle Charley, and here I was responding the same way."

The following weekend, Jimmy told June to make arrangements for a baby sitter, that they were going to the Blue Dolphin on Friday night to meet some people and play pool. June called her grandmother and dropped off Jana around eight o'clock. Jimmy was in a bad mood because he had to drive across town in the opposite direction from where he wanted to go, and reasoned that it was all Cheryl's fault.

When they arrived at the bar, Jimmy ordered two beers for himself and a Tequila Sunrise for June. Being a Friday night, the place was crowded, and by ten o'clock, it was packed. It was the type of bar where everyone knew everyone else. Jimmy's friends had not yet arrived, but his cousin Tom had, and they drank at the bar for a while before Tom headed over to the pool tables.

June had heard about Jimmy's terrible reputation for bar brawling, and after the window incident, knew how out of control he could get. But she had never witnessed the full force of his fury until this night.

June was coming back from the bathroom, and was making her way towards the bar to be with Jimmy. He had told her going in to stay near him and "not get too friendly with anyone." If he was jealous, she had not yet seen it; but the comment led her to believe that he was. As June walked toward Jimmy, a bar patron accidentally bumped into her, causing her to trip slightly but not fall. Jimmy saw the collision and instantly leapt at the man like a panther.

Within two seconds, Jimmy had the man on his back on the floor, and was on top of him pounding his face with all his might. First one fist, then a crossing blow with the other, then back again with the other. Back and forth, right, left, right, left. The man was unable to defend himself because Jimmy had straddled his chest and pinned his arms to his sides. Consequently, with each blow, the man's head flew from one side to the other as Jimmy held him immobile with his great weight.

"Stop it, Jimmy!" screamed June. "Stop it! He apologized! I'm fine!" June was leaning into him, yelling close to ears that were deaf to reason. He was too intent on the job before him to hear anything — anything except the knife that came sliding across the barroom floor.

Jimmy's cousin, Tom, heard the commotion and came running to see Jimmy embroiled in a fight; that's all he needed to see. It didn't matter who was right or who was wrong, when a member of the Briand-Norton clan was in a fight, the family backed him. This time the backing came by way of the steel blade Tom carried on his belt.

"Jimmy!" yelled Tom. Recognizing the voice, Jimmy looked up to see Tom's hunting knife spinning towards him like a helicopter rotor. He scooped it up and held it in front of his victim's glazed eyes. Up until then, the man had not uttered a word; he'd only taken punishment. Now he had just enough consciousness — and sense — to finally speak up. "I'm sorry," he managed to spit out with a mouthful of blood. "Sorry, man, sorry." Jimmy accepted the apology and ended his barrage of blows.

On the way home, Jimmy was still in a contentious mood. By now he had consumed five or six beers, and was not happy about driving back to the Jackson's to pick up Jana. This brought back thoughts of ex-girlfriend Cheryl. "Jimmy was still mad from the bar fight, and he started in about Cheryl. I saw another new side of him that I didn't know existed. And for the first time I learned what he was capable of.

"He started rambling about the time he got drunk just after he had split with Cheryl. He drove over to her apartment with his hunting rifle and sat in the bushes for hours with her in his scope sight. He said that before Cheryl finally threw him out, she filed charges of assault and battery against him, and he went to jail for it.

"Then he told me about the time they were at a cookout and she did something he didn't like. He said, 'I hit her with one punch and knocked her out cold on the picnic table.' He sounded *proud* of it. He said she landed face first on the table and was bleeding, but he didn't think anything of it. 'She got mouthy,' he said. 'I had to teach her a lesson. Then I had to drag the bitch all the way back to the house.'"

"I shuddered when he told the story. But I reasoned that these were isolated incidents where everyone was drunk and out of control. Nothing could have been further from the truth."

When Jana first arrived, June took time off from work to get organized and spend time with the baby. Now she had to get back to her job at Teledyne, and needed a full time babysitter. She looked in the classified ads and called the first name she came to. It was an older woman, a grandmother, who earned her modest living taking in infants and small children for working mothers. June was thankful that she had room for one more child, and made arrangements to drop Jana off in the morning and pick her up after she finished work at three-thirty. Since Jimmy didn't end his shift until four, June would usually drive home with a friend from work and pick up Jana on the way. This saved a couple of dollars in babysitting expenses, and gave June half an hour to tidy the apartment before Jimmy came home.

The arrangement seemed to be working fine, and everyone was quite happy — especially Jana, who was getting much-needed attention from her babysitter and heartfelt love from her surrogate mother. June finally felt settled, and once again, her dreams of a united family were becoming a reality. And again, two weeks later, they were disrupted.

"Jimmy came home upset about something that happened at work. I heard his car pull up, and went to meet him at the door as I always did. When I opened it and said 'Hi,' he shoved me out of the way. He was really mad and screamed, 'I don't need some bitch at work telling me what to do! I know what I'm doing! Women should stay home and raise babies!'

"I didn't know what he was talking about or where his tirade was coming from. What I *did* know was that he shoved me, and he had never been rough with me before. I'd seen him slug other people but he was never violent toward me — until then."

After Jimmy drank a couple of beers and calmed down, June asked him what happened. He explained that his boss — a woman — had criticized something he had did and told him that she wanted it done differently in the future. "That was all he had to hear. It was bad enough that he didn't respect women and was angry about his broken family and stepmother — who he often referred to as 'the slut' — but to be *corrected* by a woman? That was too much for him."

But June accepted Jimmy's explanation, and to some degree, it eased her anxiety. She knew his view of women was less than healthy, and reasoned that his shove was only an overreaction to a situation he did not know how to handle; she quickly dismissed it as an aberration.

The next day June saw she was wrong. If there was an aberration, it was Jimmy's calm periods. She had not lived with him long enough to know that his *normal* state was one of almost constant agitation, and his *abnormal* state was the calm one she had been witnessing during their short time together. She had convinced herself that the horrible window incident with Jana was due to Jimmy's suddenly having a crying infant around the house. And she forgave his shove, believing it was brought about by the stress of his new work situation. When he came home the following evening, however, June's views started to change.

"Jimmy was still moody about being told what to do by a woman. He just couldn't stand it; it was eating him up. When he came home the next night, I was in the bathroom, so I didn't go to meet him at the front door; maybe subconsciously I didn't want to.

"It didn't matter; we got into it again when he wanted to go into the bathroom just as I was coming out. I looked up and said 'Hi,' and he shoved me again, this time against the wall. He said, 'Get out of the way!' It was like a replay of the night before."

Once the taboo against physically accosting his mate had been broken, Jimmy's behavior toward June would never be the same. It was as if a small break had opened in a levee, and as time went on, the crack would continue to enlarge. Before long, Jimmy was shoving and pushing June whenever something disturbed him. She was the most convenient object on which to vent his rage, and he took full advantage of her quiet acceptance of his treatment. June's acquiescence only served to encourage his maltreatment, and soon it worsened.

"Jimmy was concerned about looking good to other people. His big issue was measuring up. A lot of his insecurity came from his stepfather. Even though he beat

Jimmy, Jimmy wanted to be like him: have a good job, nice car, wife, kids. But he wasn't making it and he was frustrated. Unfortunately, he took it out on me."

It didn't take Jimmy long to go beyond shoving. A few weeks later, he invited some friends from work over to play cards. He told June to make sure they had enough beer and food, and left her twenty dollars to buy what she needed. This time she didn't hear him pull up, and he suddenly burst through the door anxious about the evening get-together.

"I was standing at the kitchen sink about to wash a few dishes when he came over and asked calmly if I had remembered that people were coming over. I turned around and gave him a big smile and said yes, I knew they were coming. Then he blew up.

'Then why the hell aren't the goddamn dishes done?! This place is a fucking pigsty! You can't have goddamn dishes in the sink when *people are coming over!*'

"He went on and on ranting about the apartment: Did we have enough beer? Did I get the food? Every little thing. And the company wasn't even due for an hour. He was yelling and yelling and I said, sort of under my breath, 'Calm down.' Before the words were out of my mouth, he slapped me across the face with the back of his hand. He said, 'The goddamn sink is full of *dishes*! We've got *people* coming over! Don't you fucking *get it*?!'

"I was shocked by the slap. I took a step back and tasted blood in my mouth. I stood there holding my stinging cheek. I couldn't believe he hit me. I didn't know what to do.

"I know that Ron's conditioning me to be submissive came into play with Jimmy. Ron taught me to do what I was told, to be obedient — and I was because I needed love so badly. I thought sex equaled love. By the time I got to Jimmy, I was the perfect victim — only with him it wasn't sex, it was violence."

After the slap, June turned back to the sink and started doing the dishes. There were tears in her eyes and a sick aching in her stomach. Jimmy went into the living room and turned on the television. Twenty minutes later, he came back into the kitchen calm, as if nothing had happened, and said cheerfully, "What do you think we should give them to drink?"

Confusing as this may have been for someone else, it was not to June, and fit perfectly with her early childhood training: submit; ignore the insanity; pretend nothing's wrong, and everything will be all right. It was a formula for disaster.

The longer June lived with Jimmy, the more she saw him as an extremely fearful, paranoid man who needed not just to measure up, but to *control* the world around him. More and more, June saw how deep his insecurities were regarding his stepfather's expectations — something he brought up constantly.

"His problem wasn't just that he wanted the station wagon and the 2.3 kids and the steady job, he also wanted to hold on to his hoodlum image and hang around with his drinking buddies. He was torn between being a biker and being a family man like Randolph. He didn't know *what* he wanted to be; he only knew his cousins were buying new trucks and getting better jobs than he was. One even had a high-paying job with the city — and Jimmy was still stacking pallets."

The couple did not have much of a social life, and spent most of their time either at the Canadian Club or with Jimmy's best friend, Pete, and his wife, Susan. They had six children, and June enjoyed the visits because it gave Jana an opportunity to socialize with other kids. The two families usually got together twice a week — partly for the kids' benefit, but mostly so Pete and Jimmy could get drunk together.

Susan, who was several years older than June and a serious drinker in her own right, took June "under her wing" and taught her how to make Sombreros, a coffee-brandy and milk concoction that became their standard get-together drink.

The visits were good not only for Jana but for June as well. Having virtually no friends other than the casual friend from work who drove her home, June looked forward to the visits. She was still shy and unskilled in social situations, but she enjoyed being around gregarious Susan.

"Susan talked a lot and I couldn't hold a conversation. We were like opposites. I watched her with envy as she flitted around talking and laughing while I just sat there sipping my drink with nothing to say. Part of it was that I had never really been around adults before. Ron and I never had any friends, so I didn't know how to act. The other thing was, I didn't want to say anything that would make Jimmy mad — or worse, *look bad*. He was always worried I would, so I played it safe and didn't say anything."

June had seen how temperamental Jimmy could be, and was cautious now and watched for clues as to his state of mind. "I still wanted to run into his arms when he came home, but I didn't. Instead, I studied him: his face, the way he looked, walked. He was secretive and I couldn't always tell what mood he was in. Usually he needed a few beers to unwind, *then* I would approach him and it was usually safe. If it wasn't, he would have already said to Jana, 'Get away' or 'Get back' and she would know to leave him alone. So would I."

If June was envious of Susan, Jimmy was *more* envious of Pete. He was what Jimmy wanted to be: a family man. He had a good job, a lovely wife, six kids — everything Jimmy wanted. A few days after visiting them, Jimmy came home from work and, without taking a beer from the refrigerator (which was most unusual), he called June to sit on his lap.

"He wanted to discuss our future. He began by saying he had seen a really nice car for sale on someone's front lawn, and how he wanted to start thinking about savings so we could buy cars and take vacations like Pete and his cousins were. Then he brought up the subject of marriage.

"We had been living together quite a few months, and I always hoped he would one day say something about getting married. Even though he was grumpy and had been rough with me a few times, it wasn't very often and it was never anything serious.

"I always thought we could have a future together, so when he wanted to talk about marriage, I was thrilled. I thought many of the problems we were having were because I didn't know how to keep house or raise kids or whatever else it was that Jimmy complained about. And I figured that when I learned how to get things right, everything would be okay."

One major obstacle to getting married, however, was Randolph and Leslie. Jimmy had not spoken to his stepfather or stepmother for two years — ever since his ex-girlfriend, Cheryl, and Leslie had a fist fight at one of the weekend cookouts. Randolph had to break up the altercation, and neither side had spoken to the other since. Now June suggested Jimmy make amends.

"We can't very well have a wedding without your family," she told Jimmy. "And besides, it's time to patch things up." It was one of the first times June gave Jimmy advice — instead of the other way around — and amazingly, he listened. He wanted very much to see his stepfather again, and so, after a few beers, he called him and said he'd like to bring June and Jana over for the weekend cookout. Randolph was surprised but glad to hear from his stepson, and that weekend the two men got roaring drunk and were back to their old selves. June was the happiest of all: She knew she was going to get married, and with the Nortons back in the picture, Jana would have a whole new group of cousins to play with. Things couldn't have been rosier.

More planning went into June's second wedding than her first. This was to be a large wedding in May of the following year, 1981, with guests and relatives from several families represented. Randolph and Leslie invited all of the Nortons and their extended families. June invited her mother and her current husband, her grandparents, her aunts, and her sister and his husband. Jimmy invited his friends, Pete and Susan, and several of their friends. And someone invited Jimmy's mother, Carol.

Not anticipating any problems whatsoever with the guest list, arrangements were made to celebrate the event in a rented hall above Jimmy's favorite drinking hole — the Canadian Club. But the club owners *did* anticipate problems. They knew Jimmy and the Norton cousins well, and knew their reputation for brawling, so they required a sizeable security deposit to cover any damage that might be done to the premises. They also required that everyone "promise to be good," hoping that their personal words of honor might keep mayhem from erupting between the numerous families, all of whom had long-standing feuds with each other.

This time yellow pages were not required to find a Justice of the Peace. Randolph knew a minister, and made plans to have a simple ceremony at the man's home, then move the party to the Canadian Club. Mary Jackson came early, just as she had for June's first wedding, and again wove a white gardenia tiara for her granddaughter's hair. Ann helped her daughter back into her junior high school graduation dress, and a short time later, guests and family surrounded the couple in the backyard of the minister's home.

Pete was Jimmy's best man, and his wife, Susan, was June's maid of honor. The couple exchanged vows, and an hour later, the party at the Canadian Club was in full swing—with right uppercuts answering left hooks, and bloody noses ruining tuxedo after rented tuxedo. June and Jimmy had left shortly after the party began, and missed the grandest display of pugilism the club had ever known.

The police were called, the deposit was lost, and Jimmy had a huge bill to pay for damaged furniture and broken sound equipment. As always, the Nortons lived up to their reputations, and as usual, took full advantage of a party to get blithering drunk and punish one another for insults and infractions dating back to their childhoods.

Since June had taken off time from work when Jana first arrived, she could not take off additional time now for an extended honeymoon—that would have to wait. But it didn't concern Jimmy. On Monday morning, when he and June returned to their respective jobs, he was a new man. He now had a wife, a child, a job, an apartment, a car, and renewed relations with his family. He was on track for the first time in his life, and in better spirits than anyone had ever seen him in. He was finally measuring up to the standards by which he felt the rest of the family — especially his stepfather — judged him, and he was pleased.

But one thing ate away at Jimmy: Things were not moving as fast as he would have liked. Certainly, he had made progress by getting married; his stepfather had to be proud of that. But financially, he was stagnant. There was no extra money in the cookie jar June kept above the refrigerator — nothing left over for movies, dinners out. Sometimes June didn't even have enough money for milk or toilet paper, and would wait until Jimmy passed out from drinking to sneak five dollars from his wallet to purchase it.

The problem for Jimmy was that the next step — becoming financially successful — seemed hopelessly beyond his reach. Everything he wanted — especially the car he had been eyeing for so long — was unaffordable. He often talked about it at family cookouts, saying, "Yeah, I think I'm gonna go down next week and pick up that car I've been lookin' at." But really, he knew he hadn't put a nickel away for it, and it was nothing but an impossible dream. What mattered, though, was that Jimmy Briand always look good: make an impression; pretend to be that which he was not. And living the lie took its toll on him.

"Jimmy really wanted to be successful, but he didn't have the skills to make a lot of money. The anger I had seen before — which he had been holding back pretty well — started coming to the surface again. Marrying me was the only thing he accomplished toward his goal of being a family man. After the novelty of that wore off, and he realized he was still in a dead-end job, his frustration began to rise again. But I had an idea I thought would help."

On a warm Friday night in July, June suggested they go to the drive-in movies — partly to ease Jimmy's increasing hostility toward everything and everyone, and partly to put herself in the right mood for what she was about to suggest later that night. Though he grumbled about not having enough money for a night out, he agreed, and they drove off to the movies, and then to an ice cream parlor afterwards. June and Jana shared a banana split while Jimmy, uninterested in desserts, brooded over a cup of black coffee.

When they returned home, June put Jana to bed and came back into the kitchen where Jimmy had pulled a chair out from the table and was sitting drinking a beer. She walked over to him and climbed onto his lap, facing him, and took his beer from him. She put her arms around his neck and said, "I think we should have a baby."

Jimmy was surprised, but said nothing. June watched his face closely for a reaction, and could see his mind churning. He reached over and picked up his beer and drank deeply. June knew the idea of another baby fit into his picture of successful family man, and knew it would add to his feelings of self-worth to have a child with his new wife. His friend, Pete, had six children; his cousins had two or three each;

and now he, too, could come up the ranks. And of course his stepfather would be even more proud of him. Everything made sense.

"You want to do that?" was all he said. But it was enough for June. After living with him several months, she knew this was as enthusiastic as Jimmy ever got about anything.

"Yes, I do," June answered.

"I don't have a problem with that." That clinched it. A *double* confirmation of enthusiasm! June was elated. That night the couple went to bed and had sex, and continued to do so every night for a week, after which June discovered she was pregnant. Jimmy never talked about whether it would be nice to have a boy or a girl, what his or her name should be. In fact, he never brought up the issue again. He simply got his wife pregnant, and that was that.

With another child on the way, they would need a larger apartment in which to live, and a few weeks later started driving through neighborhoods on weekends looking for rentals. They eventually found a suitable duplex back in Hudson near Robinson Pond, and when June was four months pregnant, they moved.

Just before the move, Jimmy put on his most vivid display of temper since the window incident several months before. It occurred when he and June went to the landlord's home to get their security deposit back on the Kinsley apartment. The landlord owned a palatial home in the nicest section of Nashua, which no doubt added to Jimmy's irritation when the man said he would not return the deposit because the lease was not yet up. He did, however, offer to give back half of the deposit, but Jimmy would not hear of it.

June was waiting in the car when she heard the screaming. "I heard Jimmy yelling about something, then I saw him stomping down the driveway. His face was red and he was screaming on the top of his lungs. He kept turning around and giving the house the finger and screaming obscenities. I had seen him mad before, but never at that level — he was hysterical. I couldn't bear to look at him when he got in the car, and looked out the window. Jana was in the back seat and for the first time, I saw her, too, look away from her father."

Three trucks converged on the Kinsley apartment. Two were pickup trucks driven by the Norton cousins, and the other was a U-Haul truck Jimmy's friend had rented. It was moving day, and the three trucks had come as a convoy from the U-Haul facility. Inside the apartment, June was scurrying around with a role of packing tape and marking pen, packing last minute kitchen items and marking several still-open cartons. Jana was coloring at the dinette table, oblivious to the activity around her.

"How ya doin', June?" asked one of the Nortons as he walked in the door.

"Oh, going a little crazy but getting there," said June. Jimmy walked into the room and greeted his cousin. June had just sealed shut a carton and began to lift it when Jimmy yelled, "What the hell are you doing?! You can't pick that up!" June turned and looked at him quizzically. She smiled a knowing smile to herself and put the box down.

"Since when did Jimmy show concern for *me*? Answer: only when someone was around to see it. If his cousins weren't there, I know he wouldn't have said anything about the box. I had been lifting things all week getting ready for the move and he sat there watching television and drinking beer. *Now* he's a concerned husband; it was just like him to do that."

June and the men worked all day. After the move was complete, Jimmy broke open a case of beer and everyone celebrated. For him and June, moving back to Hudson was like going home since they were both originally from there. With a new baby on the way, June was looking forward to the move. The duplex had a second bedroom and a large yard for a dog and maybe even a garden, possibly chickens too. The old man in the home next door raised them, and when June and Jana had first looked at the duplex, Jana chased them around the yard and giggled. The man didn't mind at all, and told June that if she took the apartment, he'd help her get started with a chicken coop and a few chicks.

Jimmy, too, wanted more of a country life, and liked the idea of a vegetable garden and being more self-sufficient. He also knew that with the large yard, he could invite Pete and Susan and their six kids over to play instead of always going to their house. And he was proud that the rental came with a full cellar where he could store his hunting equipment and set up a motorcycle repair bench.

The only problem was that the move left him still in conflict about his identity. In Jimmy's mind, it gave the impression of being settled and of upward social mobility — just what he wanted to portray to his stepfather and family. But it gave the same impression to his motorcycle friends who rumbled into the driveway to visit and ribbed him about being "a family man" and "the good husband" instead of the wild and free biker he used to be — and they still were.

"What's the matter, buddy, feeling a little tied down?" they'd say. Or, "How's it feel to be a responsible, law-abiding citizen, Jimmy?" To a normal man who was breaking away from his youth and at long last growing up, the teasing would have been taken in stride. But Jimmy was not a normal man. With his loyalties divided between his family and his cohorts, this heckling did nothing to ease his anxiety. He couldn't get his roles straight and again became frustrated, confused, and *angry*. And he took it out on his wife.

"We weren't in the duplex a month when Jimmy blew up at me again. This time I was lucky though. We were supposed to be going somewhere, and Jana was making a fuss, so it took a while to get her dressed and ready. Jimmy was getting more and more nervous — he couldn't stand being late anywhere.

"Finally we were set, and we walked out the door and were just starting down the steps. Jimmy was behind me fuming. He shouted, 'I can't believe you're making us late!' and shoved me. I started to fall, but he grabbed me by the back of my coat and said, 'Oh shit, I forgot!' He forgot I was pregnant. It was the first — and the last — time he stopped himself from hurting me."

Jimmy may have moved physically, but he still stacked pallets for a living, and he resented it — especially since his boss was still a woman. He continued to come home from work complaining about "the goddamn bitch" and "I don't need that slut getting in my way." As the months went on, he expanded his criticism to the entire factory, complaining that "lowlifes work there" — as if he were from high society.

Jimmy also expanded his criticism of his wife. The worse he felt about himself, the more he complained about June — especially her housekeeping. Regardless of her pregnant condition, he demanded a fastidiously clean home at all times. Though personal hygiene meant little to Jimmy (he often lived for days in dirty coveralls and the same sweat-stained work shirt), his home had to be impeccable.

Jimmy's demands would have been comical if he were not so serious about them. One of his seminal rules was: All caps and lids must be clean of food at all times. Jimmy was particularly obsessed with plastic milk bottle lids, which he inspected closely to make sure no encrusted milk was visible. It had to be an odd sight to see a long-haired, dirty laborer with black grime under his fingernails carefully scrutinizing a little yellow milk lid. June was diligent about the lids though, and made sure that after she poured the milk, she rinsed the lid thoroughly. If the children, however, poured a glass without her knowing it, she paid the price with a tirade about how poorly she was doing as a wife.

"Jimmy took advantage of my inexperience. He knew I was married at fourteen, and then came directly to live with him and didn't know much about anything, especially housekeeping. If I did something he didn't like, or forgot something he expected me to do, he'd lace into me and tell me how every other wife was doing better than me and that I was the only one not getting it right. That was his favorite dig, telling me I was a bad wife and that I was the only one like that. I had no evidence to the contrary, so I believed him."

Jimmy made this point particularly clear one evening when he came home late from work drunk and ornery. It was past nine o'clock when he walked in and sat down at the kitchen table. June had kept his dinner warm since six, and when she asked him if he was still hungry, he snapped at her, "What does it fucking look like? Would I be sitting at the goddamn *table* if I didn't want to fucking *eat*? Jesus, you women are stupid!"

June knew it was best not to take offense to the comments, and opened the oven and brought Jimmy his meal, which was covered with aluminum foil. She quickly removed the foil, and went to the refrigerator to get him a beer, hoping it would calm him down (it usually did). She struggled to twist off the lid, but before she could manage it, Jimmy was on his feet with the plate in his hand.

"I can't believe you'd feed me this garbage," he said, and opened the front door. "This is where the garbage belongs." He flung the plate of food into the yard, stomped into the garage, and took off on his motorcycle. June quietly closed the door behind him, and vowed to do better in the future.

"He was right. I was a bad wife. I figured I had kept the food warm too long and everything was dried out. I thought Jimmy was justified in being mad and that, as he always said, I had to do better. I had to be a better wife, had to get it right. *Get it right.* He said if I could just 'get it right,' he wouldn't have to do the things he did.

"So I tried to do better by making his favorite meal the next night: steak, baked potato, and asparagus. He came home on time that night, so I was happy about that. When he sat down to eat, he didn't say anything, and he hadn't said anything when he came in, so I wasn't sure about his mood.

"My hands were shaking when I served him, and I know he saw it. I felt like I was serving a bowl of food to a vicious dog: I set the plate down and quickly stepped back. He looked at it for a moment, then without a word, took one swipe of the entire table. Everything went flying. Then he grabbed me by the back of the neck and pushed me down on the floor and told me to clean it up — clean up his favorite meal of steak, baked potato, and asparagus."

The cookout invitations continued to come, and Jimmy kept trying to work himself back into Randolph's good graces. Pete and Susan were visiting once or twice a week, and June, though growing larger every day, worked in the small garden she had planted along the side of the duplex. She relished her time out of the house, and tried to make herself feel contented, though she was always on edge, never knowing when her husband might explode again.

As winter came, June's anxiety eased. Jimmy was not only behaving normally, he was going out of his way to be nice — something June had never seen before. As her pregnancy developed, Jimmy took unusual measures to assure his wife's comfort and safety. June worked right up until the last week of her pregnancy, and during the last few months, Jimmy would pull up to the front door and help his wife into the car. Every morning when driving her to work, he would take her to the pastry shop she liked and buy her coffee and a cinnamon bun even though it was out of his way. He even carried Jana to the car, which, prior to June's pregnancy, was unheard of. "Jimmy never carried Jana anywhere, unless, of course, someone was there to see it."

Winter was a calm period. Jimmy had not struck his wife since the backhand to the mouth months earlier, which she now dismissed as "a slip from his old fighting days." She also saw that he had controlled himself after pushing her on the stairs, and saw that as a good sign as well. "I knew that after I had the baby, it might not be as quiet as it had been. But for now, I was 'fat and ugly,' as he Jimmy said, and he wasn't jealous like he usually was. He liked me big because I wasn't attractive to anybody else. I had found the key to keeping Jimmy calm: get pregnant and fat."

Jimmy was excessively possessive of June, and he worried that, being a woman, she couldn't be trusted and would one day leave him. It was this fear of rejection that would eventually destroy their marriage. He insisted that June stay right next to him, and if he suspected she was looking at another man, would ask his standard question: "Where do you know *him* from?" Though June made it clear that she was neither looking at the man nor had she ever known him, Jimmy was never satisfied, and continued to grill her for a confession. "He was completely irrational when it came to other guys. He assumed I had slept with hundreds of men, and that anyone who even looked at me had to be an old flame. It was crazy."

Now that June was pregnant and Jimmy's jealousy had subsided, she felt relatively safe. But in May of 1982, when June was entering her ninth month of pregnancy, the tenor of the relationship changed dramatically. June had assumed (or perhaps blindly hoped) that her husband's behavior was changing permanently since there had been no major blow-ups for months. Unfortunately, her confidence was ill-founded. Nothing in his emotional makeup had changed at all: he was merely a simmering kettle.

Jimmy had been holding in all the fury and anger and disappointment he felt about himself only because his wife was about to have a baby — a baby that would, in his distorted view, bring him up another notch in society's eyes. But like all kettles, he had his boiling point, and it came one night three weeks before June was to deliver their child.

"It was not an accident that a major incident occurred in my last month of pregnancy. I think because I was going to have the baby soon, and be back to my normal size, Jimmy was getting possessive all over again. I saw it coming and saw him getting upset about the little things again. He'd yell about the house not being picked up, my cooking, that type of thing; those were his signals."

The night in May when Jimmy blew up, the instigating issue was again housekeeping. Jana was about three, and had been told by her father "to keep her room clean or else." Three-year-olds, however, are not adept at keeping fastidious quarters, and this particular night Jimmy's ire was fueled when he walked into her bedroom to see toys and dolls strewn about the floor. Usually June made sure the room was picked up, but had not done so this particular day.

Jimmy came home late and did not want anything to eat. June had made dinner for him earlier, but by 8 p.m., she figured he was out drinking again, and decided to put the food in the refrigerator. When he walked through the door at 8:45, she was just finishing reading a story to Jana, who was almost asleep but not quite. June had put her to bed at seven, but Jana couldn't sleep, so she put her on her lap in the living room to read to her. Jimmy went to another part of the house, and when he came back he was furious.

"He started in about Jana's room. He said he was sick and tired of telling her to keep it clean. I argued that she was only a child, a three-year-old child, and she didn't understand about keeping a room in perfect order. Jana was so tired, she didn't even notice the argument, and kept nodding off to sleep.

"Then Jimmy started yelling directly to her: 'Wake up!' he said. And she would wake up but then fall back to sleep. He kept yelling at her, 'Wake up! Pay attention! Listen when I'm talking to you!' as if she was ten or twelve. But she couldn't stay awake; she was falling asleep and couldn't pay attention like he wanted.

"Jimmy really started yelling then. Out of control. The red face like when he wanted his deposit back. Only this time his craziness was directed toward his own daughter. I saw then something I had not realized before: He wasn't just loud and obnoxious, he was cruel and mean. For the first time since I had met him, I was scared. I saw he was dangerous, the way he was screaming at a little kid who hadn't done anything wrong.

"All of a sudden Jimmy grabbed Jana and started smacking her in the face. I pulled her away and jumped up and ran out of the room. Jimmy kept screaming in the living room, and I just opened the back door and ran out. He didn't even know we were gone he was raving so much. Jana had on her footie pajamas and I was barefoot and wearing my baseball pajamas with the elastic waist band; I had been wearing them ever since I was six months pregnant.

"All I remember was running. I wanted to get away from Jimmy, just run away from him as fast as I could. But I was as big as a house and couldn't move very fast. I got down the street about a hundred yards when Jimmy grabbed my hair from behind and pulled me backwards. I started to fall and had Jana on my hip, but luckily I had time to tuck her in front of me before I landed on my rear end.

"Now I'm crying, Jana's crying, Jimmy's screaming in the middle of the street and slapping us both. He didn't care who he hit, he was just hitting. Then he started dragging me by the arm back to the house. He was screaming and pulling me, and then he let go of my arm. I thought he was going to stop — but he didn't.

"He went around behind me a grabbed both my legs and started dragging me like he was a plow horse. I was yelling and crying for him to stop, yelling that he was hurting me, but he wouldn't. My head was bouncing on the pavement as he pulled me. I could feel the hair getting sanded off the back of my head and my spine scraping along the pavement. I tried to hold onto Jana with one hand and put my other hand down to raise off the ground but the skin on my hand was peeling off and I couldn't do it; I was getting all scraped up no matter what I did. But Jimmy didn't care; he just kept dragging us all the way back to the house."

When they got back inside the house, Jimmy shoved June in the chest and she fell back onto the couch. He was silent then for a few seconds and paced back and forth in front of the couch. Then he stopped and turned to her and said something he had never said before: "If you ever leave me again, I'll kill you. I'll fucking kill you!" After what he had just done, June had no doubt that he meant it.

"Please let me just put Jana to bed," pleaded June. "She's got to go to bed. She doesn't need to hear all this and she's exhausted."

"No!" he said. "She's got to be taught how to act!" Jimmy screamed his decree and continued to pace back and forth. He stopped again and added another new threat: "If you ever leave me, I'll take the kids away from you. I'll track them down through their school records and take them!" Now he was threatening the baby June hadn't even given birth to.

"Who's in charge here?!" he screamed.

June was in no position to argue. "You are, Jimmy."

"Whose rules do we follow around here?!"

"Yours, Jimmy, yours."

For ten minutes straight, Jimmy continued to fume and spout. By then, Jana had stopped crying and was clinging to her mother like a newborn chimp. She was wide-eyed and petrified by the frothing animal before her.

Jimmy's tirade ended with one final proclamation: "If you ever leave, it's because *I make you leave*. Is that understood?!"

"Yes, Jimmy, it's understood."

The contractions were coming regularly now. The monitor in June's hospital room showed when the next one was due and like clockwork, it would come. Jimmy hated the visual reminder. He hated his wife tensing up from the pain and crying. "He didn't want me to have any pain medication because he wanted a natural childbirth, but when I cried, he'd say, 'Stop that, you're embarrassing me.' When I saw the next contraction coming on the screen, I'd cringe and he'd say, 'Don't do that. Relax.' It was like *he* was having the baby. The lady in next room was having a bad labor and was screaming. Jimmy kept saying, 'I wish she'd shut up; Jesus, will she *ever* shut up?' It was like he thought we could control our pain."

After several "embarrassing" hours, June had an uneventful birth and returned from the hospital with another girl, Pamela Ann, swaddled in a pink and turquoise baby blanket. Jimmy seemed pleased with his new child, though he was above showing it. And enough time had passed since the violent incident three weeks before that June had forgotten about it and now focused all her attention on her newborn baby. She had set up a nursery in the corner of Jana's bedroom, and told her daughter how much she would need her help in caring for the new infant. Jana appreciated the trust her mother put in her, and looked forward to the new arrival.

June took a leave of absence from her job, and hoped that during that time she could help Jana and Pam bond. She looked forward to the special time with her new baby, and felt that for now, at least, all was going well. One evening three weeks later, when June was reading to Jana and cuddling with Pam on the sofa, Jimmy dropped some bad news: "You've only got two weeks left, so make sure you call the babysitter and tell her you're bringing over another kid."

June turned to Jimmy in shock, her jaw slack. They had quit using the sitter when June came home from the hospital, and Jimmy hadn't said anything about June returning to work—at least not for the immediate future. Now she was going to be pulled away from her infant daughter just when they needed to be together most.

June thought about bringing up this point, but knew better than to argue with her husband. She called the babysitter the next day and tearfully said she'd be bringing over a newborn and was that all right? "I was crying so much when I hung up the phone that I'm not sure she understood me. I didn't want to give up my baby so soon. But Jimmy said we needed the money, and we weren't going to discuss the issue. When we dropped Pam off that first day, I had a pit in my stomach. It was too soon to hand her over to a stranger. I felt terrible about it, and called the sitter all day long. I must have called her twenty times that day."

Because she was only eighteen, it did not take June long to lose the extra pounds she had put on during her pregnancy. She soon returned to her slim, attractive self, and when she did, her husband's possessiveness increased. "Jimmy's male friends would drop by to say hello and they'd say something like, 'June's really looking good, Jimmy.' He struggled with that. He was proud of me, but on the other hand, he couldn't stand other guys noticing me; it made him scared, and when he got scared he got mean."

Whether it was June's return to normal size or something else, Jimmy soon fell back into his old ways. The first evidence that he still had not grown emotionally as June had hoped he would came two weeks after Pam was born. Jimmy came home for lunch that day, and before leaving for work in the morning, had told June that he wanted macaroni salad with egg in it. He had been back to nitpicking about her cooking and cleaning which, by now, June was becoming accustomed to. She was still trying to "get it right," and apparently was doing quite well because she had not seen the flashes of anger Jimmy displayed in the past — until this day.

"Jimmy was more specific about everything now, and needed things done just so. Generally I got them right. That morning he gave me explicit instructions about the ingredients for the macaroni salad. He said he wanted chopped celery, onion, lots of salt and pepper, eggs, and mayonnaise. I did just as he told me, and was satisfied with myself when he finished his plate and asked for more. He was eating his second bowl when he stopped and began to pick through the macaroni very carefully. He said, 'Gee, those eggs must be cut up awfully small; I sure can't see them in here.' And I said, 'Of course you can't see them — they're raw eggs.'

"He just about threw up. He got up slowly, picked the bowl up, and threw it at the television. That's when I started backing up. I put my arms out in front of me to protect myself and then he threw the whole pot at me. It hit me in the chest and fell on the floor. Then he grabbed me and pushed my face into the floor and again made me clean up the mess *he* made.

"While I was on my hands and knees, he was yelling again that I'm the only wife like this, that all the others know how to cook and I'm too stupid to be a good wife. He said they did things right and they didn't have to pay the consequences that I did. And I believed him. All I could think about was doing better. Next time I had to listen more closely and get it right. Get it right! I should have known he wanted hard boiled eggs chopped up in the macaroni. He was right; I was wrong."

But June couldn't "get it right." Jimmy was a man who was looking outside himself for that which he lacked within. He needed to be constantly reassured that he was all right, and if things in his world were not, he became fearful, then angry, then violent.

From that point on, the abuse intensified, as did June's fear of her husband. What triggered the change is uncertain, but the level of physical and verbal assaults began to increase day by day. Even in play, Jimmy became abusive — and sometimes blatantly cruel.

"Jimmy liked to tickle me, but it wasn't a fun kind of laughing he was looking for. And he was never laughing when he did it; he was dead serious. He'd grab me and pin me down and tickle me until I was sick or crying. It was torture, and he knew it. One time he picked me up over his shoulder and I knew I was going to get hurt, so I started to cry. That didn't stop him either; he called me a cry baby and a pansy and said I was weak, then he dropped me over his shoulder on my head."

Jimmy's attacks became more and more regular now. If there was a period of calm, June knew it would not last — and it didn't. Jimmy's outbursts were cyclical and as predictable as the phases of the moon. He blew up at his wife and kids so often that the neighbors sharing the common wall in the duplex started pounding on it to shut him up. They had little children too, and they needed quiet. Jimmy's response was always the same: He'd kick the wall and yell 'Come over here, you motherfuckers!' But he'd never go over *there*.

"He was a coward like that. Jimmy Briand — the town tough guy — was tough when he had his cousins or buddies around. But he had a yellow streak a mile wide when he was alone. It was okay to beat up on his wife, but he didn't dare go next door and confront the neighbor. And he was unnerved by the fact that they heard him screaming at his wife all time; it wasn't exactly manly.

"My job was to make sure things were done to the letter. I wasn't just cautious anymore, I was scared of Jimmy. Before I wasn't afraid, but now I was. After all, he had slapped me, thrown me on the floor, threatened to kill me. Jimmy always made good on his threats, and I wasn't about to test him on that one."

June always fed Pam and Jana before Jimmy came home from work. He couldn't stand sitting at the table watching them dawdle over their food. Here too, he had rules and regulations. One rule was: no ketchup on the string beans. Jana didn't like string beans, but when June poured a little ketchup on them one night, Jana devoured them. Later, June made the mistake of doing it in front of Jimmy and he "threw a fit." He said it was "wrong" to put ketchup on string beans, and forbade its use thereafter.

"At least she's eating her vegetables, Jimmy," June had said. "What's wrong with putting a little ..."

"Who's the fucking boss around here?!" he bellowed.

"You are, Jimmy," said June, looking down at the table.

"Then why the fuck are you *arguing* with me?! You don't put goddamn ketchup on beans! It's just not *done*! And I don't *want* it done, so don't fucking do it again, *got it*?!"

June didn't answer fast enough.

"I'm talking to *you*!"

"All right, Jimmy, no more ketchup."

"I didn't say no more ketchup. Jesus, are you stupid. I said no more ketchup *on the beans*!"

"I know, Jimmy. No more on the beans. That's what I meant, on the beans."

During Jimmy's tirades, Pam would wail in her high chair while Jana ate as fast as possible and got out of the room. As Pam grew older and June started teaching her to feed herself, she would often play with her food or try to make funny faces in it. Jimmy didn't like funny faces and would yell at Pam until she started wailing again. So June eventually gave up altogether the notion of a family dinner, and simply fed the children early. When Jimmy arrived, she fed him and left the room to tend to the children; he was perfectly happy with that arrangement.

One evening after serving Jimmy, June deviated from her normal practice and did not leave the room. Unusual as it was for her to stay, Jimmy didn't notice it until he heard cupboard doors opening and closing and looked over to see June moving cans and food packages from place to place. This puzzled him because the cupboards, too, were to be kept in a particular order, and any deviation from that order would have to come directly from Jimmy himself.

"What are you doing?" he asked.

"Rearranging the cupboards."

"Why? I like them the way they are."

"Oh, I'm just, you know, keeping things straight," June replied, unable to come up with a valid reason for why she was doing what she was doing. But her mind was churning: *What am I going to do? How am I going to explain to Jimmy what happened today? Should I change my story? Or should I stay with my original story? Oh God, he's going to be furious about this.*

The only thing that mattered at that moment was keeping Jimmy interested in the cupboard project. If June had one wish in the world, it was for Jimmy to stay in that kitchen — forever. *Don't go in the living room,* she thought to herself. Please, God, let this all be a dream. Nothing happened today. It's just a dream.

But the inevitable had to happen, and it did. Jimmy finished his dinner, pushed his chair away from the table, growled once more about leaving the cupboards as they were, and went into the living room. June held her breath and closed her eyes and leaned her head against the cupboard door. She knew it was only a matter of time now. Jimmy would see what had happened earlier in the day, and he would fly into a rage.

He had been collecting miniature brandy glasses for years. His mother had given him some, others came from aunts and uncles as Christmas and birthday presents. The collection contained twenty of the inch-high knickknacks, which Jimmy cherished like expensive crystal, and proudly displayed on top of the television. Pam was now eight months old, and had learned to use a walker on wheels. Very quickly she became adept at maneuvering around the apartment, but on this particular day she bumped into the television, knocking over the display of glasses.

"Pam hit the TV and I heard glass break. She couldn't talk at her age, but she occasionally mumbled out something almost recognizable. This was the first time I heard her say something *perfectly* clear. She said, 'Uh oh.' Even though I knew I was in trouble, I couldn't help smile when she said that. It was so cute that Pam actually said something — and something that fit so perfectly! I really enjoyed that moment, but then came back to reality and knew things would be bad again. I said to Pam, 'You have no idea how uh oh this is.'"

June had set about cleaning up the broken glass and placing back on the television what remained of Jimmy's collection: five brandy glasses out of twenty. The accident happened mid-morning, so June had a long wait until Jimmy came home — plenty of time to obsess over what to do and how to explain *this* to her husband.

She came up with a story: She would say she had bumped into the television while vacuuming. Maybe he'd have some mercy on her because she was doing housework like she was supposed to. Jimmy insisted on a clean home, and liked to see it vacuumed; maybe this would help. No matter what the story, it needed to protect Pam.

The first order of business was taking the orange hand cleaner Jimmy used after work and move it from the bathroom to the kitchen. "That way Jimmy could wash his hands at the kitchen sink and not have to walk to the bathroom. To get to the bathroom, you had to pass the television; I didn't want him to do that."

Next, dinner would be all ready when he walked in the door. And bread. Lots of bread. Jimmy liked bread and butter with dinner; he would have plenty this night.

"When he came in, I held out the orange hand cleaner like I was trying to sell it to him. He just looked at me weird and walked right by me and went to the bathroom anyway. He hadn't noticed anything wrong, and then I heard him take off his pants and heard his big, brass Triumph motorcycle buckle hit the floor. My heart was pounding. Then he changed into his cutoff shorts and put his work boots back on. He had to have his boots on all the time. He didn't lace them, but he had them on with his cutoffs. It would have looked funny to anyone else, but I was used to it.

"He came back into the kitchen and washed his hands with the cleaner. He didn't say anything about it not being in the bathroom — that surprised me, and I was relieved. Then he ate his dinner, saw me rearranging the cupboards, and finally went into the living room. He sat down on the couch and turned on the television."

A minute went by as June held her breath. Two minutes. Five. Six. Suddenly Jimmy jumped up from the couch and yelled, "What the fuck happened here?" June swallowed hard and walked slowly into the living room. She started to tell the pre-planned story in a shaky voice, and just as she did, Pam appeared at the doorway in her walker and said, "Uh oh, Daddy."

June continued, rambling now, talking fast, trying to get out a suitable explanation before it was too late: "... and I know they meant a lot to you because they came from Aunt Sally and Uncle ..." June didn't finish. Halfway through the sentence, Jimmy punched her full-fisted in the cheek. She dropped to the floor and he pinned her to the basement door adjacent to the television. June clawed at it, trying to open it, trying for an escape route, but Jimmy's black boot held it shut.

"How could you let this happen?! You know what they meant to me!" screamed Jimmy. Without waiting for a response, he pounced on his wife and grabbed her long hair. He wound it around his massive fist, then yanked her head back and smashed it into the basement door. *Smash. Smash.* June screamed for Jimmy to stop, but he was in a trance and heard nothing.

Like a crippled animal, she looked about frantically for refuge, a hiding place, *anywhere* but where she was. But there was none. She was trapped, pinned tight to the basement door, and Jimmy knew it.

He stood up as if he was done with the punishment. June closed her eyes, sighed deeply, and began to pray a prayer of thanks just as the first kick landed up and under her rib cage near the solar plexus. She was temporarily paralyzed by the blow, and could neither breathe nor move. A moment later she dry heaved, releasing a low, guttural, primal groan as she doubled over into a fetal position.

The next black boot had much more force and landed squarely on the ribs. June felt something inside rip and let go. Then came the series: one, two, three kicks, hard and fast. Change feet. Now again with the other boot: one, two, three. "You miserable, fucking bitch! How do you like *this*?! How do you like it, bitch?!" And the kicks came again.

June struggled to wrap her arms around herself and protect her broken rib. She twisted to position her back towards the attack, and as she did, caught a vague, watery glimpse of her two children standing in the doorway holding each other. "Don't come out here!" she tried to yell, but the words came out as nothing more than a wheeze. It was almost impossible to breathe now, and then the pain came. Agonizing as it was, June still had the wherewithal to instruct her children: "Don't ... get back ... get back in your room!" she yelled breathlessly. They complied immediately.

But Jimmy was done. He went to the bedroom, grabbed his coat, and left the house.

June crawled to the couch and struggled to pull herself up. She sat doubled over on the edge trying to recover, but could not breathe because breathing expanded her diaphragm and triggered excruciating pain at the fractured rib. The only solution was to hyperventilate with shallow breaths and try to inhale enough oxygen to stay conscious. That in itself was a task: June was in shock — physically and emotionally. She wasn't sure what had happened, where she was, what time it was, where her children were, where her husband was. She sat and breathed as best she could until she had enough strength to lift herself off the couch and stumble off to bed, crouched over like an old woman carrying the burdens of the world on her shoulders.

At two in the morning the front door opened: Jimmy was back. He undressed and got into bed with June. She got up and moved to the living room. He said nothing and fell into a deep, peaceful sleep. She sat on the couch again, then realized she had to do something about her ribs. She had heard that broken ribs needed to be wrapped but wasn't sure what the term meant. She understood, though, that they needed support, and took a beach towel from the closet and wrapped it around her torso snugly; it relieved the pain measurably.

Though she could not sleep, she dozed on and off until six in the morning when she had to get ready for work. She was in such pain by then that she could barely move: she could not turn over or sit up, and her breathing was more labored than ever. She could not get enough air to her lungs to function properly, and became lightheaded and dizzy. The pain was now too much, and she begged her husband to take her to the hospital.

Fearing that something serious might be wrong with his wife, Jimmy gave in and drove June to Memorial Hospital (now Southern New Hampshire Medical Center) in Nashua. He parked in the hospital lot and instructed her to go in and say that she had gotten into a car accident and was thrown against the door of the car. He said he would wait in the car and, "Don't take all day. I'm hungry." June assured him she'd be as quick as possible.

When they returned to the apartment, June took off her coat as carefully as she could, wincing at the pain from moving her arm out of the coat sleeve. Jimmy was standing a few feet away, and heard June say under her breath, "I can't breathe." Jimmy took it as a criticism, and no one — especially a woman — criticized Jimmy Briand.

"What was that? Did you say you can't breathe?" said Jimmy, his guilt palpable. "I'll show you what it means to not breathe."

He came close to June and grabbed her hair again. He was not going to allow his wife to make him feel bad; it just was not something he could permit. Enough women had done that already. So to prevent further self-loathing, he would punish his wife more to prove that *she*, not he, was the one at fault, the one deserving of such punishment, the one who still needed to "get it right."

Jimmy pulled his wife into the bathroom as she stayed hunched over, trying to protect her tender ribs. She did not know what was going to happen next, but her speculation ended quickly. Taking advantage of her hunched position, Jimmy slammed his thick forearm down on June's back and knocked her to the floor. With both hands, he grabbed her head, yanked it up and over the toilet bowl, and shoved it in, holding it there without moving.

"I tried to pull free but it was no use, he was way too strong and I was in no condition to fight. I was waiting, counting, hoping. Finally, I had no choice. I had to take a breath. I inhaled and my whole body twitched violently and I coughed in more water. Then he let me go."

Tires squealed, the car engine roared, and Jimmy was gone. For the moment, he had quelled the demons that were tormenting him so. But for June, it was another story. Her demon was getting more ruthless by the day, and she now slumped over the toilet bowl in a daze. One arm hung dead off the side of the bowl while the other held her ribs. She knew she was alive, but little else. Nothing made sense. Perhaps this *was* a dream, but the pain dashed any hope of that. It was real, too real. And her husband was real when he walked in the door later that night as if nothing had happened. "What's for dinner?" he said in a congenial tone, and went to wash up in the bathroom where his orange hand cleaner was back in its proper place.

It was after this beating that June again considered — if only fleetingly — leaving Jimmy. She had given it a thought after Jimmy hung Jana out the window, and now the notion occurred to her. But as quickly as it came, it vanished. "Any rational person would have left right then, but I was not rational."

Indeed, June was already falling into what would later be widely known as Battered Woman Syndrome, a condition that includes total submission to a dominant, threatening spouse complicated by "learned helplessness," a psychological state resulting from the domination and "mind control" of the perpetrator. June was ripe for such conditioning: complete dependence on her husband, two children to care for, a minimum wage job, no friends, isolation from the world around her (she had no transportation), no parents, no money (Ron had taken that), poor self-esteem, learned submissiveness from an earlier marriage, and above all, the belief that everything that was happening to her was her own fault. If she could just "get it right" like other wives did, everything would be fine.

In June's deteriorating mental state, this made perfect sense. Jimmy wasn't mean, he was *justified*. Jimmy was not to blame, *she* was: "that was obvious." So June buckled down and promised to herself to try harder to make the marriage work. And Jimmy took full advantage of her subservience.

Now that the violence had escalated from slap to punch to full-force kick, regular beatings became commonplace. The line had been crossed now, and for Jimmy, there was no going back. He was on a roller coaster ride of emotional ups and downs. The levee had split open and pouring forth were copious amounts of venom. He no longer had the will or ability to control himself, and with his mood swings came concurrent physical swings at his wife whenever he felt the urge.

Verbal cues diminished and commands were fewer. No longer did Jimmy say "Get away" when he came home in a bad mood; it was expected of everyone to *keep* away unless directed otherwise. June was expected to know what to do and when to do it. There would be no more "I want the house cleaned": it had to *be* clean. And if it wasn't, the predictable response was now a physical assault instead of a verbal one like in the past.

Jimmy Briand didn't mind beating his spouse, but the one thing he feared most was getting caught at it. He was smart enough to know that blows to the face could easily be recognized as spousal abuse, so he wisely directed his punishment to areas covered by clothes. He took to punching his wife in the back or kicking her in the buttocks to show his dissatisfaction.

"If I was moving too slow, or did something he thought was stupid, he'd kick me in the butt or punch me in the back or in the back of the head. Sometimes he'd kick the back of my legs and say, 'There seems to be no other way I can get through to you.'"

Once upon a time, Jimmy's stepfather had said the same thing to him, but while violent himself, Randolph drew the line at women and children.

The huge black Buick was way too big for June. She didn't want a car in the first place, and with little experience behind the wheel, was afraid to drive such a massive machine. Jimmy had picked up the second-hand car for five hundred dollars, primarily so June could get back and forth to the pediatrician. He had been taking off too much time from work in order to drive his wife and daughters to their doctor appointments, and also found it a nuisance to pick up the kids at the babysitter's house on the way home from work; he preferred June deal with that.

Jimmy also felt that with June having her own transportation, he could take on more overtime work and start putting away a little money like he had always wanted. But those dreams were soon be shattered by the Briand temper.

Jimmy was still disturbed about working for a woman, and one day became irate when she told him to clean up the area he had neglected the previous day. He argued that it "wasn't all my mess," and then took out his displeasure by slugging an unsuspecting co-worker. When his superior confronted him about the assault, he began to fume at her and defend his actions. But by then, she had had enough of the insolent Jimmy Briand, and terminated him on the spot.

As always, Jimmy had to blame someone other than himself for his failures in life, and came home shouting, "The goddamn bitch is fucking her way to the top!" Not only was this not true, it had nothing to do with his termination.

Jimmy then took to the streets, scrounging menial jobs lasting from two days to two months. Now he was making less money than his wife — another source of agitation — and he was, in effect, going *backwards* rather than up the social ladder as he had hoped. He needed to find a way to stem the tide, and the first thing that came to mind was stealing his cousin's idea of making Christmas wreaths, from which the cousin was making good money each holiday season.

"It was November and Christmas was nearing. We were definitely feeling the crunch and really needed more money, so on weekends I'd put Pam in a backpack and take Jana by the hand and go into the forest with Jimmy to pick Princess Pine for wreaths. It was freezing cold and picking the pine was hard on the hands.

"When we got home, we'd dump all the pine on the floor and sort it by size. It got pitch all over the floor but it was the only way. After the kids were asleep, we'd take the wire and make the wreaths. Then we'd set up a picnic table by the side of the road and sell it.

"We were doing pretty well until Jimmy tried to get in with the florist his cousin was selling to; that caused friction between them, and when we went to the annual Norton Christmas party, there was a big riff between the two and another fight broke out. If it hadn't been about business, it would have been about something else. Christmas with the Nortons was nothing more than an excuse to get drunk and pound one another."

Besides, Jimmy hardly needed holidays as an excuse to get drunk. The worse he did financially, the more he drank. Soon, he was drinking copious quantities of beer on a daily basis. Eight beers in an evening was not unusual; two six packs was a normal Friday night's intake. If he didn't come home drunk, the refrigerator was always well-stocked with beer, so it wouldn't take long to change the situation. One of his favorite concoctions was "Red beer" — a combination of tomato juice and beer which, on weekends, he would drink from dawn until dark. If he wasn't sufficiently inebriated from Red beers, he'd quaff two more beers at dinner, then drive off to a local bar to finish the task.

Though Jimmy was insulting and beating his wife on an ever-increasing basis, most of the assaults occurred when he was cold sober; he didn't need alcohol to fuel his fury. June saw this clearly after an appalling, unprovoked incident occurred with a stray dog Jimmy had befriended. June thought it odd — and dangerous — that Jimmy could turn instantly violent without a drop of alcohol in his blood (even though he was clearly an alcoholic), but after the dog incident, she felt there was "something wrong with him," that he had "a mental illness of some kind," so violent was his behavior.

The incident occurred after a black Labrador mix without a collar came sniffing around the duplex a few times. Since Jimmy loved to hunt, he took to the dog, and even mentioned to June that he might keep the animal and teach him how to retrieve ducks. After feeding him some table scraps, the dog stayed at the duplex. Jimmy finally let him in the house one cold night after he spotted the dog curled up and shivering under a tree. He soon became one of the family, and being a docile, well-tempered dog, the children took to him as well, riding him around the yard like a horse and brushing him with an old hair brush June had given them.

A few weeks later, Jimmy was in the cellar storing boxes. Lying next to him was the Labrador, calmly watching his new master do his work, and looking thoroughly contented to have found a warm new home replete with kids who loved him very much. Jimmy yelled up for June to bring him the last of the boxes, and she came downstairs to deliver them. On the way back up the stairs, the dog tried to run past Jimmy and got tangled in his legs, almost tripping him.

"He didn't fall but he almost did. It startled him and when Jimmy gets scared, he goes crazy. He began screaming at the dog and then did the most vicious thing I'd ever seen anyone do: he kicked the dog as hard as he could right in the testicles. The dog howled in pain and collapsed onto its hind legs. He couldn't get up and turned in circles crying and crying. It was terrible. I couldn't believe what I saw; it was way too severe a reaction to being tripped. No normal person would have done that. Then Jimmy opened the door and kicked the dog out of the house. The poor thing ran away and never came back."

A constant thorn in Jimmy's side remained the living situation at the duplex. He was uncomfortable with neighbors living a wall's width away. Not only did he know they heard the commotion and crying from the other side of the wall (the neighbor's banging was returned with Jimmy's high volume threats through the sheetrock), but having them in such close proximity hampered his ability to freely discipline his wife "when she needed it." Consequently, after a year's residency at the duplex, Jimmy asked his landlord if he happened to have another rental available. To his surprise, the landlord said yes, one had just become available on Central Street in Hudson.

Believing he would have more privacy in such a unit, Jimmy immediately drove over to take a look at the rental. Before going in to inspect the apartment, he noticed an auto repair garage directly across the street, and walked over to inquire about work. The owner said that, as a matter of fact, he could use an extra mechanic since he was getting backed up with work. Without bothering to look at the apartment, Jimmy drove back home, called the landlord, and told him he would take the unit.

There was no need for an inspection. The locality was too perfect to pass up. Certainly, it would be convenient getting to work, which would entail nothing more than a thirty second walk directly across the street from his apartment. But it wasn't the convenience that excited him — it was the vantage point he had from the garage.

Having become more and more possessive of June after she had the baby and slimmed down, and less trusting of women in general after being fired by one, Jimmy relished the idea of having even more control over his wife and her daily activities. At any given moment, he could look out from the garage and see clearly his apartment and driveway, and essentially watch every move his wife made. If she was going to cheat on him "like all women do," it would be awfully hard to do right under his nose.

Jimmy signed the lease that afternoon and told June about the new apartment. She didn't care that she wasn't consulted: she was *never* consulted such matters. And besides, she welcomed the change. The ever-present tension from the wall-pounding neighbor (which provoked many of her beatings) would now be eliminated. She hoped the move would ease Jimmy's tensions, and the with his new job, things could only get better for everyone. The following month, in January 1983, Jimmy again called his cousins to help him move, this time to the last apartment he would ever rent.

Steep, narrow stairs led to the two upstairs apartments. Downstairs, on either side of the staircase, were two more apartments. Outside, a yard larger than that at the duplex offered the children even more room to play and ride their bikes. The last tenants had left behind a swing set, picnic tables, and a rope swing with a plastic seat hanging from an oak tree. Attached to the building was a large garage where Jimmy could work on his motorcycle.

The shabby fourplex, built around 1900, was closer to town than the duplex had been, and in a rare bit of luck, one of the downstairs units was occupied by Jack Spiller, an old friend of Jimmy's, with whom he could now drink and spend time with again. Though her hopes for happiness had been dashed many times before, June again mustered enthusiasm for the new apartment, praying that with it would come a more settled family life.

It was a prayer unheard.

Walking up the dark stairway for the first time, June saw garbage bags everywhere. The stairwell was smelly because of the tenants' habit of leaving the refuse outside their apartments, but Jimmy didn't seem to notice. June had, and thought it might be an omen of some kind, but quickly dismissed it when she reached the top of the stairs. She was thrilled with what she saw in the entryway: a washer and dryer. She had never had her own before, and for years had trudged back and forth to the laundromat; now she was going to "live in luxury."

Her joy, however, was premature. Upon entering the apartment, June was less enthusiastic. The six-by-six entryway had seemed a bit cramped with the washer and dryer taking up almost all of the room, but at least she could do laundry at home for a change, and didn't mind the scant space. The living quarters were another story: there was less room here than at the duplex, and with the girls growing fast, she wondered how they would all manage.

Directly in front of the entrance was a small bathroom. The shower stall was even tinier than the Kinsley apartment's, and there was no bathtub, so Jana's pink plastic toy box would have to suffice for the children's baths. To the right of the bathroom was a ten-by-ten kitchen with an antique stove vented by an exposed black stovepipe. The original pine kitchen counter had been replaced with white Formica speckled with gold flakes. Shoved up against one wall was a small, folded, drop-leaf dinette table — the only type that would fit in the cramped quarters.

The children's room was next to the kitchen, and was so small that it could accommodate only one twin bed and a children's dresser. June later bought a set of used bunk beds at a second-hand furniture store, and asked the landlord to paint the room lilac (Jana's favorite color) to cover the dirty, cracked walls that had yellowed from years of cigarette smoke. The one and only closet in the entire apartment was in the girls' room, so June saw at once that she would have to use the musty attic for all of her storage, and rotate summer and winter clothes from closet to attic every six months.

Climbing the ladder to the attic the first day they moved in, June stood on the top rung and poked her head through the hole in the ceiling. She shined her flashlight into the space to consider how to best utilize it, and came upon an odd sight ten feet in front of her: pasted to the brick chimney, which ran from a lower apartment up through the roof, were old newspapers dating back to the 30s and 40s. For some reason, someone had taken the time to carefully arrange a collage of now-yellowed news stories, and then varnished them over to preserve them. Had June taken the time to look at them more closely, she would have seen all of the stories were tales of disaster and tragedy: wars, plane crashes, fires — and murders. Another omen, perhaps, but one to which June paid no attention, so great was her desire to make things work out. For her children, for herself, and for the man she was still trying desperately to love.

The bedroom was not a bedroom at all, and was really more like a cubbyhole extension of the kitchen where the roof rafters slanted down at a severe angle allowing just enough room to bend down and slip into a bed pushed against the sloped wall. One could not stand without moving to the outside edge of the bed, and there was no door separating the room from the kitchen.

The living room, however, was more generous in size, allowing Jimmy to arrange, face to face, both of his old couches. One was a well-worn, brown leather model with several tears that had been taped over with grey duct tape. The other, brown and tan plaid fabric, had a matching overstuffed chair that Jimmy placed in front of the television.

In between the two was a large redwood burl table, glossy from several coats of thick polyurethane.

On top of the television, Jimmy displayed a small stuffed fox on a driftwood stand, replete with snarling flews and menacing teeth. Jimmy was a hunter, and was particularly proud of this trophy; the girls, however, were terrified of it, and would not go near the television. Later, when Jimmy would leave the apartment and the girls wanted to watch television, June would put the dead animal behind the television and replace it when she heard Jimmy coming up the stairs.

Several of Jimmy's hunting weapons and trophies graced the walls of the dingy apartment: Bows and arrows on one wall; a mounted deer head on another; a row of ducks in flight on another. Displayed directly across from the deer head, in a large, eight-by-ten gun case, were Jimmy's ten rifles, numerous handguns, hunting vests, hats, duck calls, and ammunition, all in perfect order behind glass doors that June had to be keep immaculately clean.

"No fingerprints. No fingerprints. Jimmy harped on me about not having any fingerprints on his gun case. But how do you tell a one-year-old to keep her hands off the glass?" Such logic was of no interest to Jimmy, and June knew not to bring it up. Instead, keep a sharp eye on the glass, and whenever the children leave the room, run for the glass cleaner and hope to avoid a slap. It didn't always work.

When one of the downstairs apartments was about to become vacant, Jimmy called Frank Norton, another cousin of his who was looking for a cheap apartment to rent. He was married with two children, and needed a place with a larger yard for the kids. Jimmy thought the Central Street fourplex would be just the place for Frank and his family, and Frank agreed, signing the lease that day.

Shortly thereafter, another tenant moved in, this one causing June a new round of angst. He was Tom Weaver, Frank's brother-in-law, who had heard of the growing party potential at Central Street. Word had gotten around that Jack Spiller was looking for a roommate, and it happened that Tom needed a new place to live. So he moved in with Jack, and that night the two men went up to Jimmy's apartment for introductions. When June opened the door, she gasped.

"Tom was my first boyfriend. Well, not really a boyfriend — I was only twelve — but we liked each other in seventh grade for about two months, and used to walk and hold hands and sometimes kiss a little. I hadn't seen him since then, and there he was, standing at my door! I didn't know what to do, but I knew Jimmy would go crazy with jealousy if he found out about Tom. So I pretended I didn't know him; I just let them in and disappeared into the bedroom."

June had to be particularly careful now that she was hiding a secret that, innocent as it was, if exposed, would surely lead to a beating — or at the very least, another confrontation on "whoring around." Later, if Tom stopped by the apartment to borrow a tool or a beer when Jimmy wasn't there, both he and June would instinctively take a step back from each other as June opened the door. Tom, like everyone else, knew of Jimmy's notorious temper and was not at all interested in provoking him.

"It was nerve racking having Tom living downstairs. I worried that if he got drunk with the guys, he might say something about us, like the time my grandfather looked through the cellar window and caught us kissing. I prayed that Tom had forgotten about it, or if he didn't, would know enough to not say anything."

On the other hand, having Frank and his wife Deena in residence was a bonus. Their two children were about the same age at June's, and Frank adored Pam. "He would melt when Pammy was around, and Jimmy worried that when she began to talk more, she might tell Frank what was happening to us upstairs. But that would be a while yet. Now she could only saw a few words. If it wasn't so pathetic, it would have been comical that Pam's first perfectly clear word wasn't 'Mama' or 'Dadda,' it was 'Bitch.'"

Though Frank drank his share of alcohol, he was never violent toward his wife or children. Jimmy teased him, calling him "pussy whipped" and "a pansy" because he didn't "discipline" his wife enough, and was "soft" for letting Deena make decisions that "should be made by the man."

The first few months at Central Street were generally tolerable, thanks mostly to the distractions Jimmy had from his drinking buddies — Frank, Jack, and Tom — and the weekend parties they held. "I wouldn't say he was *happy*, because Jimmy was never *happy*. It was more like he was steady, more emotionally level, without the dips and peaks.

"And the kids were doing better too. Jana and Pam were having a wonderful time because they had Frank and Deena's kids to play with. And on weekends, Frank's brothers and cousins would bring over even more kids. They'd make Kool-Aid stands and charge a penny a glass. It they had any left over, they'd freeze it into homemade popsicles. Watching them have such a good time, I had a glimmer of hope that everything would be all right, that the kids might have a normal childhood after all.

"With all the activity around us, Jimmy paid less attention to me. At the parties, he'd play horseshoes and drink; other times he'd work on his bike. I was more social too. I wasn't as isolated as I'd been. I was meeting other women, learning how to talk and relate. I was feeling pretty normal, but I knew not to get too confident. Jimmy still controlled everything I did, and though he wasn't beating me as much, he was unpredictable.

"For example, if we were going to have a party, he might say, 'Wear that blue halter,' if he felt like showing me off; other times it was, '*Don't* wear that blue halter.' Sometimes

I could drink or play horseshoes; other times I couldn't. Sometimes he'd trust me to go get more beer; other times he'd tell me to sit where he could see me and not move without asking him. There was no way to know what he wanted."

One thing Jimmy *did* want, badly, was more money. Now that he had a new apartment, a new better-paying job, and a broadening social life, he liked the "adrenaline rush" he was getting and didn't want to "come down." But it wasn't enough. He still had his eye on that new car, and was considering buying a camping trailer a friend had for sale. He would need more money for these things, and one day came up with what he thought was a novel way to get it: commit welfare fraud.

Jimmy heard from a co-worker that all a woman had to do was apply for welfare saying her husband had left her and she didn't know where he was. "It'll be a piece of cake," the worker had said. "You guys will have it made."

Jimmy liked what he heard. It would be simple: the welfare department would give June money, food stamps, daycare, "hell, they'll even pay for her mileage," the worker had said. And it all was true.

"When I applied, all they asked me for was my birth date and social security number and I was on welfare. It was easier than Jimmy had said. To stay on, all I had to do was bring in a slip of paper every week showing where I applied for work."

June immediately quit her job at Teledyne and became a full-time mother — something she had always wanted. She had not, however, bargained for full-time slave, which soon became the more descriptive term. Though June hoped that Jimmy had really turned himself around, she secretly knew it was more likely that his buoyancy was temporary and he would return to his former abusive self. Her optimism quickly faded when she found the latter to be the case.

"Now that I was not working and had more free time, Jimmy turned more paranoid about where I went and what I did. When I used to go to work, he didn't worry because he knew where I was. Now he was watching me from across the street, and quizzed me the minute I came back from running an errand. Sometimes I'd leave without him noticing and he'd go nuts. He'd stop work and run across the street the minute I pulled in the driveway, demanding a complete itinerary of everything — even the route I took.

"To keep better tabs on me, he started leaving me long lists of chores I had to complete everyday: take the screens off the windows and vacuum them; wash the windows; pull out the drawers from under the bunk beds and dust behind them. It wasn't about cleanliness, because he wasn't clean — he was greasy and smelly. It was about control. He got to the point where he was even telling me how he wanted the *beds* made. Beds? Jimmy never made a bed in his life!"

The welfare scam was working beautifully: June pretended to look for work while making it obvious to her prospective employers that she was not interested in employment — she was making too much money on the program. She continued to collect check after check and food stamps whenever she needed them. For the first time in years, money began to accumulate in the cookie jar. (Because there had been so little surplus every week, the cookie jar served as the bank. Jimmy said he didn't trust banks and didn't need a checking account; in fact, he had applied for one and was turned down).

Five months into the program, June came home excited after meeting with her welfare case worker. She had told June that the department was going to send her to vocational school and teach her "a marketable skill." She would finally be able to earn a decent living and be free from the limitations she had lived with all her life. She would be educated, and Jimmy would be proud of her. She would be a contributor and help him realize his dream of prosperity; it even said so in the pamphlets she clutched as she ran across the street to tell Jimmy the news.

"School? They want to send you to school?" asked Jimmy, wiping his hands on his overalls.

"That's right, Jimmy. Isn't it great?"

"Let me see those pamphlets."

June handed them over proudly, smiling broader than she'd smiled in months. A moment later they were in shreds on the garage floor.

"You're too stupid to learn this shit!" said Jimmy as he tore up the last pamphlet. "And you need to be home with the kids anyway."

June forgot who she was dealing with. Even though the welfare scam was moving him ahead, and allowed him to put enough money away to buy another hunting rifle, he was willing to let it all go to keep his wife from learning anything but total dependence on him.

"He would have rather starved than seen me educated. And now I know why: he feared that if I learned about the real world, about how people really live and how other wives relate to their husbands — rather than bow down to them — it would be too threatening. I know he thought I'd leave him; it was his biggest fear. First, his mother left him; then Cheryl dumped him; then he was *fired* by a woman. He couldn't handle it — he *hated* women.

"He hated women so much that once, in the middle of the night, he woke up out of a deep sleep screaming, 'Women suck! They're goddamn whores! They all suck!' Then he fell fast asleep again and didn't remember a thing in the morning."

June turned and ran from the garage. She ran to her children who were playing in the yard and hugged them close. "I wanted to cry, to really let go and weep, but I couldn't. It's not just that I didn't want to upset the kids, it's that I was beyond crying by then. I *couldn't* cry anymore. I was cried out.

"I was tired of hoping and praying and being let down. I promised myself right then and there that I would never cry again because of someone hurting me. And I kept that promise."

The next day Jimmy made June call the welfare office and say that her husband had returned and that she didn't need welfare anymore. He was so unnerved by her desire to educate herself, that he took a new measure to assure that she stayed sequestered in his controlled environment: he banned all books — including the phonebook.

"He took the phonebook and threw it away. He said I didn't need it. Why did we need a phonebook? I knew which pizza parlor and Chinese take-out he liked, and that was all I was supposed to know. He wanted me to have as little contact as possible with the outside world. If he saw a book around, he'd pick it up and say, 'You don't need this junk' and throw it away. He wanted me stupid like he was, and tried to make me believe I was. When he got mad, one of his favorite things to say was, 'You're stupid, right, June?' And I'd answer, 'Yes' — and believe it!

"Jimmy controlled the television too. He would only allow the shows *he* selected. Educational shows were out. Once when *Jeopardy* was on, I was kind of half watching it and mumbled the right answer to a question. It got him so mad that he jumped up and said, 'That's it! No more! I don't know why you watch this shit; it's not like you can understand it!' and turned off the television. It was obvious that he was talking about *himself*, but he was too unaware — too stupid, really — to know it.

"He also liked to belittle me in front of the kids; show them I was stupid or an 'airhead.' That was one of his favorite terms: airhead. If the kids were making too much noise, he'd say things to them like, 'Shut up or you'll be just like your mother — no good; you won't amount to anything.' They didn't know what he was talking about, but *I* did, and I knew he was talking about himself again. He was throwing on me all the hate he had for himself."

June's quitting welfare was a double-edged sword for Jimmy. By forcing her to quit the program, he felt he lessened the chances she would leave him (though in reality, she could not conceive of it after all the death threats he had made). On the other hand, without the additional income, he had no way to acquire the material possessions that were so important to him, or the social status he so craved. Therefore, he determined that it was June again who was cramping his style, keeping him from getting ahead, causing him unneeded anxiety. "It's the women, always the goddamn women who fuck things up!" he said over and over. "They need to stay home with a kid on their tit! They need to *stay put*!"

But June was a mother and a wife. She couldn't "stay put" all day long; she had to go shopping and run errands. Jimmy's earlier interrogations of his wife's whereabouts began to take on a greater intensity. His fear level was rising, though June had done nothing to cause it. He was getting worse, not better.

Evidence of his ever-increasing paranoia came the day after June quit welfare. His new command was: "You are not to leave this house unless I *tell* you to leave. And don't forget: I know where you are all the time."

"But Jimmy," protested June. "Sometimes I've got to run to the store to get milk and bread and ..."

June didn't finish her sentence. Jimmy leapt at her and grabbed her by the throat and yelled, "You obviously didn't hear me! What did I just say?"

June struggled to get out an answer but could not because she was being choked. She tried to spit out an answer but it was indecipherable. And Jimmy became more enraged.

"*What did I say?!*" he demanded.

"Not ... to ... leave ... home," she sputtered.

"*Wrong!*" he said, and slapped her with the back of his hand. Her head snapped from one side to the other. "That's what I said *before*. What did I *just* say?"

June thought quickly. He had said a lot of things. Which one was he referring to? She'd try again and pray it was the right answer. "You said you know where I am all the time."

"*Finally,* you dumb bitch. Fucking *finally!* Now repeat it!"

"You know where I am all the time."

"Again."

"You know where I ..."

"All right, all right! Shut the fuck up. I hope you've got it this time, because next time I'll keep squeezing your goddamn pencil neck and I won't stop. You got it?"

June tried to nod that she understood but under Jimmy's vice grip, she could not move her head. She quickly gurgled out the words, "Got ... it" and Jimmy released his grip.

Cut off from welfare and with no source of income, June would have to find work again. Jimmy knew it and was torn. He ardently wanted to keep his wife isolated from outside influences, but he desperately wanted the money she could bring in — especially after getting used to her welfare income.

"The conflict was torture for Jimmy. At this point, he was the most anxious I had seen him. But he knew I had to work, so he gave me explicit instructions to drop the children off at Grandma's house, go directly to my job interviews, pick them up, and come straight home. I did exactly as he said, and then I found a job."

After a week of searching, June saw an ad for an opening at New England Microwave, this time making PC boards for computers. Again, she lied and said she was experienced at the work, and again she was hired on her word and learned quickly what to do while on the job.

One of the things she had to do was "not talk to anybody." As always, Jimmy was afraid that someone would find out he was beating his wife and report him. And it was more likely to happen if June got friendly with her co-workers. Thus, the command: "Keep your mouth shut."

"I was shy to start with, but now that I knew how violent Jimmy was and how he'd interrogate me about every little thing I did, I thought it best to do *exactly* what he said, and that meant not talking to anybody at work. When I first took the job at New England Microwave, I took a station at the far end of the room so I wouldn't have to interact with anyone. It was just as well because the older women — the ones who had been there forever — didn't like me because I used to work for the competitor, Teledyne.

"I didn't even go to the bathroom because I knew I might have to talk to someone. At lunch I would go to my car and drink soda. I wouldn't eat because I was too nervous. I tried the cafeteria one time and it was too overwhelming. People tried to talk to me, ask questions. I couldn't take it and got up and left.

"Jimmy said not to talk and I wasn't going to take the chance. He had ways of finding out things, and if he heard I talked to someone, it would mean a beating. Later, they moved a woman from another area to my station. But there wasn't any problem. She talked constantly; she loved to talk and talk and talk. It didn't matter if I listened or not, or if I didn't answer. That was okay with her, because then she could talk more."

June's new job started at seven in the morning, while Jimmy's started at eight. June welcomed the hour difference since she went to work about the time Jimmy was getting up, leaving no time for dialogue. She took the children back to the babysitter, but now Jimmy gave explicit instructions not to talk to her either.

"How can you take your kids to a babysitter and not *talk*? Plus, Jimmy had me prep the kids and tell them, 'Now remember, anything that happens at our home is family business. You're not to talk about it to anyone, even the babysitter, okay?' That didn't make any sense to them at all, but it's what Jimmy wanted me to tell them. They were confused but nodded their heads even though they didn't know what in the world I was talking about.

"The babysitter must have thought it was odd that I was suddenly so cool to her after all the time we had been using her. I'd pop in, grab the kids, and leave. It was obvious I didn't want to talk to her; I know she knew something was up."

When June returned from work every day, Jimmy quizzed her on who she had talked to and what was said. "I worked, Jimmy. I didn't talk to anybody," she would say. And she didn't. Nor did she dare lie about it — or anything else. She had already learned her lesson one Saturday evening, a few weeks after starting her job.

Very casually, while taking a beer from the refrigerator, Jimmy had asked June in a nonchalant tone where she had gone that day. June didn't know it was a trap, and absentmindedly, rattled off various stops she had made: "Oh, you know, the post office, the supermarket, the gas station. Oh, and I stopped by my grandmother's to pick up a pie." June had her back to Jimmy, and he suddenly spun her around, grabbed her by the shoulders, and slammed her into the refrigerator.

"What about Maple Street? What were you doing on *Maple street*?! he demanded. "Who did you *talk* to, goddamn it?! I want some answers!"

The donut shop. June forgot about the donut shop. Yes, the kids had asked for treats and she had driven them to get glazed donuts and cartons of milk. Somehow, Jimmy found out.

"I didn't talk to anyone. Honest. I forgot about the donuts. Honest, Jimmy, I just forgot. The kids wanted ..."

"Why didn't you mention the fucking donut shop? You were *there*. I just *asked* you where you went. Why didn't you say the donut shop?"

"Because I forgot, I just forgot."

"You forgot? You *can't* forget! I'm warning you, bitch, if you ever forget again, you'll get a beating you'll never forget, understand?"

June understood, and from then on was alert to every stop, every day. She didn't know how Jimmy knew where she was, but from that day forth, she started believing he was invincible, that he had awesome powers with which he could control her. "Up until then, I didn't pay all that much attention to every detail of my day. I'd be thinking about whether or not I needed more diapers, which store had what on sale, things like that. Now I was worried that if I had to stop to wipe Pam's nose, and it was in front of some guy's house, Jimmy would find out about it and accuse me of having an affair with him; that's how irrational he was getting."

June began to see her world as "a tiny cubicle" that was controlled at all times by her omniscient husband. She had heard him boast often enough that he could "take down" five or six "fucking pigs" (cops) at a time, and had heard from others how "bad" Jimmy Briand was in his youth, never losing a fight and never ending one until the man on the receiving end was bloodied beyond recognition.

Now she was afraid to take a wrong turn, to "make a mistake" while driving and end up on the wrong street or on a block where she had no business. He'd find out, she was sure, and he would grill her for hours, even days, about what she was doing and who she was *really* going to see. Then he would punish her.

At this point in her relationship, June was falling into what psychologists refer to as "learned helplessness" —

a complex psycho-social condition that leaves a woman powerless to do anything to stop her attacker. Being battered over and over again, particularly within a short period of time, diminishes a victim's ability to respond, and convinces her that there is nothing she can do to help herself.

"Such beatings are like shock waves," said one psychologist and expert in domestic abuse who later examined June. "They envelop a person totally — physically, emotionally, mentally — and seem inescapable no matter what she does. The worst of it is, since her perception is altered — and June's was particularly distorted — she believes she has no way out of her situation, and thus her motivation to do something to change it dissolves.

"People in June's situation become passive because their ability to perceive accurately is changed. They find that when they take certain actions, they do not get the expected results. When this happens often enough, they begin to believe that there will *never* be a favorable outcome to anything they do. This is exactly what happened to Ms. Briand — her *perception* became her *reality*, and she was crippled by it."

As Jimmy's paranoia grew, and his dreams of prosperity died, his neuroses became more intense, and took on weird qualities. Orderliness now became an obsession with Jimmy. The cupboards in the Central Street apartment were larger than those at the duplex, and Jimmy took advantage of the extra room. In the past, it was acceptable to leave the cold cereal on top of the refrigerator. The children ate it almost every morning, so June kept it handy. That habit had to change, as did the general arrangement of everything else in the cupboards.

Cold cereals were to be kept on the left, hot cereals on the right. "Don't get them messed up; I want them separate."

All labels were to face outward and be perfectly straight. "I don't want to see the back of no goddamn cans of soup; I want to know what I'm lookin' at." Large cans and boxes in the back, small ones in the front. "If people come through here," Jimmy said during his instructions to June, "I want them to see things are *right*." To this, June's immediate thought was *Who would look?*

Stricter rules were imposed for the rest of the housekeeping as well. Vegetable bins were to be removed from the refrigerator once a week and washed. *All* food was to be removed from the refrigerator every other week and the racks wiped down. The washing machine in the entryway was noticeable to people entering the apartment, so after each use, the soap dispenser was to be rinsed with boiling water in order to wash away any caked detergent that may have accumulated after the last load.

In January of 1984, about a year after moving to Central Street, Jimmy's violence reached a new height. His obsession over orderliness was more intense than ever, and June was becoming more and more submissive, trying harder each day to do things the way Jimmy wanted. At the same time, Jimmy was becoming more moody, and less satisfied with himself. He was drinking more than ever. Even in the morning, his breath reeked of beer.

"I was not infallible. I couldn't be everywhere watching everything at every moment, but that's exactly what Jimmy expected. One day when Jimmy came home for lunch, he went to the refrigerator and poured a glass of milk, but I was doing something and wasn't watching him. I heard him say, 'What's this?' and then I held my breath. I thought he was looking at the milk lid and saw some dried milk on it. I knew I'd get hit for that. But he was just asking about some leftovers. I was so relieved.

"Then he told me to make him a peanut butter and jelly sandwich. I grabbed the jars and opened them on the wooden cutting board and made the sandwich. I had just screwed the lid back on the peanut butter when Jimmy grabbed the jar and held it up to the light like he was trying to look through it. Then I saw what I did wrong: the lid was on crooked.

"In a flash, he picked up the knife and stabbed me in the back of the hand. He caught me in the web between my first and second finger. I couldn't move my hand; it was impaled on the cutting board. I just looked at the knife sticking out of my hand. It wasn't the pain that was so bad, it was seeing my hand stuck to the board. I felt sick to my stomach. Then he said, 'If you can't get the lid on right, maybe you should stand there and think about it for a while.'

"I was beyond crying by then. And I still didn't think he was mean; that's how crazy I was getting. I thought, as usual, that it was my fault for not getting the lid on straight and that if I had done like I was supposed to, if I had been a better wife, this wouldn't have happened. It was *never* Jimmy's fault."

The closest Jimmy ever came to giving an apology for anything came later that night when he walked in and saw June sitting quietly at the kitchen table with a bandage on her hand. She was gazing at the wall, looking at nothing. Jimmy passed by her on the way to the refrigerator. He took out a beer, closed the door, twisted off the cap, and stood there for a moment. He looked at his wife and said, "I wish you would stop making me do these things to you." Then he took a swig from the bottle, burped loudly, and walked into the living room to watch television.

Jimmy's dream of success was no different from June's dream of a happy marriage, but neither were materializing. Even Jimmy's beloved job at the garage wasn't working out as he had hoped, with the owner often sending him home, supposedly for lack of work, but really because of bad attitude. As a result, Jimmy began drinking more and staying out later in the evening. Sometimes he was too hungover in the morning to work even when his boss wanted him, and he made June call across the street to say he was sick and wouldn't be in.

Then a new pattern developed: About once a week, Jimmy wouldn't come home at all, or he would come in at two in the morning after closing down a bar. With June working long hours at New England Microwave, she didn't see her children nearly as much as she wanted, and welcomed Jimmy's new behavior pattern. She took advantage of the calm, peaceful evenings to play with Pam and Jana, and began hoping Jimmy would stay away longer so she could give her children some semblance of the normal home life she longed for.

After spending hours drinking and fighting, Jimmy would often bring drinking buddies home from the bar. Once, at two-thirty in the morning, he brought four of them home for breakfast, and woke up June to cook it. In the process, he woke up the children. "I had to get up and get dressed and make breakfast, but Pam started crying so I stopped and gave her her bottle. Jimmy's yelling at me to get cooking, Pam's wailing, then Jana starts crying; it was chaos.

"The guys felt bad and said they'd leave, that they didn't need breakfast. Jimmy said, 'No, she'll cook it,' and turned to me and gave me the order: 'We want fried eggs, bacon, and home fries.' But that wasn't the end of it. He stood right behind me while I cooked. He squeezed my shoulder and kept saying, 'Don't break the yokes,' or 'Don't make the bacon too crisp.' I didn't cry, but tears came to my eyes. I was just so tired, so tired of everything — the way we were living, Jimmy's craziness, his violence, just everything. After I served them, I put the children back to bed, and when I came out again, everyone was gone. The food was just sitting there; they hadn't touched a thing."

With more time off from work, Jimmy started going hunting more often and staying away longer. His stepfather was a hunter, and the two would occasionally go off for long weekends during the season. If it was winter, they'd go ice fishing and sit in their little shack and get drunk. Jimmy would often test June, saying he was going to be gone several days, then show up back home the following morning.

"He thought he was going to catch me with some man in my bed. Or off whoring around. He never did, nor did I ever give him the slightest reason to think I would. But he still didn't trust me; he didn't trust *any* woman."

Jimmy was more possessive than ever now, and before leaving on trips, would give June explicit instructions to not leave the house. "You have everything you need," he'd say. But many times she didn't. If she ran out of milk or cereal, she had to buy it, and, knowing her husband was far away, didn't see any harm in running down the street to the convenience store to pick up the items. Usually she got away with such violations, but on one occasion Jimmy caught her.

He had just returned from a trip, and opened the refrigerator door for a beer when he spied a bottle of Coca-Cola that had not been there when he left. "Where did this come from?" he asked June.

"Where did what come from?"

"The Coke. We didn't have any Coke when I left. Where did it come from?"

"Jimmy," June said, more exasperated than afraid. "The kids wanted soda. We didn't have any soda. So I ran across the street. I was only gone *five minutes*." Jimmy walked close to June and looked her in the eye. She looked at the floor. He made a slight body movement and she flinched, expecting the sting of a slap.

"What are you so nervous about?" he asked, smiling. She didn't answer. "Hey, I'm talking to you. *Look* at me when I'm talking to you."

"I'm not nervous," she said nervously, looking up from the floor and then back down. He grabbed her chin and wrenched it upward. She had no choice but to look in his dark, pitiful eyes.

"What are you *scared* of, huh? I told you not to leave the house, and you did. But I'm not going to hit you this time. What do you think about that?"

"That's good, Jimmy."

"Damn right that's good. But don't ever leave again unless I *say* leave, got it?"

"Got it."

"Who's the goddamn boss around here?"

"You are, Jimmy, you are."

"Damn straights I am."

June was relieved that her momentarily-benevolent husband did not feel the need to discipline her for her infraction, but the reprieve only served to put her further on edge. "There was no telling with him anymore. Sometimes he'd say, 'Why aren't you looking at me?' Other times it would be, 'Why *are* you looking at me?' I couldn't win, and I could no longer predict what to do and when to do it. The rules were constantly changing now and without the clues he used to give me, I just had to know. And I didn't always."

June also had to know things Jimmy should have known, like where particular pieces of his clothing were at any given moment. Before one hunting trip, Jimmy was rummaging through the pile of clothes at the foot of the bed, trying to find a plaid flannel shirt he wanted to take on the trip. He yelled to June and she responded, "I think it's out here by the dryer. I'll find it and dry it; it'll only take ten minutes." Jimmy was in no mood to wait, but had no choice and grunted his agreement.

A few minutes later June came into the apartment, looking scared. Jimmy was in the bathroom when June went in and said, "I can't find it." She knew the news would not sit well with Jimmy, and it didn't. Without saying a word, he shoved her backwards and she tripped and fell into the shower. That brought down the shower curtain, whose rod separated into two pieces. That incensed Jimmy further and he grabbed the loose end and began the whipping.

He struck June first on her side, then on her neck, and then on her head. And there he stayed. Over and over, he whipped the steel rod down onto June's head and shoulders, cutting her hands with one stroke and her scalp with the other as she tried futilely to protect herself. Blood suddenly spurt from a gash behind her ear. He had gotten through the frantic hands that flailed wildly about the head, trying to predict where the next blow would fall. And it seemed to drive him to more fury. He was like a mad horseman trying to force a dying horse to move, a horse tied in the corner of a corral with no place to go.

When the beating was over, Jimmy got up silently, looked down at his bleeding wife, said nothing, and left for three days. In pain and severely bruised, June felt a new, strange sensation. Inexplicably, it was one of elation.

"The beating was terrible but it wasn't what I focused on. I thought about the fact that he would stay away for several days again; that was his pattern. And that's what I found so relieving: being away from him. I started looking forward to those weekends when he left. It was the only thing I *did* look forward to — being away from my husband.

"When I thought about that, I realized that more than being afraid, I was very, very sad. I *wanted* a husband and a family. And here I was hoping my mate would stay away as long as possible. If I could have cried I would have, but I couldn't anymore."

To keep from setting off her husband, June learned not to flinch, not to cry, not to look at her husband unless he demanded she do so. He was like a cloud of gaseous vapor ready to explode with the tiniest spark. June was not about to provide the friction for those sparks, and began to slowly shut down. So did her children.

Jana's first day of school should have been a happy time but it was not. It was September 1984, and the family had been at Central Street for almost two years. Jana was five and a half, and both her and June's relationships with Jimmy had greatly deteriorated. Pam still didn't know any better than to run to her father when he came home from work, and was oblivious to his stench of grease and beer. But Jana had long since given up greeting him at the door.

The day she was to go to school, Jimmy got up early and called work, saying he'd be late, that he had some "family business" to attend to. Mornings were never a good time for the girls because Jimmy was there, and he was usually in a foul mood due to a hangover, or because things weren't being done precisely according to the Jimmy Briand doctrine. This morning, he was even more of a nuisance than usual.

"He needed to inspect Jana's backpack to make sure she was taking everything she needed; he couldn't trust that I might be able to take care of that. He pulled out her favorite jacket — the one she had packed special and wanted to take with her on her first day of school. Jimmy threw it aside and said, 'Get the windbreaker I gave you; that's the one you're taking.' Jana protested but all that did was bring a threat: 'You want something to complain about? I'll give you something to complain about. Now get the windbreaker!'

"Then he started in on this pathetic lecture about how she wasn't supposed to talk to strangers. Strangers. Who were the strangers? Her classmates! It was an odd way to characterize little kids. He said she should not to talk to them or discuss anything that goes on in our house, that it was private business. Here was a little girl going off to her first day of school all excited, and her father's telling her not to *talk* to anybody. I felt so sorry for her."

Jimmy's obsession with family secrecy took its toll on Jana. She was utterly confused at school, not knowing how to relate to others and always remembering her father's stern warning: "Don't talk to strangers." Consequently, Jana failed miserably in school.

"She couldn't focus on her work. Every night when she tried to tell me about her day or do a simple first-grade assignment, she'd break down crying. She got so frustrated because she couldn't concentrate or explain herself. When she had a problem with an assignment or had done poorly on a project, Jimmy would call her a retard and say, 'If that's what you want to be, go ahead.' When I tried to help her, he'd yell, 'No! Get away from her and let her be a retard.' Then he'd add for my benefit: 'After all, she's only female.' That was one of his favorite digs. If the girls were hurt or crying about something, he'd say, 'Stop being so *female*.' He'd say me and my kids would never amount to anything because we were female.

"And because Jana was the one who reacted, she was the one he picked on. When he was in a nasty mood, he'd walk up to her and tap real hard on her head and say, 'You're going to be just like your mother, an airhead.'"

Jimmy was upset not just because Jana was doing poorly in school, but because he could not get any information out of her. He could not determine what she may have revealed to her schoolmates about the family. "When she got home from school, he'd ask her, 'Who did you talk to today?' as if she could possibly answer such an absurd question. She's at school; there are kids all around her. He'd ask, 'Who did you sit with at lunch time? What did you talk about?' She'd look at me, not knowing how to answer, and I'd just shut my eyes."

One night after grilling Jana without success, he showed to what depths he had sunk and how vicious he could be even to a small child. It gave June yet more insight into the man she was living with. "Jana was afraid of the dark, so I'd leave the bathroom door open and the light on for her. This one night she was crying because she didn't know how to answer her father's questions; they weren't making any sense — to her *or* to me.

"He kept at it though, and kept badgering her about what she did that day and who she talked to. But she wouldn't answer him, and got so frustrated that he picked her up and took her into her bedroom. Then he went to the bathroom and turned off the light. That really got her screaming. After that, he went to *her* room and slammed the door shut. He yelled through the door, 'There. Now you've got something to cry about.'

"I've never heard a child scream in such terror. Jimmy stood by the door blocking it so I couldn't get near it and just let her scream. Ten minutes went by, then twenty. She was banging on the door and screaming so much she was getting hoarse. She was terrified! After a half an hour of torturing Jana, he walked away and I ran to open the door. She was pale and shivering and her nose was all runny. I couldn't believe he did that to his own daughter."

The more volatile Jimmy became, the more apprehensive June became. Like a wounded animal walking through the woods, she'd watch and listen for every sound, hoping to spot danger before being attacked again. One sound she came to rely on was that coming from the stairwell.

"The stairs were a big cue. I could tell from the creaking on the stairs if Jimmy was coming or going. I learned to listen carefully because sometimes he would play tricks on me. One time he left and started down the stairs. I tiptoed over to the door and put my ear against it. It didn't sound like he'd taken enough steps, so I waited for a while and kept listening at the door. Finally I decided I was being silly, that he must have gone, so I opened the door — and there he was glaring at me. He'd been standing there for ten minutes. He looked up at me and said, 'Where do you think you're going?'"

June also became more aware of time. The kids loved to "play tents" in the kitchen, and June would often pull out

Pam's old baby blankets and make an entire fort, complete with six-foot tunnel and an area for eating. "We'd play in the tent with flashlights, then have dinner on plastic plates. Everybody would be having a ball until I looked at the clock on the wall. The kids couldn't tell time, but they could read my face. I'd get serious and they would get tense; they knew it was time to clean everything up before Jimmy got home because he didn't like the mess in the kitchen."

When June heard footsteps coming up the stairs and say, "Daddy's coming," Jana would run to the bathroom and look through the space behind the door to watch the entranceway. If Pam ran to Jimmy without being told "Get away," Jana knew it was safe to come out.

"Pam had a way with Jimmy. He didn't pick on her the way he did Jana because she was more bold. If he yelled at her, Pam didn't react. But Jana was hurt. Once, when Pam was almost three and just tall enough to reach the door knob, she saw Jimmy slam me into the coat rack and start hitting me. She was fearless, and walked over to the door and said, 'I'm going down to tell Uncle Frank.' Jimmy stopped immediately."

As the months went on, June continued to shut down. She was doing everything right, leaving no openings to incite her husband, and still it was not good enough. Even her nervousness was a sore spot with Jimmy, a constant reminder of what he was doing to his wife and family. But rather than atone, Jimmy succumbed to his guilt and his behavior worsened; he now turned to weapons to terrify his wife.

Jimmy kept his Buck knife in a pouch on his belt unless he entered a bar; then he hid it in his boot. He had modified the latching device so that when he flipped the knife a certain way, the blade would fly open and lock like a switchblade. One night before Jimmy got home, June was busying herself in the kitchen, and as always, kept one ear on the stairwell. The children were in bed, and June had just checked the refrigerator to make sure she had several dishes from which Jimmy could select a meal. Then she heard the steps creaking.

"I knew he was going to be drunk. Usually the best thing to do then is feed him. When I met him at the door, I said hello and asked if he wanted something to eat. He lunged at me and grabbed me by the throat and pinned me against the door. He had choked me many times before, but this time I heard the snap on the Buck knife pouch; then I heard the blade flick open. I couldn't see it but I heard it and my mind went into high gear. I tried to think quick: Where did I go without telling him? Was it the milk lid again? Fingerprints on the gun case? I couldn't think what I had done wrong.

"I wouldn't look at him, I couldn't. He was too crazed to look at. Then he screamed, 'Look at me, goddamn it! Look at me!' But he didn't want me to look at *him*, he wanted me to see the knife. He held it right in front of me — two inches from my eyes. But it was *his* eyes that were scaring me: they were red and bloodshot; he stank of booze and grease and looked like the mental patients I used to see at the state hospital — only crazier.

"Then he stuck the point of the knife to my neck. I knew he was going to slit my throat, I just knew it. And the only thing I could think about was the kids. What about the kids? They'd be left alone with *him* — a madman. He'd kill them too!

"I could feel the point digging in and it hurt. I thought this time he was going to do it—he was going to give it a quick shove and kill me like he always threatened to do. I was waiting to die when he said, 'All you women *suck*! I don't know why we keep you around. I could stick you like a pig and no one would know, no one would *care*! No one would even come looking for you!'

"Then he let me go and went to the bathroom. I stood there not moving. He flushed the toilet and went to the living room and turned on the TV. I still stood there, not knowing what to do. Five minutes later, he walked back in and calmly asked, 'What do we have to eat?' I listed off, 'Chicken, pizza, hamburgers, meat loaf ...'"

The knife incident disturbed June deeply. She had been beaten over and over by her husband, but he had never gone this far before. With the introduction of a lethal weapon, whose point was poised to sever her jugular vein in a mad instant, June now saw a man out of control, and for the first time, contemplated the forbidden: getting away from him.

She did not, however, see herself leaving her husband. He had threatened often enough that if she ever tried, he would find her and kill her. Now she knew he meant it; he was getting closer. Perhaps as a coping mechanism, perhaps as a deep-seated, unconscious desire, June started fantasizing about Jimmy being the one to die. "In my mind I saw every detail: the hospital; the funeral; how the kids would take it; how I'd work for a while, then move to another area and try to forget everything. The only thing I didn't see was how he died; that was never clear."

June also fantasized many times about calling the police, but each time the idea arose, she quickly dismissed it as out of the question. Asked later why she hadn't called authorities (indeed, this was often the *first* question people asked) she said: "Two things kept me her from lifting the receiver: One, Jimmy said if I ever called the authorities, he would beat me so badly I would never talk on a phone again. And two, he had always taught me that the police were the enemy. Look what they had done to him in jail: the handcuffs and the black hands. The times he and his cousins were arrested — supposedly without justification. The treatment he got in jail. He taught me that the police were no good and that they'd never believe a word I said anyway."

June had one other fantasy that came and went, one which she eventually acted on. Against her better judgment, she slowly and cautiously began stashing away small amounts of money in a secret hiding place. She was well aware of the threats Jimmy had made about her ever leaving him, but as things continued to deteriorate, all she could do was think of her children.

"I didn't know how bad our lives would get, and I didn't want to be left unprepared if I saw we had to leave in a hurry. I didn't know *how* we would leave but it was a fantasy that kept coming up for me. Jimmy was getting more and more unpredictable, and I thought that one day I might take my sister up on her offer to have me and the kids come live with her in California. She said it would take about three thousand dollars to make the move, so little by little — a dollar or two at a time — I started saving up."

Though June had fantasized about leaving, and was putting away small amounts of money, in her heart she was just going through the motions. She knew she had no intention of leaving her husband and no desire to test his resolve — particularly after he returned from one of his hunting trips and made it clear just how much danger she was in living with this man. If the knife to the throat was not convincing enough, the incident following his return was.

Jimmy had long ago made his first threat to kill June, and ever since then, such verbal taunts increased in direct proportion to the physical assaults, which were becoming more frequent and more forceful. The day he returned from hunting, he decided to clean his rifle and several of his handguns, and had laid them out on a towel on the coffee table. The girls knew never to come near the guns when

Jimmy was cleaning them — not so much for safety's sake, but so Jimmy would not worry about them picking up and misplacing a gun part.

On this particular afternoon, the girls ran inside carrying their plastic swing seat, which had broken off from its rope. They complained to June and said, 'Ask Daddy to fix it.' Without thinking, June walked into the living room and said, "The girls want to know if ..." and then cut herself short. She could see Jimmy was concentrating on his guns, and didn't want to bother him. "Oh, never mind," she said, and turned to walk out of the room.

"No, tell me," he said.

"It can wait," she said, leaving the room.

"*Get in here* and tell me what the *problem* is!" he screamed. With that, June picked up the broken seat and brought it to Jimmy. Looking right at it, he again said, "What's the problem?" June took this as a bad sign. He was looking for a confrontation, and she didn't know how to avoid it. So she simply said, "The kids brought this in and wanted to know if you could fix it."

"Does it look like I can fix it right now?"

"No, it doesn't. That's why I said never mind."

"But you *knew* I was cleaning my guns, didn't you?"

"Yes, but ..."

"So you *knew* I wouldn't be able to fix it right now, but you had to bring it in anyway, didn't you?"

"Jimmy, I just ..." June made the mistake of not answering the question immediately and specifically. She knew better, but "wasn't thinking."

Jimmy leapt from his chair and screamed, "When I'm doing this shit I can't be bothered with ..." He was too enraged to finish the sentence. He snatched a gun from the table and grabbed June from behind. He put her in a headlock and pressed the muzzle to her temple and said through gritted teeth, "Why do you keep *pushing* me?! Huh? WHY?!" Then he placed his lips to her ear and whispered a threat she had heard before: "I could kill you right now and no one would know; no one would care. I could blow you away and that would be the end of you."

Jimmy eased his grip and June broke away and ran to the bathroom. She slammed the door and refused to come out the rest of the night. But it didn't matter; Jimmy had already seen the effect of this attack on his wife, and he liked it. This time she was particularly shaken — even more than she had been during knife threat.

"After the first gun incident, Jimmy began threatening me with them more and more. On several occasions he would open his gun case, pull out a rifle, sit back in his living room chair as if he was going to clean it, but instead, point it at me while he sighted through the scope, just like he had done with Cheryl. He'd laugh and repeat his usual threats, but it wasn't at all funny because I never knew if the rifles were loaded — and I *did* know how unstable he was."

By adding weapons to his repertoire of torture, Jimmy broke his wife down further. Soon there was a noticeable change in the way June carried herself. Over the years, she had been coming out of the introversion she had suffered in childhood, and was gaining confidence as she met more people at parties and family get-togethers. Then everything reversed itself.

As the verbal, physical, and psychological abuse increased, June's self-esteem regressed to its pre-teen stage. Now she looked constantly at the floor to avoid people's gaze — especially her husband's. Her shoulders started rounding forward, and her eyes became watery, with dark grey circles under them. She was more sensitive to noise, and jumped if a motorcycle backfired or the children slammed a cupboard door.

Tense, nervous, afraid, June became more and more uncertain of herself in an uncertain world. Because of her dysfunctional childhood, she never developed the coping skills required to deal with the life she was now leading. Finally, it became too much, and she began to succumb.

June became fearful of everything — both inside and outside of her home. She was often confused and could not think clearly. She felt shame for having endured the acts of abuse she had, and guilt for "letting" her children see them. She often felt dizzy and disoriented, and drifted into deep depressions for weeks at a time. Then, for no apparent reason, she'd snap out of them for short periods, only to return to her sorrowful state shortly thereafter.

Exacerbating June's plight was her inability to communicate to anyone about her home life. She was utterly alone in a cage with a beast — a beast she loved and feared at the same time. Many days June would wander around the apartment without purpose or direction. Her perception of reality was becoming warped, and she saw no possible way to escape the man who said over and over he would kill her if she ever tried.

June's eating habits began to suffer as well. At five-foot-five, she was usually a thin one hundred pounds. By late 1985, she had dropped to ninety-five pounds and virtually stopped eating. (Two years later, she would be down to ninety pounds — only ten pounds more than her nine-year-old daughter.) She nibbled at a cookie or cracker after the children were off to bed, and in the morning, took an apple to work and ate it alone in her car during her lunch break.

If it weren't for Jimmy's increasingly frequent excursions away from the house, June's physical and mental deterioration would be have been more rapid. "Jimmy was gone a lot, so it gave me time to recuperate. I'd play with the kids more, and pretend to be like any other mother. I hoped it would make them feel normal too, but I could see it wasn't.

"They were antsy all the time, and they weren't sleeping well. When Jimmy went hunting or camping, they did better, but they didn't let their guards down much because they knew he'd be coming back soon. When he did, things would be fine for two or three days, then everything would fall apart again."

With Jimmy gone more, June enjoyed brief reprieves from the violence — "time outs" that made life "more like a roller coaster than a nosedive." It was these ups and downs that kept her holding onto the relationship, hoping that it still might be salvageable or that one day the ups would outweigh the downs. "Had it been *all* downhill it would have been easier to deal with. But Jimmy had a way of keeping things going, sort of dangling a carrot of hope. I wish he hadn't."

"Look, kids, a yard sale! And they've got a television for sale," said June excitedly as she drove home from the grocery store one day. She knew better than to stop and look at it without her husband's permission. Even stopping to call him from a payphone was risky, but June decided to take the risk this time. The kids had been asking for a television of their own, and Jimmy had said he would allow it if he could find them a cheap used model. When June called him at work and told him about the set, his first response was, "Where are you calling from?"

"The corner of Main and Grove," she answered.

"Main and Grove? That's a busy intersection. I don't hear any cars. Why aren't there any cars in the background?"

"Because I'm in the drugstore, Jimmy."

"What are you doing in the drugstore?"

"I'm using the phone to call you."

"Why didn't you use a phone outside?"

"Because there *isn't* one outside. There's a sign saying phone, but it's *inside*. You know, one of those little blue signs?" After a few more inane questions, Jimmy gave his consent for June to buy the television provided it was no more than ten dollars. With that, June returned to the yard sale and bought it with the understanding that if it didn't work to her husband's satisfaction, she could return it. For ten dollars the owner wasn't going to argue, and made the sale.

For two weeks, the television sat on a bench in the garage. The kids had cautiously asked their father several times if he could *please* bring it in and hook up the cable so they could watch it, and he had said yes, yes, he would "as soon as I've got a goddamn minute."

On the last request, he blew up. The kids made the mistake of throwing the question at him just after he pulled in the driveway after being turned down for a car loan. He was in a terrible mood. "Get the hell away from me! Get in the goddamn house, *now!*" he yelled. The children scampered up the stairway to their mother, complaining that the television was *never* going to be hooked up; they weren't there long.

Jimmy got out of his truck and stomped into the garage. He hoisted the television onto one hip and walked back to the front of the building. He looked up to his second-floor apartment and yelled to June, "Get your ass down here and get those kids' asses down here too!" They all obeyed, but the kids sensed something was wrong and walked down the stairs as slowly as possible.

When everyone was assembled at the front of the building, Jimmy said, "Watch," and walked twenty feet to the street where a construction ditch had been opened for a new water line. "You want your motherfucking TV? Well go and get it!" With that, he threw the television in the ditch where it exploded into a hundred pieces of flying glass and plastic.

"As I stood there with my two weeping daughters — unable to even *start* to explain the cruelty they had just witnessed — I couldn't help thinking how similar my marriage was to the television. A piece of me died along with that set. The hope I had been holding onto for so long just vaporized like the television had."

Whatever remained of June's hope faded a few weeks later. It was nearing the end of the summer, and to celebrate, the extended families were having a big party at a friend's barn out in the country. Over a hundred people turned out, including Jimmy's stepfather, stepmother, and dozens of his cousins. Even here amongst friends and family, he was jealous and worried about his wife cheating on him and had warned June to "stay close and don't talk to anybody." Only three days earlier he had interrogated her about a man who was looking at her from the car next to them at a traffic light. It was one of Jimmy's regular insecurity sessions, and the quiz always took the same form:

"Where do you know him from?"

"I *don't* know him, Jimmy."

"Look at the way he's looking at you. Who is he?"

"I don't know. I don't care."

"You know him! Don't let me find out you know him or you'll get hit."

"I don't know him, Jimmy. The light's green."

At the barn party, kids and dogs ran everywhere, beer flowed from two kegs, and June got drunk. She rarely drank enough even to feel woozy, but with the festive atmosphere and the warm day, June had a second beer. And then a third. Midpoint through the party, she was completely out of her shell and having a wonderful time. She spotted a chair and pulled it into the center of the barn and stood up on it. Seeing Randolph and Leslie in the corner, she directed her announcement towards them. It lasted about ten seconds.

"Attention!" June shouted in a slurred-but-steady voice. "Everybody listen!" People stopped talking and turned to hear June. She was talking to the crowd but looking right at Randolph. "Let me ask you something about your precious

Jimmy. How do you feel about someone who beats his wife and kids?"

End of speech. June saw Randolph's face suddenly turn white — not red from embarrassment, as might have been expected, but white from fear. "As drunk as I was, I knew what his face meant. It meant: 'You're in trouble.' And he was right.

"The next thing I knew, I was in midair. Jimmy had flown through the crowd and scooped me off the chair; my feet didn't even touch the floor. He carried me out of the barn and threw me in the truck. The girls got in the jump seat behind us and crouched down and didn't say a word. He burned rubber out of there and as soon as he was out of sight of the barn, he grabbed the back of my head and slammed my face into the gearshift. He was screaming every possible obscenity you could think of and slamming my face into the gearshift.

"For the whole ride home — it was about twenty minutes — he kept punching me in the face and head, and smashing my head into that gearshift. When we pulled into the driveway, he leaned over, opened my door, and kicked me out onto the ground; then he threw Pam out. Fortunately she was little and landed on top of me. Jana scooted out the door and up towards the woods."

June lay in the driveway, uncertain whether to move or not. She heard Jimmy's door slam shut and braced herself and her daughter for another round of beating — this time expecting kicks. She quickly huddled into a fetal position, with Pam tucked well inside and protected by June's arms. But he walked right past her and into the apartment. Seeing that it was safe, June got to her feet. But she was dizzy and had to grab the car door handle to steady herself. She put Pam down and called for Jana, who came running from a thicket of trees behind the garage.

"Mommy, you're bleeding, you're bleeding!" screamed Jana. June looked in the truck mirror and saw that her lower lip was split wide open and full of dirt. Her left eye was pooled with so much blood that it looked like a crimson lake without its iris island. Just then she heard another car pull into the driveway. Turning from the mirror with blurred vision and a head aching from the blows, she saw a woman and a man get out of a car and walk toward her.

The man seemed not to notice that anything was the least bit wrong with June, and grabbed her by the shoulders and yelled, "Goddamn it, June, why the hell did you keep it from me all these years? How could you do that?! You're a liar! A goddamn liar!" It was her brother Dan, now eighteen, and he had come with Aunt Margaret who decided that at eighteen she was going to tell "her son" the truth about where he came from. But Dan didn't blame her, the woman who had raised him and demanded that his true identity be kept a secret. And he didn't blame his mother, who had dumped him at her sister's doorstep in the first place. He blamed *June* for not breaking everyone's trust and telling him who he was, and it was her he was railing against as she wiped the blood from her mouth and tears from her eyes.

PART III: THE CRIME

In total, June Briand would be married for five years and nine months. It was later determined by a forensic psychologist that by the time she had entered her fourth year of marriage, in the spring of 1985, "Ms. Briand had been severely beaten by her abusive husband no less than fifty times and probably much more." By the time her marriage would end, on February 12, 1987, the figure swelled to over a hundred.

In 1985, before the most intensive onslaught of brutality was to come, June was convinced that the savagery of the attacks could not possibly get any worse. By then, she had been kicked in the ribs so often that her husband forbade her from going back to the hospital. After one kicking episode, June had struggled to her feet, again unable to breathe and knowing better than to say so. Jimmy looked at her and said simply, "You know what to do," and she went off to the bathroom to again wrap her ribs as she had done so many times before.

Over the years and on Jimmy's insistence, June had switched back and forth from Nashua's St. Joseph's Hospital to Memorial Hospital to avoid arousing suspicion. She had been in both ERs numerous times for myriad of injuries, the most recent being a urinary disorder brought on by Jimmy's kicks to the kidneys and stomach. "The pain in urinating got so bad that I put off going to the bathroom until the very last second."

No, things could not possibly get any worse, June believed. She had been punched hundreds of times; routinely choked to the point of passing out; stabbed through the hand; nearly drowned in the toilet; and told over and over again that if she tried to leave, she would be "tracked down, captured, and killed" — not unlike the animals Jimmy proudly displayed on the living room walls. To make sure she understood the messages, Jimmy had driven home the threats — first at the point of a knife, and then at the end of a gun barrel.

But June was wrong: the worst was yet to come.

The longer the marriage went on, the more fearful and possessive Jimmy became, and the more ferocious his attacks. And with the increased brutality came increased frequency. It seemed that the longer he was married, the more frightened Jimmy became that his wife might leave him. And the more frightened he became, the meaner he got.

Though he was having a terrible marriage, after five years, the relationship had become important to Jimmy. If for no other reason than because a defeat now would be humiliating — a family disgrace and one more failure to add to all the rest.

The problem was June had power. She was a woman, and women were the ones who had always hurt Jimmy: the ones who had left him, fired him, and made him look like a fool. He needed June but he feared her, and his mind was forever jumping between the two ideas like a toad on a skillet. Jimmy Briand was now hyper-paranoid, wary, suspicious, and constantly afraid — and when he was afraid, he did unthinkable things to those weaker than himself.

The first of a series of three deranged acts, all of which came in rapid succession, occurred shortly after the barn party. It was as if the humiliation he suffered there was eating him alive, and to exorcise the cancer inside, he had to hurt someone or something very badly. He had to show that *he* was boss and *he* had control of his world again, and to do that, he resorted, as always, to abject violence.

Unfortunately, the audience for Jimmy's control exhibition was not only his wife, but his two young daughters as well, who were to witness cruelty beyond their most horrible nightmares — nightmares that, by mid-1985, they were having on a nightly basis. Jimmy's new strategy was not just to attack his wife, but attack those things most dear to her. He was still beating June regularly, but now added to the mix the things she loved.

"The first thing that happened came on a Saturday morning after I went shopping with the kids. They loved going to the grocery store because, for one thing, Jimmy wasn't around and we could laugh and have a good time. They'd ride in the cart, eat cookies from the package — things they could never do if their father was there.

"When we got home it was still early, about nine in the morning. Jana wanted to carry the milk, and Pam took the box of cereal. I told them to be quiet because Daddy might still be sleeping. They went tiptoeing through the kitchen trying not to laugh, then out into the backyard to play. They were very happy for a change.

"When I peeked in the bedroom, Jimmy wasn't there. But what I saw gave me a chill. All my stuffed animals — I had about ten of them — were ripped apart. My panda bear, Tweety Bird, Sylvester, the Cat in the Hat, my penguin — all of them were ripped up and their stuffing was everywhere. This was something completely different; it was pure viciousness, craziness. I didn't know what to make of it, but suddenly I felt sick — and terribly scared."

June quickly took the animals outside and placed them deep inside the garbage can under the other bags. She knew that the sight of the torn animals might bring up guilt in the miscreant she was living with, and guilt could then turn to rage. She wanted to prevent any further escalation of *this* new trend, but her wishes would go unheeded.

"The worst part was not knowing what I did to deserve this. Did we wake him up too early when we left? Is he mad about something from yesterday, last month, *last year*? There was no way to know, but ripping things to shreds was new, and it made me wonder when he might do it to *me*. One day he might not hold back, and literally rip me apart — either with his knife, or his gun, or his hands."

Destroying inanimate objects was like a warm-up, a prelude to Part II of Jimmy's three-part Symphony of Terror. In his next performance he went further, and it convinced June that she was, indeed, living with a madman who was very, very dangerous.

"I had gone shopping again the next weekend, and when I came home Jimmy was gone again, just like the weekend before. I immediately sensed that something was wrong, something was different, but I couldn't tell what it was. Then I heard Jana screaming from the backyard. 'Fluffy's gone! Fluffy's gone and all of her babies are gone too!'

"Fluffy was the girls' pet rabbit, and they had gone to feed her some of the lettuce we had just bought at the market. The first thing I noticed was that her cage door wasn't open, so I knew someone had taken her and her babies out and closed the door again. I ran to check the gerbils in the old fish tank, and as I suspected, they were gone too. I knew what happened."

Jimmy's next act of insanity left the girls deeply traumatized. It came a month later, and Pam had nearly forgotten about the rabbit by then. Jana, on the other hand, missed her pet, but was comforted by the fact that she still had her "favoritest" pet of all — Patches.

Patches was a black and white cat that came around the apartment one day and never left. She had a wild streak in her though, which Pam learned one night when she lifted her up by the tail and got a slash in the face that took three stitches to close. The kids loved her nevertheless, and grew particularly attached to her after she gave birth to kittens. They watched them being born, and with old towels and pillows, made a cozy home for them in the bottom drawer of their bunk beds.

Jimmy, on the other hand, hated the animal, and often swatted it off the kitchen counter. The day of the incident he had said, "If I see that goddamn cat on the counter one more time I'm going to take it out back and shoot it." June had no doubt that he would, remembering that he once told her that when he was a little boy, he had seen his stepfather kill a litter of kittens by stuffing them in a pillow case and slamming them over and over against the house.

"I had taken the kids and gone down to the post office and then to the pharmacy to pick up some cold medicine for Pam. When we came back and opened the front door, Patches was right there waiting for us and she was crying. She was really upset, but we didn't know why. Then we looked in the bunk bed drawer and saw that her kittens were gone. She was crying for her kittens. I figured they had gotten out and were somewhere in the apartment, so we started looking everywhere.

"I said to her, 'Don't worry, Mommy, we're looking for your babies.' She was looking too. She jumped in the shower searching for them, while we moved furniture and looked under beds. I kept telling Patches we would find her kittens, and then I suddenly stopped. It dawned on me that we wouldn't; I knew what happened to them. And when Jimmy came home silent, I knew I was right.

"Two days later, the kids and I were having lunch. I didn't hear Jimmy coming, and when he walked in, Patches was on the counter. I didn't think anything of it until Jimmy grabbed her by the neck and went to the gun case for a rifle. He wasn't talking, which was a bad sign. The kids put down their sandwiches and watched their father.

"The worst part was that Jimmy took Patches over to the old oak tree. He could have taken her anywhere — around the side of the house, up into the woods — but he knew we could see the tree from the kitchen window, and that's where we all were — at the window praying he wouldn't hurt Patches.

"He walked up to that tree and with all his might, threw Patches against the tree trunk. It only took one throw and she dropped to the ground without moving. Then he put his foot on her neck and shot her in the head. The kids screamed and Pam covered her eyes with her hands. Then he picked up the cat and put her in a fishing bucket and walked into the woods.

"An hour later he came back. Me and the kids had been crying and tried not to sniffle when he came in. He looked at me and said, 'I guess you'll keep the fucking cat off the counter now.' For a quick moment I had a feeling of guilt, as if it were my fault she was killed. But it was only for a moment; that's what was different this time. I always thought Jimmy was right and I was at fault. Finally I was starting to see things differently, starting to see that it wasn't *me* that couldn't 'get it right'— it was Jimmy."

A month later, about two in the morning, June heard Jimmy get up. He often got up in the middle of the night to eat. This time he was looking for snack crackers in the cupboard. June heard him slamming cupboard doors, and finally he came back to the bedroom. He said he couldn't find the crackers; she told him they were behind the oatmeal. He got up again and looked behind the oatmeal, but still couldn't find them. So he ripped open the oatmeal tube and threw it all over the floor. Then he opened *all* the cereal—and all the other dry goods—and dumped them on the floor as well.

"When I got up and walked into the kitchen, Jimmy was stomping on everything like a child having a temper tantrum. He was all red in the face and looked like he was drooling. He turned to me and screamed, 'Clean it up!' He had that crazed look in his eyes and I wasn't about to argue.

It took me an hour to clean everything up. Usually after an hour he's calmed down, but not this time.

"He came back in to inspect my work and found a few flakes of cereal I missed under the kickboard; that set him off all over again. This time he opened the other cupboard and opened the liquid goods with a can opener: tomato sauce, beans, soups. He poured all that out too; then he got dressed and went across the street to the garage at three-thirty in the morning."

June was tired now — tired of the constant vigilance, the watching for clues and signals like her husband's tone of voice, the way he walked, moved. She had never felt so tired in her life. The last few months of her marriage found her listless, underweight, hypersensitive to sound, pain, movement. "I got to the point where, if Jimmy moved his arm in his sleep, I'd be instantly awake and covering my face to protect myself."

When he left in the morning, had he *really* left? Or was he standing behind the front door waiting for June to open it? How long would it be until he woke in the middle of the night screaming, only this time with a club in his hand and beat her skull in as he had threatened to do so many times? All this cognition took energy — energy June no longer had.

"My mind never stopped. I was now in survival mode. I was going insane and doing insane things like checking under the couch for people who might be hiding there; drawing maps of *exactly* which route I would take to the market and back even though I'd driven it a hundred times.

"I wanted so badly to not hear his, Jimmy's, voice anymore. I wanted him to just go away. *I* wanted to go away too, but I didn't know how. And I knew Jimmy would find me.

"I looked in the mirror one day and said, 'I'm never going to get it right.' The cooking, the cleaning, laundry, food, clothes — everything was perfect now; I was doing everything exactly as I was told and still it wasn't right. Or it wasn't good enough. Or it was *too* good. I couldn't win. Now Jimmy would come in and run his hand over the stereo cabinet looking for dust, but when he didn't find any, he'd get mad and say, 'Get me a beer.'

"That day after the food dumping, a little piece of me died; the piece that said, 'My actions can change things.' I knew then that *nothing* I did could change things. Hope died too. I was sure that I'd never make it to the end of the year. I was sick of everything and wanted it to end, for him to go ahead and kill me and get it over with. But I kept thinking about the kids. What about them? The thought of leaving them with Jimmy always stopped that kind of daydreaming."

It may have been June's physical and mental state of exhaustion, or just an accident that would have happened anyway, but late in the fall of 1986, while working at New England Microwave, she turned to leave the bathroom and slipped on a puddle of water. She fell backwards and hit the base of her skull against the sink and blacked out. When she regained consciousness, two of her co-workers were holding cold compresses on her forehead; she was uncertain where she was, and her vision was blurred.

When June left work, she assumed she would be taking off the rest of the day and return the following morning. As directed by her manager, she went directly to a Worker's Compensation doctor who examined her and determined that she had suffered a fairly severe concussion in the accident. She would have to leave New England Microwave for an extended but yet undetermined period of time.

On the way home from the doctor, June stopped at the pharmacy to fill the prescription he had given her, then stopped at the local market to pick up a few groceries before going home to rest. While there, she saw the young clerk who had recently taken a cashiering job at the store and who, on occasion, made small talk with June.

Her name was Helen Lewis, and after June explained what had just happened to her and why she was not working in the middle of the day, Helen promised to visit her at home and keep in touch by phone. June still did not engage in much conversation with anyone, and kept mostly to herself for fear of revealing something about her home life that Jimmy was certain to discover. Nevertheless, she let down her guard with Helen.

Helen was younger than June, just eighteen, and had a child out of wedlock who was now three months old. Helen was a tall, thin girl, standing five-foot-ten but weighing only one hundred and fifteen pounds. The loose jeans and baggy sweatshirts she wore to give her bulk did nothing to flatter her figure, and her thin, drawn face seemed forever unwashed. What would have been attractive, oval-shaped blue eyes were diminished by dark, greasy hair and straggly bangs. The cheap perfume she slathered on herself daily did nothing to increase her appeal.

When Helen had first met June, the first thing she asked was whether or not June had a child. June responded that she had two, and they immediately started talking about babies and childrearing. June steered clear, however, of husband talk since Helen didn't have one and hers was a wife-beater.

Another store clerk, Jill, who was a friend of Helen's but had worked at another branch store, asked to be moved to Helen's store and was granted permission by the manager. She, too, was young — only nineteen and a half — and also had an illegitimate child. Though both girls still lived at home, it was Jill's mother who cared for their infants. Helen's mother refused the duties, saying, "You had the kid, you take care of him."

Jill joined Helen in discussing the pleasures and pressures of raising children. June enjoyed having someone to speak with, but when the conversations turned to the women's relationships with men, June discreetly kept the focus on the young ladies' lives instead of hers.

As they got to know each other better over the months, Helen and Jill would ask June to join them for a trip to the beach or a picnic, but she knew Jimmy would never allow that type of unchaperoned socializing, and always made excuses, saying the kids were sick or they had to go to the doctor's. When they asked June to accompany them out for Friday night bar-hopping, June told them she had made an agreement with her husband that after they were married, "neither of us could go out without the other." This was, in fact, all Jimmy's idea rather than some agreement on which the two had concurred, but now it came in handy when talk turned to Friday evening carousing.

The women eventually discovered that Jimmy often went away on weekend hunting trips, and suggested that June slip out with them when he was gone, that she needed a little diversion now and then. "And besides," said Helen, "you're not going to *do* anything with anybody, so what's the problem?"

If only June could enumerate. One obvious problem — obvious to June, at least — was Jimmy's surveillance system, which included several phone calls a day, especially around ten o'clock on Friday and Saturday nights. Not only did Jimmy possess a "sixth sense" about June's whereabouts, she knew she couldn't beat his surveillance system — nor would she ever try.

The headaches started the day after June's accident. She woke up in the morning with a terribly stiff neck. The lump on the back of her head had not gone down much from the previous day, and was tender to the touch, as was her upper thoracic spine. And her thinking was still somewhat confused. Jimmy was concerned about only one thing: how much would Worker's Compensation pay while she was off work?

Jimmy was relieved to hear that June would be receiving maximum benefits while she was off work, but conversely, he was concerned — as he was when she was on welfare — about the freedom his wife would have if she wasn't sitting in a factory all day. It only exacerbated his concerns when, a week after the accident, Helen Lewis pulled into the driveway.

"Helen first came to the house about three o'clock on a Friday afternoon. Jimmy was like a hawk. He could have his head buried under a car hood and still see everyone who came to the apartment. Helen had her three-month-old with her, and wanted to show him to me. When Jimmy saw her get out of her car, he shut down the garage and came home.

"I met him at the door and he asked, 'Who's that?,' like Helen wasn't even there; he didn't say anything to her at all. I said, 'She's a girl I know from the market.' Then he asked, 'How does she know where you live?' I pulled him into the other room and explained that I never gave her my address, and only said that I lived on Central Street, and that I guess she saw my car. I told him I didn't know she was coming over, and I didn't."

They walked back to the kitchen where June tried to introduce Helen, who was standing there with her baby. But after June said, "I'd like you to meet Helen," Jimmy turned and walked out the front door, slamming it behind him.

"He's tired," said June, embarrassed. "He doesn't like to talk when he comes home." Helen nodded and said maybe it was better if she came by some other time. June agreed, and she left. Ten minutes later, Jimmy burst in the door.

"Why'd you tell her where we live?!" he demanded again.

"I said I *didn't* tell her, she knew we ..."

Jimmy cut her off, screaming, "I don't want any goddamn single white welfare trash around here!" It was an incomprehensible statement, and one that again projected Jimmy's own legacy — this time onto someone who, in fact, was *not* on welfare and was a good, hard-working employee of Hudson Market. Had he known Helen was earning more than him, he no doubt would have outright banned her from ever coming to the house again.

With June's headaches and body aches continuing, the doctor told her she would have to stay off work for the foreseeable future. Because she was not stopping by the market anymore, Helen started dropping by the apartment more and more often.

Before, when Helen had asked if she could come by with her child, June made up excuses like she had for the beach and picnics. Now Helen felt it was her duty to check on June and see how she was feeling. She admitted once that she had no other friends besides Jill, and June suspected the visits were more out of loneliness than sympathy for her ailments. She may have also been attracted to the apartment by the wine and beer Jimmy allowed her to drink when he was in a good mood. Yet even when he was on his best behavior, Helen had an inkling that all was not right in the Central Street apartment.

"Helen had seen Jimmy enough times to know he was an overbearing husband. She saw him slam doors and yell. Once when she was telling me something, Jimmy called from the other room and I said, 'Just a minute.' He didn't like that at all, and came running in and said, 'Who the fuck do you think you're talking to?' After he left the room, she asked me if he ever got out of control and took things out on me. Of course I said no, but she wasn't convinced."

Helen continued to come by the apartment to see June and watch videos and play with the kids. Sometimes she would bring over a horror movie, and the two women would watch it late into the night, screaming and holding each other when the scary parts came on. It became clear that Helen was a thrill seeker (indeed, all of the movies she rented were either action thrillers or horror films), but June didn't make anything of it at the time.

Jimmy eventually got used to Helen being around, but he never liked her. "He was threatened by her independence and used to tell me, 'I don't want her coming here.' But for some reason, he never put his foot down." It appeared that one reason he tolerated Helen's visits was that he enjoyed tormenting her as much as he did his wife. It didn't take long for him to start referring to Helen as an airhead too.

"He would often come home and say, 'What junk are you two airheads watching on TV?' On one occasion he made an intentional cut at Helen when he said, 'Women are lost without a man; they can't do anything by themselves — especially raise children.'"

Outwardly, Helen appeared to ignore the comments, but inwardly, she came to detest Jimmy — not only because of his insults but because of the way he treated June. "When Jimmy wasn't around, Helen would tell me he was mean, and that I shouldn't take it from him. She heard him call me disgusting names, like the time we were sitting in the kitchen and he yelled to me from the living room, 'Hey, cumbucket, get out here with a beer.' She couldn't believe it. She saw him shove me a few times, and once asked about a black eye I had. I said Pam kicked me by accident when I was changing her, but she didn't buy it."

In November 1986, three months before the Briand marriage would end, Lynn Holmes of the Hanley Insurance Company called the Central Street apartment, inquiring as to why June had missed so many physical therapy appointments. Therapists had been working with June since her fall at work, and were trying to relieve the back pain and headaches that were not improving with therapy.

Lynn was a rehabilitation specialist who now was assigned to the case, and was quickly losing patience with June because of several missed appointments during the past six months since the accident. When she missed yet another one, and Lynn saw in the appointment book another

No Show notation, she felt it was time to schedule a home visit to see if she could sort out what the problem was. June knew this was not something Jimmy would approve of, and grew anxious with the prospect of having "a stranger" in the home.

After June gave another feeble excuse for not making her last appointment, Lynn threatened to cut off her benefits and drop her from the Worker's Comp role. June then accepted Lynn's next available appointment for a home visit on November 4, 1986.

When Lynn arrived at the apartment that day and knocked on the door, no one answered. She went to the other apartments and knocked on all their doors with the same response. Having been through this deception before and suspecting June was home, Lynn went to a payphone and called her. June answered.

"I've been banging on the doors over there for the last twenty minutes," said Lynn.

"I didn't hear you," June said unconvincingly.

"I'm coming back right now. Meet me downstairs in five minutes."

June did as she was told her, and met Lynn at the bottom of the stairs. "The stairs were littered with garbage," Lynn later reported. "The place was a mess. June's apartment, though, was clean. But she was obviously upset with my presence. She appeared overwhelmed that I was there. She made no eye contact the entire visit; she only looked at the floor. I told her she had to continue therapy if she wanted to get better, but she didn't talk much. I wasn't getting anywhere and thought it would be better to just leave my card. She seemed like she needed to talk but not face-to-face — it was too much pressure for her.

"That night I got a phone call. But it wasn't from June — it was from Jimmy. He was irate, and he questioned my presence in his home and said 'bullshit' every other word. He said it was bullshit, all bullshit — whatever 'it' was. I calmed him down and explained that I was there to help June get better so she could get back to work. I suggested that he be present at the next meeting, and he said he would be."

That meeting was scheduled for November 13. One of the reasons for Lynn Holmes' intervention — one that she had not enumerated to Jimmy — was that the doctors and medical professionals who had been examining June were puzzled. According to one doctor's note, "the origin of Ms. Briand's ailments remains unclear."

June had gone to enough therapy sessions over the months to relieve her pain, but still it persisted. She also had other injuries that came out during her medical evaluations, such as a numbing of her left arm and hand; a swelling around her right eye; tenderness about the ribs; pain while urinating; intense headaches that came and went seemingly without reason. Medically, these symptoms did not match the trauma: they could not have all originated from a slip in the bathroom. There had to be "more pieces to the puzzle."

Lynn's observations during the November 13 meeting reveal a great deal about June's and her children's states of mind while living under the tyranny of Jimmy Briand. "When I went to the Briand apartment the second time," Lynn later reported, "I met Jimmy. He was big and fat and greasy. He looked like he never stepped into a shower. He acted macho, and was overbearingly nice. I got the distinct feeling he was trying to impress me. He talked more about himself than his wife. He talked about his job as a mechanic, and about the trailer he was planning to buy. He even talked about his own ailments.

"When I tried to turn the conversation to June and her problems, he would cut her short and did all the talking for her. He was overbearingly nice and said he wanted the best for her, but it was not convincing in the least. He went so far as to say *he* was the one living with June's pain, and that I didn't know what it was like.

"June was the most nervous person I've ever had to interview. She sat there cross-legged on the kitchen chair looking at the floor. She was so nervous that at times she visibly shook. It was difficult for me to distinguish what she was feeling — or if she was feeling *anything*. She was like a lump on a log.

"Her two young daughters were neatly dressed but there was something about them. They were too quiet; they never said a word, and just knelt by the TV and stared. June was good with them and stroked them a lot. When Jimmy sat down and June got up from her chair, both children immediately ran over to her and clung to her. Jana said over and over, 'I love you. I love you Mommy, I really love you.' You could tell they were afraid she would leave them."

Jimmy was on edge after the meeting. He didn't like "goddamn authorities stickin' their noses into my life." And he particularly didn't like it when the authority was a woman. "They suck," he said after Lynn left. "These bitches suck. All they know how to do is fuck up other people's lives."

To assuage his anxieties, June suggested they go to the Chinese restaurant around the corner instead of staying home. She told Jimmy she had talked to one of his cousin's wives during the week, and the woman had said that several of them were going that night and that June and Jimmy should too.

Jimmy agreed, and at seven o'clock they walked the short distance to the restaurant via a wooded pathway. June was right. Two of Jimmy's cousins and their wives were there, as were several friends of the family. But the company did not put Jimmy at ease. During dinner, he barked at the young Asian waiter when he got one small part of the order wrong, and he kept harping about people minding their own business, and how he didn't like strangers coming around the apartment.

The group broke up earlier than usual that evening. The cousins had work to do early the next morning, and left soon after eating. One them and another friend, however, stayed to talk with Jimmy. The wives soon tired of the men's conversation and decided to go to the bathroom together. As they were returning to the booth, someone from across restaurant whistled at them.

"Who the fuck's the wise ass?" Jimmy shrieked, jumping up from the table and looking around the restaurant.

"*I'm* wise, *you're* the ass," said a patron sitting three booths away. With him were two other men, both bearded and wearing work shirts and jeans. They were big, tough-looking men in their late twenties, and they laughed uproariously at their friends comeback, looking not the least bit troubled by the brouhaha that was starting.

Jimmy flew from his seat and leapt at the man taunting him, who had not expected such a sudden response. Immediately, Jimmy was on top of him, flailing his arms one after the other, landing five or six punches before the other two men could grab him. Four Asian waiters ran over and tried to pull Jimmy from his foe but he tossed all of them away with one fling of his powerful forearm.

The men in the booth, however, were good friends with the restaurant owner, and told Jimmy to take the fight outside; he stopped punching and agreed. It was a mistake. Outside were three more of the men's friends, talking and smoking cigarettes. They were all every bit as big and violent as Jimmy was, and with three of them and one of him, he had a problem.

"I never saw Jimmy lose a fight until that night. Jimmy's cousin and his friend were fighting the three guys from the booth, while the other three got a hold of Jimmy. He looked over at me and yelled, 'Go home!' Right away I started running back up the path. When I got to the top, I looked back and saw that the guys had Jimmy on his back on the hood of a car. Then they broke off the radio antenna and jammed it through his ear. They knew who he was, and they wanted to show him he wasn't as tough as he thought.

"When Jimmy got home he was a mess. His knuckles were all skinned and pushed back, and two of them were dislocated; they were horrible to look at. When I pulled the antenna out of his ear, I knew not to show any emotion because he was enraged and embarrassed. He could hit me even with his knuckles all broken up."

Three days later, Lynn Holmes called June with a new idea. June had told her not to call during lunch because Jimmy was usually there, so the call came in about ten in the morning. Lynn had contacted Sandra Cook, a biofeedback specialist with the Biofeedback Corporation in Nashua, New Hampshire, and told her about June's uncontrolled muscle contraction headaches. Sandra checked her schedule, and found that she had an opening the next day, November 17, at nine-forty-five in the morning. Lynn said she would contact June and get back to her to confirm the appointment, which she did.

This turn of events greatly disturbed Jimmy. With the intrusion of hated authorities into his life, he feared the worst: he would be found out. With doctors and therapists involved, it was certain to be revealed to the world what a monster he was. The repercussions of what this two-hundred-sixty-pound motorcycle thug was doing to his emaciated ninety-pound wife would be too much for him. One and all would finally know that the *real* Jimmy Briand was not strong and brave and in control but rather, a coward who beat and coerced and degraded women behind closed doors where no one could see.

Now that "the authorities" were involved, it looked imminent that Jimmy's dark secret might be exposed; he could not let it happen. Likewise, he could not afford to give up the money his wife was receiving from Worker's Compensation. He had to make a decision, and his desire for wealth and success overshadowed his fears. Grudgingly, he consented to June's continued course of medical attention.

If there was any peace amidst Jimmy's his eternal fury, this decision cost him the last of it. Now his apprehension was palpable. He was worried and edgy all the time. The more appointments June went to, the more irritated he became. June saw the danger signals but didn't know what to do. She had to continue seeing the medical people or risk losing benefits. But continuing meant living with a seething, unpredictable husband who could explode at the slightest — even nonexistent — provocation.

Nevertheless, June kept her appointment with the Sandra Cook, the biofeedback specialist, who later described the meeting in detail. "June was very quiet, very withdrawn. She seemed timid and uncomfortable with people. She clutched herself and held herself close. She made no eye contact and was mostly nonverbal, giving simple yes and no answers to questions. She was fidgety and nervous and had a hard time relaxing. She seemed overwhelmed and afraid. She was so tired that while waiting in the reception room, she fell asleep.

"June brought her youngest daughter, Pam, with her. She was clingy and didn't want to be away from her mother at all, and when she wanted something, she would whine meekly. The two of them seemed pale and undernourished, and looked like their home could have been a shack somewhere. They looked fatigued and depressed."

Sandra Cook asked June to come into the treatment room, and explained the rudiments of biofeedback and how it could help a person learn to relax by learning to control muscle contractions. She explained that this aids in alleviating headaches and other ailments. She then asked

June how she rated her headaches on a scale of zero to ten, and got a startling response. June said that sometimes her headaches were zero, other times they were ten — but nothing in between.

"These were extreme and unusual ratings, and suggested that anger and fear were involved, and that the headaches were almost certainly home-related, not work-related."

Following up on her hunch, Sandra hooked June to the electromyographic machine (EMG), using sensors that measure muscle contractions. She attached the sensors to June's head and began asking a series of questions while watching the EMG meter. The questions, at first, were of a general nature and the meter responded accordingly at normal readings. After June was accustomed to these questions, Sandra tried another one, this time more direct: "Is everything all right at home?"

"I felt pretty good at first, and the beeper was beeping at a steady pace until then. Then the thing went wild; the needle flew into the red zone. I ripped off the sensors, grabbed Pam, and ran out of the room. I knew that if it got back to Jimmy that the needle went crazy, I'd be in big trouble. All I could think about was getting out of there."

It did not get back to Jimmy, but June was in trouble anyway. When she returned from the appointment, it was late morning and Pam had not eaten breakfast yet. It was not that she wasn't hungry earlier — she was. It was that June forgot to feed her. She wasn't thinking clearly anymore, and it simply slipped her mind that her child had not eaten breakfast. Now Pam asked for oatmeal and June set a pan of water on the stove to heat up. When she turned around, Jimmy was staring at her with crazed eyes.

Without a word, he grabbed her arms and locked them behind her. With one hand he held them high up on her back like a policeman does when restraining a troublemaker, and with the other he shoved the pan off the burner and bent June's face over the gas flame.

"Jesus, Jimmy, don't!" June screamed. She was looking at white-orange flames inches from her face and she thought of hell. Satan himself had seized her. He said nothing as he pushed her face closer to the heat. She struggled against the massive hand on the back of her head. "Don't, Jimmy, don't! Oh God, STOP IT!"

"What the fuck did you tell her?!"

"Nothing. I swear it, nothing!"

"You fucking lying bitch! What did you *TELL HER?!*" He pushed her closer; she felt the heat singe her hair and she smelled it burn.

"Nothing, Jimmy! I'd didn't tell her anything. Stop it! You're going to burn me! I didn't even stay for the appointment. We left! We left! Now let me go!"

With that he released her and she ran to the bathroom to put a cold towel on her face. He had not burned her face, but her heart was scorched. There was nothing left now. Jimmy was going to kill her. She was sure of it. He was coming progressively closer, and she knew it would only be a matter of time.

Looking in the mirror at her reddened face and burnt hair, her escape fantasy returned. She vowed to start stashing away more money. She would increase her saving from a dollar at a time to five and ten that she would steal from Jimmy's wallet after payday. She'd wait until he passed out from drinking, then filch the bills. He would never miss them, she figured, and before long she would have enough to get away from him forever. She wouldn't go to her sister's house because that's the first place Jimmy would look. She'd go somewhere else. Where, she didn't know, but she would go. The thought of her being killed didn't trouble her — but the kids. What about the kids? How in the world could she leave them with this ... this ... *thing?* She could not. She *would* not.

Sandra Cook called Lynn Holmes and reported what had happened in her office. Lynn listened silently and became more concerned than ever that something was amiss in the Briand household. June was languishing physically and mentally, and was not responding to therapy and not making appointments. It appeared that she was trying to hide something, but what? She didn't appear to be battered though she showed all the classic signs of an abused woman.

The following day Lynn called June and asked her and Jimmy to come down to Nashua Memorial Hospital and meet "the treatment team" to see if they could help determine how best to help her. She was no longer going to play games. She intentionally called in the evening, knowing Jimmy would be there and able to set a time for the meeting. She told June point blank that the meeting was required in order to retain her Worker's Compensation benefits. In fact, there was no such requirement.

Lynn had concocted the story in order to get Jimmy to come to the hospital so her colleagues could assess him and ask him questions. The treatment team she referred to included four doctors, a lawyer, Sandra Cook, a note taker, and herself. This was not revealed during the phone conversation either. The team was interested in "sorting out whatever underlying issues were present," chief amongst them psychological issues.

On December 10, Jimmy strode into the meeting with June behind him. He was so huge that when he entered the room, June was not visible and Lynn thought he had come alone. Then June peeked out from behind him and gave a little wave.

The team was assembled around a conference table, and Lynn told the couple to sit beside her in the two remaining empty chairs. Jimmy pulled out his chair and sat down. He was on his best behavior and had even replaced his jean jacket with an old tan corduroy sport coat that was two sizes too small for him.

June had been seeing these people for months and knew them all; they were not going to pull any punches. Lynn started by saying, "There is more going on with June than her injury from work." She did not look at Jimmy, but she did pause to let the statement sink in. Jimmy showed no reaction.

"We're here to help," she continued. "We think its best if we set up a treatment plan." She went on to describe the various components of the plan, all of which Jimmy supported. "He came across as overly supportive," she said later. "And backed the program one hundred percent." Lynn felt he was disingenuous at best, and suspected he was downright lying. Her hunch proved correct when she got to the pain management part of the plan.

"I sat there not saying anything while Jimmy was nodding his head and agreeing to everything. They were talking about continuing my physical therapy and biofeedback, and he nodded in agreement. Then they said they wanted me to try some other forms of pain management, including psychiatry. That's when Jimmy flipped."

Jimmy held his hand up and stopped the meeting. "No psych," he said. "She don't need no psych." Lynn turned to him and started to argue the point. Suddenly he grabbed June and said, "We're outta here!" and jumped up, throwing over his chair. He grabbed June by the shirt, and started dragging her out of the meeting.

Jimmy had gone along with everything else — the benign, routine modalities that could detect nothing about the true nature of his wife's ailments. But psych? This was too close to home; it was going *into* his home, and he would not hear of it. No one was going to probe his wife's mind and discover the truth.

Before reaching the door, June turned to the people who, for months, had been trying to sort out what was wrong with her. She mouthed the words "I'm sorry" just before the door slammed shut with the kick of Jimmy's black boot.

Five days later, on December 15, June called Lynn Holmes at Jimmy's insistence. He told her to cancel her upcoming appointment — one supposedly for physical therapy, but which he suspected was for something else. (It was not.) He didn't trust anyone after the team meeting, and told June to make up an excuse, say she had a babysitter problem. Though he would have preferred to tell everyone to go to hell, he still needed to play the game because he still needed June's benefit payments. He was only buying time though, and eventually his ego and his fear would overpower him.

"I was talking to June," said Lynn, "when I heard Jimmy yell in the background, 'Give me the fucking phone!' I heard some muffled sound and more yelling, then a fumbling of the phone. Jimmy got on and started screaming. He screamed at me nonstop for ten minutes; he was in a rage.

"He called me a fucking cunt and said that he'd snap me in two, that he didn't want any fucking shrink. He said his wife wasn't going to have any psychological treatment. 'That's all a bunch of bullshit,' he said. When June finally got back on the phone, she could barely talk; her voice was cracking and she was extremely upset. She said she was sorry, and that she had to go, and hung up. I shuddered to think what it would be like living with someone like Jimmy Briand."

Up until this call, she had not been afraid of Jimmy. She had seen a glimpse of his temper at the meeting the previous week, but had no idea he harbored this much wrath or could unleash such a barrage of contempt as he had. After the call, she "felt shaken" and said, "I wouldn't go back to that house under any circumstances."

Likewise, the babysitter June had hired to take care of the kids so she and Jimmy could attend the team meeting said she, too, would not go back to the Briand house. Though withdrawn and quiet, the children were suffering deep, psychological scarring from witnessing all the violence around them, and they acted out these fears and frustrations on the babysitter.

When June had tried to leave, both girls clung to her — hanging on dearly to each of her legs. By the time June extricated herself and slipped out the door, both girls were hysterical. And when they realized their mother was really gone, their hysteria turned to rage. "They pummeled me," said the babysitter. "They lashed out with such frustration, such vengeance — it was scary. They refused to sit down and eat their lunch, and instead, went into their rooms and threw books and clothing everywhere. They were so nervous and uptight.

"So was June; she was a wreck. She had a black eye, her head would shake, she was teary-eyed. I've never seen anyone like that before. She looked like she was ready for a nervous breakdown."

Like their mother, the girls' looks had changed drastically by the end of 1986. No one was eating now, and both of them had dark circles under their eyes like June. They were listless and stayed mostly in their room and no longer played around the house, which became eerily quiet.

Partly to blame for their decline was Jimmy's most recent restriction: No playing with your cousins. He had now isolated his children from their own cousins — who lived in the same building. Back when the plastic swing seat broke, Jimmy had gotten into a fist fight with Frank because apparently, Frank's children had jumped on the seat and broken it. Though it was only a five-dollar item, it was excuse enough to punch Frank in the mouth when he made the mistake of saying, "Your kids are just as responsible as mine."

June, however, disregarded the restriction as often as she dared. "It was terrible that the kids had to be kept separated. Jimmy was punishing the kids for problems *he* created. He told Pam and Jana to *ignore* their cousins! How can kids ignore each other in the same yard?

"When Jimmy went away, I'd tell the kids they could play together but not to say anything about it. They understood and were delighted — partly because of the danger of it, I think. I told them to keep a watch for Jimmy, and when he drove up, separate — quick!

"They'd meet under the stairs and play in the sand box because you couldn't see it from the kitchen window. The kids would ask each other, 'Is he gone yet?' And when they were playing in the yard and heard the rumble of his motorcycle, they'd dive back into the sand box or scatter in all directions. That's how we lived; that's how the kids grew up; it keeps you on edge."

June continued to fall into deeper and darker depressions. Her sleep was erratic and disturbed, and she walked around the apartment "in a daze." As the kids became more and more withdrawn, she foundered along with them. She stopped brushing her long, dark hair, which became knotted and unmanageable, as did the children's. Lynn Holmes later reported, "The children's clothes were clean but their faces were dirty and their hair was uncombed."

Jimmy no longer needed an excuse to beat his wife, and continued to hit and kick her whenever he felt the urge. He gave up altogether speaking to her or his children. Except for screaming like a lunatic at the television, he now communicated mostly in grunts, and simply shoved whomever was in his way as he trudged to the refrigerator for another beer or lumbered off to an intoxicated sleep in the cubby-hole bedroom.

When Jimmy demanded sex, June knew better than to resist — even if it was midday and the children were eating lunch in the kitchen, five feet away. On more than one occasion, the girls would hear activity in the door-less bedroom and start to come in. June would say between breaths, "No! Don't come in! You can't come in here. Go play, Mommy will be out soon."

Fortunately, the sessions were usually no more than a few minutes long, except for when he was drunk and took longer to satisfy himself. For these sessions June resorted to her old coping mechanism. "There is no place else you can go but in your head. Just like Ron before him, when Jimmy was hurting me or forcing me to have sex, I'd think about things — specific things — like which groceries I had to buy and what their prices were, the school project Jana was working on, that sort of thing.

"I'd concentrate on smells too. My face was on the floor so often that I clearly remember the smell of floor wax. Jimmy demanded that the floor be shiny and waxed every week, so you could always smell the wax. And the Lemon Pledge. He made me polish the redwood burl table with it and you could always smell Lemon Pledge in the room. Smells are all that's left when you try to turn off all your other senses."

Helen Lewis continued to visit June. By Christmastime, she was a common fixture around the apartment — so much so that Jimmy let down his guard, and more and more, demonstrated how abusive he was to his wife. When he'd leave, Helen would say, "I wouldn't let him talk to you like that," or "Are you gonna take that from him?" But June knew better than to respond.

Helen was beginning to see how volatile Jimmy really was. Once, while she and June were sitting in the kitchen talking, Jimmy called for June to come into the living room. When she did, Jimmy was sitting looking at a blank wall. He said vacantly, "Talk to me." June looked at him not knowing what to say, and did nothing. Again he said, "Talk to me June. I said talk to me."

"What would you like me to talk about?" she asked.

"That's it!" he said, and threw over the redwood burl coffee table, spewing beer bottles, glasses, and ashtrays into the air. Helen heard the commotion and came running.

"What the fuck are *you* looking at, airhead?!" he said brusquely as he stomped past her and out of the room.

After he left, Helen helped June clean up the mess. While the women were down on their knees picking up cigarette butts and broken glass, Helen looked over to June and said, "You've got to get rid of him." June stopped what she was doing and looked at Helen. For a moment, she held very still, as if she had just had an epiphany, as if she had just heard the sweetest words from a deity who spoke a great truth. But the moment passed quickly and she went back to cleaning the rug — and cleaning it well, for she knew it was bound to be inspected.

The following Saturday was the annual Christmas party at Randolph's house. As always, it was to start at four in the afternoon, and June was looking forward to it as a diversion from the pressure she was under. It would also be a treat for the children who needed desperately to socialize with someone other than their "stranger" classmates and their dictator father.

About three o'clock that afternoon, June finished bathing Pam. Jana already had on her blue velvet holiday dress and patent leather shoes, and was sitting quietly on the couch watching cartoons. Pam was cranky and uncooperative, and didn't want to get dressed, even though June had bought her a lovely second-hand dress at the Salvation Army outlet. To inspire her, June walked to bedroom closet and pulled down a box from the top shelf. Pam had never seen the box before, and was curious. She ran over wearing only her underpants and a little towel around her wet hair, and excitedly peered into the box.

Inside was a dress made of a beautiful cream satin material, with a high neck and lace yoke across the front. June's sister Diane had sent it from California, and the price tag still hung from the sleeve: $250, marked down to $150. June had received the present the previous week, and had kept it hidden away — ostensibly to surprise the children, but really, to keep it from Jimmy.

A present from "the outside" was threatening to Jimmy; *anything* from beyond his controlled domain was viewed with great trepidation. June hoped that on the day of the party, his fears might somehow magically disappear, and decided not to reveal the gift from her sister until then. Jimmy hated Diane, so it followed he would hate the dress she had sent. And June's logic was sound.

Though the dress was modest and "not too sexy," June looked radiant in it. Despite her sallow appearance and the fact that the dress hung on her emaciated frame, she was delicately beautiful in it — and Jimmy noticed this. She looked *too* good.

Pam loved the dress too, and upon seeing it, immediately ran back to her room. She wanted to be "pretty like Mommy," and quickly wriggled into her own new dress and shoes. June brushed Pam's hair and told Jana to get her coat, that they were leaving.

Jimmy was impatient, and had been cursing all morning for "you females to get your asses in gear." Now the three ladies started down the back stairs. Jana was first, Pam second, then June, and behind her, Jimmy. When the girls reached the bottom stair, they had to step gingerly around the icy slush puddle at the bottom. June was on the third stair from the bottom by then, and holding up the hem of her dress in anticipation of the puddle. She hesitated a moment in order to lift the hem higher, and as she did, Jimmy yelled, "Get going, we're going to be late!" and kicked June in the rear.

"I fell face-first into the slush puddle. I couldn't move. I wasn't hurt, but I just couldn't move. In the past I would have made light of it; I would have made a joke of some kind so the girls wouldn't be disturbed. Now I couldn't even get up. I just laid there. I was too tired to move, too tired of everything. I just wanted to lie there. Then I heard little Pammy say, 'Are you all right, Mommy?' God, I wanted to cry when I heard that. It was the saddest part; my little girl coming over wanting to help me. But she couldn't. No one could help me.

"I was tired of the abuse. I didn't want it anymore. I didn't want the children subjected to this anymore. Something inside me said, 'Okay Jimmy, you win. Kill me, I don't care. I just want to get away from all this.' But every time I thought like that, I thought about the kids, and it would bring me out of it. Then I started thinking about what Helen had said: 'You've got to get rid of him.' That thought would go away too, but it would come back. It kept popping into my mind every time something like this happened."

June finally picked herself up and headed back up the stairs to change. Jimmy merely stepped around her and walked off to have a cigarette, seemingly pleased that he had accomplished two goals with one kick: He had done away with the symbol of the outside world, and he had stripped his wife of her beauty, which, particularly at a party, was too threatening to permit.

June removed the dress and put on a pair of jeans. She didn't try to wash it or even save it. Nor did she attempt to keep the dripping mud from dirtying the floor as she would have in the past. She simply walked slowly to the trash can and dropped in her Christmas dress. And that was all. It hung over the side of the can, but she took no notice; she was too tired now to worry about keeping everything perfect. She had no energy left. She wanted it all to end.

The children's power of recovery was remarkable. By the time they got to the party and saw their cousins and other kids playing, they immediately joined in, forgetting the horrible incident they had witnessed an hour earlier. June, too, took solace in the company. She had been through so much with Jimmy that nothing seemed to phase her anymore. Soon she was dancing with Jana.

June absorbed the convivial energy of the party like a wilted plant absorbing much-needed nutrients. What was once lifeless now sprang to life, and she blossomed as the music enveloped her and her daughter. She blocked out everything else and danced with abandon, feeling momentarily free of her despot. She was ecstatic to have a taste — a tiny, teasing taste — of joy. She closed her eyes as she twirled Jana in circles, around and around. When she opened them, she caught Jimmy's glare. He was standing by himself in the corner of the room watching her, and he was not happy with what he saw.

Unusual as it was, Jimmy did not drink much at the party; neither did June. She had one Sombrero, and then switched to ginger ale, which she drank with her daughters. Nor did they stay long. Usually, when Jimmy was around the Norton clan, he was in his element and drank hard, fought hard, and didn't want the party to end. This day, however, he was not having a good time — and his wife was; it was an intolerable situation.

At seven o'clock, they left the party and went home. Since they had eaten at the party, June fixed Jimmy only a light meal around ten, and they went to bed. As was now the norm, he hadn'tsaid much to June, but he did want sex from her. She complied, and Jimmy fell off to sleep immediately afterwards. June cleaned herself in the bathroom, checked on the kids, and came back to bed. Though she normally slept fitfully, she was less anxious after the party, and immediately dropped into a deep sleep.

An hour later, she awoke with a start, unable to breathe. Jimmy was choking her. He had awakened and rolled over from the wall side of the bed and grabbed June by the throat. Now he got to his knees and lifted her off the bed by the throat, standing her straight up. He was still kneeling, but he was so much taller than she, that in this position, their eyes were perfectly level. He looked at her and said, "You fuckin' bitches. I don't know why we put up with your shit. You all suck!" He said the last three words over and over and over. "You all suck! You all suck! You all suck!"

As Jimmy screamed, he tightened his grip on June's throat. *This time it's going to happen*, June thought. *This time he's going to kill me.* But she wasn't going to go without a struggle. With both of her hands she clutched his one mighty paw but it was like fighting King Kong; it was no use. And she was beginning to lose consciousness.

Still gripping as tightly as he could, Jimmy stood up. He raised himself to his full height, now towering over his wife, and shoved her against the wall. With his free hand, he grabbed a fistful of hair from the top of her head. Now he had a grip on her throat and one on her hair. He brought her head forward to his chest as if to hold her tightly and say how sorry he was, then smashed her head through the wall.

Luckily his placement was perfect: her head broke through the wall right between the studs. The gaping hole left sheetrock and paper and nails hanging in all directions. But Jimmy wasn't finished. June stood dazed with her head still in the wall like a victim in some sick carnival game. With his massive hands, he reached into the opening, grabbed either side of June's head and pulled it out. Then he smashed it back again. And again. And again. Sheetrock went flying, electrical wires snapped, and all the while he was screaming, "You all suck! You all suck! You all suck!"

In the apartment below, Frank and Deena were rousted out of bed by the shock waves resounding throughout the building. Deena threw on a robe and Frank grabbed for his pants, and the two ran up the stairs. They had no idea what was going on, but they knew something was terribly wrong. Their first thought was of the kids: Were they hurt? Had something heavy fallen on them? Whatever it was, it was right above them and they hurried to rescue whoever it was that might be in trouble.

When Frank burst into the apartment, Jimmy was still yelling at the top of his lungs. Frank bolted into the bedroom and grabbed Jimmy from behind. He looked quickly at June who was in shock and not moving, still standing as if glued to the wall, her arms limp at her sides like doll's.

Frank pulled back on Jimmy's arms, locking them behind him. "Come on, bro," he said. "Come on. Let's go outside. Come on." Jimmy did not resist though he could have. He was a much bigger man than Frank, but he allowed his cousin to guide him away from his victim.

Deena appeared next. She approached June and asked an idiotic question in light of the circumstances: "Did he hit you?" Still dazed, June responded with her usual cover, not realizing that this time it wouldn't cover anything. "No," she said, and then collapsed in a heap on the floor.

After this last attack, June dropped further into the depths of learned helplessness. Psychologists would later describe her as having been suffering from "psycho-paralysis," whereby she could neither fight nor flee because she had lost the ability to perceive success of any kind. There was no way for her to change her "failure expectancy" because that was all she ever experienced — failure. One later psychological report stated, "Like most battered women, June saw herself as powerless to escape the control of her batterer, attributing to him the power he repeatedly worked to convince her he had."

By this point in her relationship, June was, indeed, convinced of Jimmy's power, and believed she had nowhere to go and no way to get there. "Leaving was never an option; it wasn't even a *consideration*. Living with the fear of death was one thing; *precipitating* it, causing your *own* death by doing exactly what your spouse forbids you to do, well, that would be suicide. I hadn't sunk that far yet."

Psychologists would later explain how Jimmy's cycle of violence perpetuated itself, saying that aggression towards someone creates a need in the abuser to justify that violence by degrading his victim further and further. This leads to more violence because he then sees his victim as somehow "deserving" of the punishment, and the cycle continues unabated.

One incident just after New Year exemplifies this cycle. It occurred a few weeks before the marriage would terminate, and was one of the final acts of insanity that would lead to that abrupt ending. Jimmy had just come back from a weekend of ice fishing and was cleaning his fish in the kitchen sink. He had filled the sink with cold water to keep the fish fresh as he gutted and beheaded them. Before leaving the previous Friday morning, he had attacked June again, and again honed in on her ribs with his heavy boots. She had wrapped her arms around her body the way she had learned, trying to protect herself from the wicked black pendulum that kept coming and coming, but the blows got through and this time, tore the cartilage on June's left side between her last broken rib and the one below it.

Seeing her husband at the sink, June knew better than to ignore him, especially after a long weekend away. Helen had come over both Saturday and Sunday, but June was not about to tell Jimmy that. Too likely to incite him. She thought it best to simply greet him and see what he wanted to eat.

When she walked into the kitchen and over to Jimmy, she looked down at the bloody water filled with floating fish guts and decapitated bass floating belly-up. The stench from the entrails was vile, causing her to take a quick step backwards. As she did, she winced in pain from her tender ribs and Jimmy caught it.

"What's the matter with you?" he asked. June didn't have time to respond. As psychologists would later explain, Jimmy was hypersensitive at this stage of the relationship. His guilt about what he had done to his wife now turned to self-loathing, which then precipitated attack — the usual response in this cycle of violence.

Like a coiled snake with lightning speed, Jimmy sprang at his wife and shoved her head into the sink so fast that she had no time to react. She struggled to get free and was successful — for a moment. Jimmy laughed a maniacal laugh as he let her come up for air. He wanted to see the look on her face, the greenish-red slime dripping from her chin and nose. June turned just enough for him to see this — and see that she was petrified; then he shoved her under completely and held her there.

He held her head longer than he had during the toilet incident. Longer. Longer. He wanted *reaction,* goddamn it, and June refused to give it to him. "I stopped struggling and held my breath. I thought if I stayed under long enough, he would let me go. But he didn't. I held on longer, hoping he would let me up. I wouldn't dare open my mouth with all the guts and filth in that water. He had to let me up, but he wasn't. Finally I was out of breath. I had no choice. I knew what he wanted, and I did it: I inhaled a mouthful of bloody water. Then he let me go."

That night Jimmy went out drinking and Helen came by to visit June. She seemed to have nothing else to do in life but come by to see June. June didn't mind though, and this time, she did something she had never done before: She told Helen about the sink incident — and the kicking as well. She knew Helen suspected she was being beaten, and this time she couldn't hide how hard it was for her to breathe.

When Helen asked June what was hurting her, and why she couldn't stand up straight, June lifted her shirt to reveal a huge purple bruise that extended from just under her left breast, around her side, and halfway across her back. Helen gasped when June pulled up her shirt, and instinctively reached to touch the spot but then pulled away, realizing how tender it must be. June spoke with short, soft breaths to avoid expanding her lungs. When Helen asked why Jimmy did this to her, she shook her head and looked at the floor, offering no explanation because there was none to offer.

The pressure on Jimmy did not ease. Walking out on the team meeting did not eliminate the doctors and other professionals who were determined to help June. Nor did it result in June losing any benefits. Jimmy had threatened to get a lawyer and sue. Who, he didn't know, but sue *someone* so he could keep June's Worker's Comp payments coming in. The members saw, through Jimmy's vivid exhibition at the meeting, what was obviously the root of June's problems, and were not about to "hang her out to dry." They did, however, rescind their requirement that she see a psychologist, knowing how intensely Jimmy was opposed to it. But they still required June to continue physical therapy and biofeedback treatments in order to maintain benefits.

Jimmy was suspicious though. He didn't believe that the appointments were just for physical therapy and biofeedback, and suspected that "the fucking shrinks" were "messing with her mind." To Jimmy, that meant they would soon discover he was beating his wife, and his worst fears would be realized. But *not knowing* — that is what caused his anxiety to soar. He accused June of hiding the truth, and demanded that she admit she was seeing psychologists (which she was not). She implored Jimmy to believe her, but his retort was always the same: "You're a lying bitch!" followed by a slap, punch, choke, or kick.

Evidence of Jimmy's heightened state of apprehension came near the end of January 1987, in a totally unprovoked act of internal rage. It was, to date, the most outrageous of his attacks — and the most unexpected. This time, it wasn't until the last moment — just before he grabbed June — that she realized the mistake she had made. And it wasn't even her mistake: it was Pam's.

"All Jimmy said was, 'Come here.' That was about as much as he ever said anymore. One or two words, the bare minimum. He was standing in the bathroom doorway. I didn't have any idea what the problem was this time. Then he said, 'What did you do today?' I thought it was an odd question because by this point in our relationship, he had stopped talking to me and didn't care what I did. I thought maybe I forgot to tell him where I had gone and he found out — but where was that? I hadn't been anywhere. I thought it had to be something else — and it was.

"He was standing there, waiting for me to answer, and then it dawned on me. Pam had used the bathroom earlier, and I didn't remember hearing the toilet flush. At that moment, Jimmy grabbed me by the back of the neck and shoved me down toward the toilet bowl. In the same motion, he reached in the bowl and scooped out Pam's bowel movement and threw it on the floor. Then he smashed my face into it and held it there with all his might. He didn't say a word and just pushed my face down with all his weight. It was at least twenty or thirty seconds before he let go."

June moved very slowly after her husband left the bathroom. She picked herself up slowly, washed her face slowly, changed her clothes slowly. She was at the end of her limits. She was now utterly and completely exhausted. Something had to change. She could not go on like this any longer. Something had to happen, and soon.

June heard Jimmy's truck tires burn rubber on the pavement as he sped away from his latest deranged act. That night, Helen came over again, and June was happy to see her. After what she had been through, she needed someone to keep her company, but did not want to explain what had happened that day. She didn't need to. Helen was way ahead of her.

"I've got something to show you," said Helen as the two women sat on the couch.

"What's that?" said June.

"Look," said Helen, opening her purse. She withdrew a small, brown plastic prescription bottle and opened the lid. She tipped it toward June. "Glass. Ground glass. That's how we can do it. I saw it on TV, in a movie about World War II. The Japanese women poisoned the men by putting ground glass in their food. That's how we can get rid of him. Put glass in his food."

June was stunned. She stared at Helen. Helen stared back with an odd smile on her face. What stunned June most was the idea that this young woman, with minimal knowledge of the abuse taking place, took it upon herself to plot to kill Jimmy Briand.

"We never had any long conversations about anything that was happening in the house. I was conditioned not to say anything about it, and was too afraid that if Jimmy goaded Helen enough, she might burst out with something that would get me in trouble. And we never discussed *killing* anyone. Helen only said that I should get away from Jimmy and that 'we should get rid of him.' But I didn't know what she meant by it until that moment."

June told Helen to put the ground glass away, that she was talking crazy. Helen complied, and the two women started to watch television. But June wasn't concentrating on the program: she was thinking about Helen's suggestion.

"She had no idea what my state of mind was or how horrible my life was. She didn't know I feared for my life or that Jimmy had constantly threatened to kill me or had done such terrible things. What struck me was, the idea of killing Jimmy sounded *possible*. I had never thought of it before, and now, all of a sudden, it was like a little ray of hope peeking through the clouds; then I dismissed it."

But June didn't dismiss it for long. She sat there trying to forget what Helen had said, trying to watch the television show, but she couldn't. It kept coming back. She kept thinking about it and thinking about it. In the days to come, she would think about it some more, then a little more, and a little more. Eventually she came to *rely* on the fantasy.

"It never seemed real, but in the end, it was the only thing that got me through the day. When I thought I couldn't go on anymore, I'd think about what Helen had said. 'We should get rid of him.' I heard those words over and over in my head. And my little ray of sun would come out again."

The other thing that puzzled June was how Helen so casually used the term "we." She had said, "Here's how *we* can do it" and "*We* should get rid of him." She included herself in a plan to murder a man she barely knew, who had done things to her friend that, for the most part, she knew nothing about. It didn't make sense. Not until June analyzed the situation a little further.

"Helen had no life. She had no friends. She had no fun. She was a thrill seeker. That's why she always brought over horror movies. She constantly needed to be thrilled. She wanted to go bar hopping and meet exciting men. She wanted everything, but she was too overweight and unattractive to get anything. That's why she was always over at my house. I was her captive audience; she knew I wasn't allowed to go anywhere.

"She came over even though she hated Jimmy. And he got to her. It had to be his taunting and insults that started her fantasizing about killing him. But it was crazy. You don't just decide to go kill somebody because they tease you."

Later that night, while the women were watching television, Helen came out with a non sequitur: "You could just blow him away." June again turned to Helen and stared. This time Helen didn't stare back; she kept her gaze on the television — but she was thinking about murder.

"You could say someone broke in," said Helen, looking straight ahead, as if envisioning the perfect crime.

"What are you talking about?" asked June.

"You could shoot him, and your alibi can be that someone broke in the house. You can say that someone came up the back stairs, shot Jimmy, and ran away. That can be your story. No one would ever know." She looked at June now, extremely pleased with her plan.

Indeed, this was more than a fantasy for Helen. She had been thinking about her idea a great deal. She detested Jimmy, and though she wouldn't show it, seethed quietly every time he belittled her or called her "just another airhead like June." She was an overly sensitive woman who had been made fun of as a pudgy, uncoordinated youth, and consequently, suffered from a deep inferiority complex. She didn't need Jimmy — "an asshole we don't need around here" — deflating her ego further.

Jimmy knew he upset Helen, and with torture as one of his specialties, needled her as often as possible. As a result, she came to seek revenge. And, as always, she wanted thrills. The combination of the two would prove lethal.

The next day, Helen put a plan into action. Unexpectedly, she came by the apartment at ten in the morning. This was unusual as she always came over in the evening. But she knew Jimmy was gone, and June had said, based on past experience, that he'd probably be gone a few days. It was a Wednesday, and she should have been working, but was so excited about what she had to tell June that she called in sick for work and drove directly to June's apartment.

When June opened the door, Helen barged right past her and stalked straight into the living room. She didn't say anything and walked over to the gun case, took the key off the top of the case, and unlocked the glass door. She withdrew one of Jimmy's revolvers, then opened her purse and pulled out a box of bullets she had purchased at a Nashua gun shop on the way to the apartment.

Helen looked at June. June looked at the box. She knew what it was. Jimmy had similar boxes of ammunition around the apartment. "I got these," said Helen, "in case that's what we decide to do." But in Helen's mind, the decision was already made. June watched as she loaded the gun. When she finished she said, "Let's go," and headed toward the door. Like a robot, June obeyed.

Helen drove with purpose. June was in the passenger seat, and Jana and Pam were in the back seat. They were going to Mary Jackson's to drop off the kids, then they would be "taking a drive." June didn't inquire where, and Helen didn't offer any information.

After leaving the kids at the Jackson's, Helen drove to the outskirts of town, toward the woods. It was a five mile drive to the wooded area Helen was intent on, and when she reached it, she drove another mile or so to a dirt road. She slowed the car and drove a hundred yards down the road, then pulled over and got out; June followed.

"We walked through the woods not talking. I knew Helen had the gun with her, but other than that, I was in a daze. I felt no connection to reality, like I was walking through some ancient world of make-believe. I had an overwhelming sense that something bad was about to happen. Not there, not that day, but soon. Then I heard an explosion: Helen had fired the gun. She looked at me, then put the gun back in her purse and walked back to the car."

This time, Jimmy did not return home for four days. It was February 4, and the next day was garbage day, the day Jimmy "made the rounds" of each and every room, making certain all the garbage had been bagged and placed on the stairwell, and the waste baskets sprayed with Lysol. He had not seen his wife or children for four days, yet upon waking in the morning, the only thing he concerned himself with was garbage.

Jimmy Briand was more than just a cruel man who physically assaulted his spouse. He thrived on humiliation and degradation. It was as if merely inflicting pain on his wife was not sufficient to quell the demons screeching inside his mind — he needed more.

"We had trash bags at various places in the house, and on trash day, I had to remember to take all of them out to the garbage can. Just as Jimmy started his rounds that morning, I realized I had forgotten the bag under the sink. I knew I'd be in big trouble if he discovered it. Sure enough, that's the first place he looked.

"I instinctively started backing up as he looked under the sink. He turned toward me, waited for a second like he was building up steam, then lunged across the kitchen and grabbed me by the head. He was huge, but he could move fast when he was mad. He dragged me over to the stairwell, opened the door and threw me down the stairs.

"There were sixteen stairs, and I remember sort of catching myself every five or six stairs, then losing my balance and falling a few more steps, then catching myself and falling again until I hit the landing at the bottom. Then he came down after me. And he had the trash bag with him.

"When he reached the bottom of the stairs, he swung the bag over my head and it broke and all the kitchen trash poured out on top of me. Then he starting smushing it into my chest and face. He screamed at me, 'Pick it up, pick it up, you fucking lazy bitch!' But I couldn't because I didn't have a bag to put it in anymore; it was split open. He was screaming about that too.

"So he dragged me back up the stairway, and when we got to the top stair, he bent me over and started pulling off my jeans. I tried to crawl into the kitchen, but the garbage was slippery and I couldn't get any footing; plus, I had a deep cut in my hand from a soup can lid. He pulled me back and kept tugging at my jeans. He wanted to have sex right there, right there on the stairs with the garbage still in my hair and all over me and the floor.

"When I was on my stomach and he was on top of me, I turned my head and saw Pam and Jana watching from the living room. They didn't move; they were clinging to each other and just stared while Jimmy had sex with me, screaming 'Whore!' and 'Pig!' at the top of his lungs. When he was done, he called me a whore over and over again. He said I was a slut for letting him have sex with me."

After the attack, June ran to the bathroom and locked the door. Jimmy ran after her and pounded on the door, screaming, "Open the fucking door, you whore! Open up! Open up or I'll break the fucking thing down."

Jimmy didn't have time to act on his promise. There came a knock at the front door. "Who the fuck is it?!" he yelled from in front of the bathroom.

"Police. Open up, Briand."

A neighbor had called the police after hearing the commotion in the stairwell. "Go fuck yourself!" Jimmy growled. The knocking persisted. "Open the door, Jimmy. Hudson police department."

Jimmy thought for a moment and decided to answer the door. Before he had it completely open, he lunged at the officer.

"He came after me," Officer Brown later reported. "He put his hands around my throat." Frank from downstairs had seen the police cruiser drive up and came out of his apartment. Seeing the attack, he immediately helped pull Jimmy off the startled policeman. For reasons that remain unclear, Jimmy was not arrested for assaulting an officer, and the policeman left without further incident.

June had stayed locked in the bathroom the whole time, knowing better than to come out and reveal her situation to the "enemy." That night June slept on the couch. It was something she rarely did, mainly because she did not want to incite her husband by "guilt tripping" him. She worried he would interpret such an act as a rejection and take appropriate action. But June didn't care about that anymore and took the risk; Jimmy was too vile an animal to get into bed with any longer, and the thought of being next to him under the sheets gave her the creeps.

The following morning Jimmy got up earlier than usual, went to the garage, and didn't come home that night. June assumed that that would be the case, and called Helen as soon as he left for work, saying she needed to talk. It was atypical for June to be making the call, and Helen was delighted to hear from her. She said she was planning to come over anyway, and an hour later arrived at Central Street.

Since the beginning of the week, Helen had been coming over much more than usual. Vernon Jones, a neighbor, confirmed this when he later told authorities, "The Lewis girl used to come by occasionally for short visits. But during that last week, she spent a great deal of time at the Briand apartment — days and nights, with June."

In fact, during most of January, Helen Lewis had come to visit three or four days of the week, arriving around six in the evening and leaving about eight. In February, she visited even more, and often came by the apartment during the day as well as in the evening.

"Helen came over more and more. Maybe she sensed I needed someone to talk to. She may not have had any friends, but then neither did I. She was my only friend in the world. I was so isolated by not working and not being allowed to go anywhere that I was grateful for her; and after the previous night, I really needed some company.

"When she came over, I let everything pour out. She knew enough already, so what was I hiding? I told her about the trash incident the night before, and then I told her all the rest. When I was finished, she was dumfounded. She had no idea it was as bad as it was. She sat there for a minute not saying anything. Finally she turned to me and said, 'I think we should do it.'"

June had continued to stash small amounts of money in her secret hiding place under Pam's old baby blankets. The cache did not amount to much — just over a hundred dollars — but it kept alive a glimmer of hope that someday, somehow June would be able to escape the nightmare she was living. It was not so much the actual savings but rather the "going through the motions" that kept June hanging on to what was left of her sanity. When she told Helen about her plan to "leave one day" and the amount she had amassed, Helen looked glum. Then she snickered.

"You can't leave with that amount of money," she said.

"Oh I know," said June, trying to hide her embarrassment of her paltry savings.

"I'd loan you some money, but all I've got is about fifty dollars. That's not going to help much."

"That's okay. It'll build up. I'll have enough eventually."

"Eventually? Eventually you'll be *dead*. You don't have *time* for eventually."

Helen was motivated now. She had the whole story, and knew that her instincts — and revenge — were thoroughly justified. This man was dangerous. "He's like a disease; he's got to be stamped out," she said.

Helen did not stay long this particular day. After hearing June's story, she said she'd call later in the day and left abruptly. "Later in the day" came forty minutes later. Helen was calling from a payphone and sounded excited.

"I've found a place where we can dump the gun. It's perfect," she said, and went on to explain that she had "scouted out" a spot near a bridge where they could fling the gun after shooting Jimmy. June listened incredulously.

"Helen was really bent on getting rid of Jimmy. I mean, she *really* wanted to do it. My mind was blank as she was talking. It was like when we were walking through the woods the other day. I couldn't focus on what she was saying; I couldn't focus on *anything.*"

Jimmy would soon change that. A few days later, on the evening of February 10, 1987, Jimmy came home late — and drunk. Normally, his being drunk did not present a threat since most of his beatings came when he had little or nothing to drink. When he drank, he would usually come home, eat something, throw it all up, and pass out. This night was different — as was everything else that was happening in June's life.

Coming through the front door, Jimmy tripped on Jana's plastic roll-up sled and it incensed him. He picked up the sled and stomped into the kitchen with it under his arm looking for someone to blame. He started yelling, "How many times have I told you to keep ..." Then he stopped. He spotted June on her way to the bathroom. She was wearing only a towel wrapped around herself. He threw down the sled and yelled, "What are you doing running around naked?"

"He was mad about that too. I told him I was about to take a shower. I guess he didn't believe me and figured I had just finished being with a man or something equally ridiculous. Whatever it was, he grabbed me and put me in a headlock. I don't know if his being drunk kept him from realizing his strength, but it felt like my head would burst, it was so tight. Then he threw me on the bed. I landed face up, and hoped it would just be a quick sex thing like it usually was.

"Then Jimmy lowered his pants but he didn't take them off. That was strange. He was standing there and then he grabs me and pulls me up to my knees. He wanted oral sex. I didn't want to do that; I didn't like it and I told him I wouldn't do it. He didn't care. He grabbed my head with both hands and pulled me into his crotch, but I wouldn't open my mouth. Then he slapped me across the face. I knew I had to do it or I'd get a beating.

"I started but he couldn't get an erection. He got real mad about that. I was trying to get him stimulated and get it over with but nothing was happening. He held my head with both hands and moved it back and forth real quick, like he was helping me. But it didn't matter, he couldn't do it. Then he got furious.

"He was frustrated and pushed me back on the bed and jumped on top of me. He still had his pants just down to his thighs, and his big, brass Triumph motorcycle belt was in between us. The hook was digging into my thigh and I said, 'Your buckle is hurting my leg' but he wouldn't stop.

"And he still couldn't perform. He was getting madder and madder. Then he flipped me over on my stomach and pulled my hips back toward him: he wanted anal sex. I said, 'No! No! You can't do that. That's terrible, stop it!' The next thing I felt was the belt buckle again, only now it was gouging into the back of my leg. I knew he was doing it on purpose. I started bleeding and yelling that it hurt. *Then* he got his erection; I guess that's what it took.

"He forced himself into me and started moving side to side as hard as he could. I forgot about the pain from the buckle then; this was horrible. He was *trying* to hurt me — and he was succeeding. He was holding me by the buttocks real tight and pulling me onto him and reaming all around. I started bleeding there too. I thought it would never end."

This time the tears came. June hadn't cried in years; she had vowed not to. But this attack — the most brutal and dehumanizing to date — broke her. She had absolutely no coping skills left. And the tears rolled uncontrollably down her cheeks.

The following day, February 11, was cold and the roads were icy after a recent snowfall. June got Jana off to school, then bundled Pam in her hooded "Lil Bear" parka and drove over to visit her grandmother. Seeing June walk into the kitchen, Mary Jackson commented, "You don't look like you've been sleeping very good." In fact, June had not been sleeping or eating for months by then, but it took two vicious rapes — one only hours earlier — for Mary Jackson to notice her granddaughter wasn't looking particularly well.

June and Pam visited for about an hour. June didn't give any reason for the drop-in, but inside, she wanted desperately to talk to someone — someone besides Helen Lewis — about the horrible life she was leading. It seemed she was at "a turning point," but she didn't know where to turn. She had no idea where her mother was at the moment, and so she came for help to the least likely of candidates. After making small talk for a while, she decided it would be absurd to "go into it" with her grandmother. She thanked her grandmother for the cookies she had given her, zipped up Pam's coat, and left.

When June walked into the apartment, the phone was ringing. She ran to answer it and was startled by the caller on the other end. "Where's Jimmy?" said the voice.

"Who's this?" asked June. The caller didn't answer the question.

"I said where's your asshole of a husband?"

"He's at work."

"Tell him this is Scott, and I've got a message for him. Tell him I'm going to kick his ass, and he better watch his back." And the line went dead.

Scott. Scott. June remembered now. He was the one at Randolph's Christmas party. He was the boyfriend of one of Jimmy's cousins. He and Jimmy had argued about something during the party, and Jimmy knocked him down. Others had pulled the fighters outside, where Scott tried unsuccessfully to defend himself. He ended up with seven stitches above the eyebrow and a loose tooth. Like Jimmy, Scott didn't take kindly to losing fights, and had just as big an ego as Jimmy's. He said to him after the fight, "I'll get you, Briand. I don't know when or where, but I'll get you."

It was the second such call in less than a month. The first one, however, was from someone else. Apparently, Jimmy had been making a whole round of new enemies as of late. That call, too, was short and to the point. Someone phoned and asked, "Is this the Briand house?" When June said that it was, the man on the other end of the line said, "Tell Jimmy his time is limited." It was a prophecy that would soon be fulfilled.

June was upset by Scott's call. She didn't know what was going on, or why people were calling with threats, but she thought she had better inform Jimmy. She called across the street to the garage and told Jimmy about the call. He instructed June to get his revolver out of the gun case, load it, and put it under the couch; he would be home for lunch.

June didn't like being in the apartment alone after the threatening call, and called downstairs to Jack Spiller, who was home nursing a broken leg. The previous weekend he and Jimmy had gone out drinking, and Jack, as always, couldn't handle his liquor. It drove Jimmy crazy that Jack lost control when he got drunk, and this particular night he went really wild, yelling at everyone in the bar, even urinating his pants.

Losing bladder control was the final straw. Jimmy yanked Jack out of the bar, shoved him up against the side of the building, and punched him in the mouth. This was one of Jimmy's best friends, a long-standing buddy who had ridden motorcycles with him, gone hunting with him, loaned Jimmy money when he was short. None of that mattered. What mattered was Jimmy thought Jack made him look bad, look like a "pansy" for hanging around with a guy who couldn't drink six beers in an evening without "losing it."

And for Jimmy Briand looking bad was intolerable; so he punched his friend in the mouth. Then he broke his leg.

Jimmy had grabbed Jack by the neck and threw him to the ground. The man was so drunk he barely knew where he was, but he knew he had been hit in the mouth because he was holding it and yelling, "Jesus, Jimmy. What the hell did you do that for?"

Jimmy answered, "For the same reason I'm doing this," and then stomped on Jack's leg, fracturing the tibia and fibula bones of the lower leg.

June arrived at the bar at midnight after receiving a call from Jimmy to come and get him and Jack. When she pulled up, she saw Jack lying in the street. Jimmy opened the rear car door and started hauling Jack into June's car, but June yelled for him to stop, that Jack should not be moved without medical assistance.

"Fuck him," said Jimmy, and continued lifting his friend into the back seat. Jack was not speaking, and had a glazed look on his face. June wanted to drive directly to the hospital, but Jimmy had her drop him off at the apartment first so he wouldn't be involved. "Say he fell" was his three-word directive to June as he got out of the car and slammed the door.

Instead of remorse for what he had done, Jimmy would later tell others, "If Jack doesn't learn how to drink like a man, I'll break his other leg for him." That was Jimmy. Never an apology; never an admission of wrongdoing.

Now Jack came limping up the stairs to June's apartment, his leg in a cast and his mouth still with the brown scab from where Jimmy had punched him. He took a seat at the kitchen table while June explained about the call and how she was nervous about being there alone. Jack understood, and tried to calm her down with small talk and jokes. An hour later, Jimmy came bursting into the room.

"What are *you* doing here?" he demanded.

Jack had to think fast. He knew Jimmy's hair-trigger temper only too well, and also knew of his legendary jealous rages — rages that could ignite over something as harmless as a friend sitting in the kitchen with a cast on his leg talking to his wife. Jimmy might consider that socializing. And socializing could lead to warm feelings. And warm feelings could lead to... well .... he decided to lie.

"I was fixing the cable on the TV," he said. Jimmy didn't respond for a moment, then sat down at the table too. June let her breath out slowly, knowing Jack was in the clear. She almost leaped to the refrigerator and retrieved a beer for Jimmy. She unscrewed the cap and placed it in front of him, hoping it would keep him calm. There was no telling yet what his state of mind was because he had given no clues. Would he be fuming about the phone call? Would he explode any second and break Jack's other leg?

June and Jack watched Jimmy drink his beer. June was standing at the kitchen counter where the two lengths of counter met to make a right angle. She usually avoided this spot, knowing from past experience that if Jimmy decided to go for her, she was trapped. With Jack present, she had forgotten about her defensive positioning. But she had alcohol as an ally: the moment Jimmy finished his beer, June replaced it with another. She was hyper-attentive to such details by now, and knowing beer usually relaxed him, hoped against hope that he would not "flip out" about Scott's call. So far so good.

Apparently, the beers were effective. Jimmy ate his lunch quickly without discussing the phone call. He pushed back from the table and got up, saying he had a car coming in for a road test and had to get back to work. Wisely, Jack rose at the same time and said he, too, had to be going. He followed Jimmy to the door, and as Jimmy started down the stairs, Jack turned to June and gave her the *okay* sign with his thumb and forefinger. She smiled weakly and closed the door behind them.

The aging yellow school bus stopped in front of the Central Street fourplex just after two o'clock that afternoon. June heard the breaks squeal and the big diesel engine slowing to a stop just as the phone rang; it was Helen calling to say she would be over later that afternoon. June said fine and hurried the phone call, saying she wanted to meet Jana at the bus and help her carry her books upstairs.

At a quarter past four, Helen arrived at the apartment. June fed Pam and Jana about four forty-five. When their meals were over, June told the children to go to their rooms and put their pajamas on. She expected Jimmy to be home any minute, and prepared his meal and placed it in the oven. But he never showed. Five o'clock came and went. Six. Seven. June removed the meal, wrapped it in foil, and placed it in the refrigerator. She knew that if Jimmy was not home by this time, it was likely that he went out drinking and would not be home for hours. This gave her a feeling of relief, and put her in a relatively good mood despite the recent attacks she had suffered. She told the girls they could play tents again that evening, and they screamed with joy.

As her excited children watched, June pulled out Jana's old baby blankets and began setting up a tent camp. To avoid spoiling the festive atmosphere, June decided not to say anything to Helen about the threatening phone call earlier in the day. She told Jana to run back to her room, that she forgot her flashlight and how could she go camping without a flashlight? Pam trotted alongside her sister and fetched her doll to bring back to the camp as well. When they returned, June shut the lights off and the campout officially began.

"The girls were giggling and singing and we were having a wonderful time. This was the type of thing that, if Jimmy saw us, he'd call us dumb females and airheads. I was happy but sad at the same time knowing the fun wouldn't last, that sooner or later Jimmy would come home and everything would be the same as it was."

The girls were up past their bedtime, and June, amidst their protests and whining, finally turned the lights back on and told them to brush their teeth. Grumbling, they followed instructions. Afterwards, June tucked them into bed, read them a short story, and kissed them both goodnight. She then went out to the kitchen where Helen was starting to take down the tent city. June told her not to worry about the blankets just then, that she was thirsty and wanted to make a pitcher of Kool-Aid. Helen put down the blanket she was folding and went to the living room to turn on the television while June made the refreshments. June carried the pitcher of Kool-Aid into the room to join Helen, who had tuned the set to the show *The Tortellies*.

The women had been watching the show and drinking Kool-Aid for about an hour when they heard something at the doorway. It was Pam. She was up. And she was smiling. She knew her father still wasn't home, and decided to risk sneaking out to the living room to see if she could rekindle the "campfire."

June waved Pam in and plopped her on her lap with a big kiss. She was hugging and kissing her when Jana appeared at the doorway. Seeing Pam on June's lap, she ran directly to Helen, who scooped her up and cuddled her like June was cuddling Pam. Jana liked Helen, and once when she was about to go home, had told her, "Take me with you; I don't like it here." Helen had given June a knowing smile, and looked down to Jana, saying that she couldn't take her home, that she had her own child to take care of, but that she would come visit "all the time." Jana looked glum but accepted what Helen had said.

Now everyone was at it again. The giggling started, the laughter that was so rarely heard in the Briand apartment resounded throughout, and all was well on Central Street. But enough was enough. June knew not to press her luck, that Jimmy could come home any minute and "throw a fit" about the kids being up. Plus, the kids had been up late enough. The next day was a school day, and it would be impossible to get them moving if they stayed up any longer.

Still, June didn't want the fun to end too abruptly, so she told the girls to get down on their hands and knees. She grabbed hold of their waistbands and "played kangaroo," lifting the girls as they hopped along on all fours toward their bedroom. She tucked them back in and said that if they were good and stayed in bed, they'd have another fun night next week. When she walked back into the kitchen, Jimmy was standing there glaring at the remains of the tent city.

It was ten-thirty, and sure enough, Jimmy had been drinking since five. He was thoroughly intoxicated, and teetered back and forth as he stood in the middle of the kitchen. With bloodshot eyes, he looked at the blankets, then looked at June and said, "You're so fucking stupid. How old are you, two?" June did not give him an answer, and, as unusual as it was for him, Jimmy did not demand one. He preferred to continue with his drunken babbling. "You're a bad mother. You're a slut. No one will ever want you. No one wants a slut."

June was not hurt by what her husband said; she had heard it so many times before. And she didn't believe it any longer. Jimmy seemed to sense that, and headed for the living room. There he encountered Helen.

"I see we're in front of the TV again," he said sarcastically as he slumped into his chair. Helen did not respond but only frowned her disapproval and continued watching *The Tortellies*. Looking at the television, he continued: "I can't believe you're watching that shit. Airheads, you're just a couple of fucking airheads."

June walked into the living room and said, "What do you want to eat?" She did not ask *if* Jimmy wanted to eat; by then she knew the routine.

"Pizza" was the one-word response. Enough said, no further instructions necessary. June knew what to do: call Antonio's and order a large pepperoni and mushroom. Ten minutes later, she and Helen were putting on their coats and boots for the thirty-second car ride down the block to pick up the pizza. It was too cold and icy to walk, and June wanted to make sure the pizza was hot when she delivered it to her picky customer. Helen wasn't about the stay alone with Jimmy in the apartment; plus, she needed a pack of cigarettes from the mini-mart next to the pizza parlor.

After picking up the pizza and cigarettes, the women hopped back in the car and drove back to the apartment. June pulled into a different spot from where she had been parked, and as she and Helen got out of the car, they found the ground slippery with ice and impossible to walk on unaided. Using the pizza carton as their common bond, the women held onto it and tried to walk without falling. They laughed as they slid on the frozen patches, and Helen joked that Jimmy would be "a little pissed" if they brought him a pizza that was ripped in half. That made them laugh all the more. (Vernon Jones, the neighbor who observed all this from his window, would later tell authorities that he thought the women were drunk because of their laughing and carrying on. In fact, they had been drinking only Kool-Aid the entire night.)

June delivered the pizza and poured Jimmy a glass of milk. (While eating, Jimmy preferred milk to beer). She left him alone to eat his meal, and returned to the living room to watch television with Helen. She also returned to her "normal" state of emotional despair. It was true that the women had had a rare laugh, and June felt good while outside slipping about on the ice. But back in the apartment, her mind scrolled through everything again: the constant abuse, the brutal rape the night before, the threatening phone call that day, her utter and total exhaustion with it all.

Nothing had changed. Her drunken husband was in the other room, and any day — or minute or second —he would, without warning or provocation, attack again. Would it be a mere punch in the face, or would it be a protracted assault like the night he dragged her down the street when she was pregnant? Or next time would Jimmy poke the knife point not just *up to* but *into* her frantically pulsating jugular vein, "just to watch the blood spurt all over the fucking place"? *Not knowing* was what kept June's nerves frayed.

When Jimmy was finished eating, he went to the bathroom, then to bed. It was past eleven o'clock, but because he was so drunk, Helen decided to stay longer than usual. She knew how violent he could become, and thought it best to stay around this particular night until Jimmy went off to bed. Her son was long ago in bed, as was her mother, so she saw no reason to hurry home. A few moments later, she saw every reason *not* to leave June.

Jimmy had just gone to bed when June heard him coughing in the other room. They were not coughs one gets from a cold. June knew them well: Jimmy was about to get sick. She immediately ran to the refrigerator and pulled out a can of soda water; it was the only thing that soothed Jimmy's stomach when it was this upset. She walked into the bedroom to give him the glass she had poured, but he did not take it from her, and waved her out of the way as he stumbled to the toilet and vomited. She had just returned to the living room when Jimmy called for her.

"I thought he wanted help after all — the soda water or more milk. But when I went to him he was standing in front of the bathroom, wiping his mouth with one hand and pointing at me with the other. He stood there pointing his finger and said, 'I know what you're doing, and don't think you're going to get away with it.' Then he grabbed me by the shoulders. I could smell the vomit on his breath; it was sickening. I didn't know what he was talking about, but I knew I was going to get hit. When he grabbed me like that, I *always* got hit.

"But instead, he did something he had never done before: he let me go. That's when I shuddered. I felt sick in my own stomach and wanted to vomit like he had. *He let me go.* He had never done that before. Then it dawned on me. I knew exactly what he was talking about: he must have found the money I was stashing. That's all it could be. And if it was, I was dead. That's the only reason he would have let me go without hitting me: he found the money and knew I was plotting to leave him. If he had, it meant that he already decided to kill me, so why hit me now? It was over. He was going to do what he always promised he'd do if I ever tried to leave him."

Jimmy turned and went to bed. June stood frozen where she was. She stood for five minutes. Ten. Then she heard him snoring. He was asleep. She dashed to the closet. *The blankets!* They weren't hiding anything! They were draped over the kitchen chairs! She had forgotten their primary purpose: hiding her getaway money.

The small stack of bills with the rubber band around it, the stack that was under the pink blanket on the bottom of the pile—it was gone. June clawed at the rest of the cupboard like a crazed animal. She ripped every towel, sheet, pillow case from the shelves. Nothing. Had she moved the money? Of course not. It was under the pink blanket. It was *always* under Jana's baby blanket. The pink one was the good luck blanket. Put the money there, and maybe some good fairy would come along and double it. Maybe even "take me away from this hell." It worked with the tooth fairy, didn't it? Why not "to save me and my kids"?

Unbeknownst to June, when she had pulled the blankets out for the tent party, she had, indeed, left the stack of bills naked and glowing green like a menacing beacon of betrayal on the bottom of the shelf. In plain view, Jimmy had to see it. June's secret was unveiled, and her husband would now sleep peacefully knowing exactly what he was going to do with a cheating, lying, wife who would never again make a fool of him.

Jimmy had vowed that the humiliation he suffered at the barn party was the last time he would allow such personal desecration by a "disobedient female." The beating he had given June on the ride home was a warning to his wife: Don't ever again make me look bad in front of people. Now June was planning to do exactly that, and he knew it.

Like a zombie, June shuffled into the living room and slowly lowered herself to the couch. She stared blankly at the dark, dead eyes on the deer head across from her, and they stared back at her. Helen had not noticed June come into the room, too engrossed was she in the late night television thriller.

"I sat there waiting to die. And you know what? There was a little piece of me that almost wouldn't have minded. I remember thinking, 'I hope he does kill me; I don't care.' But then I thought about the kids again. Where would they go? Who would get them? Jimmy's parents or — God forbid — *Jimmy*? Would he kill Jana? She was the weak one, the one he beat on. I always protected her before. Who would protect her when I was gone?

"I sat on that couch — right on the edge of it — for two hours. I was numb. I knew I was going to be killed — that was a given. I looked at Helen and thought, 'Jimmy's waiting for her to go home so he can come out here and kill me. Then he'll kill Jana. Or he'll kill Jana *and* Pam. I don't know! I don't know what he'll do, but it will be bad!'"

June looked at Helen again, and this time Helen looked back. The women stared for a long moment at each other. It was late, one-fifteen in the morning, February 12, 1987. June reached under the couch and pulled out the gun Jimmy had directed her to hide there earlier in the day. June looked at Helen again. She raised her index finger to her lips to keep Helen quiet. Helen's eyes were huge and black and interested. She stood up. June stood as well, and walked toward the bedroom. Helen followed close behind her.

When June reached the doorway to the bedroom, she stopped. She was approximately eight feet from the bed, but could see nothing because the kitchen light was off. It was black. "I couldn't see the bed or Jimmy or anything. I stood there for about ten seconds, then I turned toward Helen who was just to my left. I said under my breath, 'I can't do this' and started to step away. She took a step toward me and cut me off. She said, 'Do it. Do it. Do it.'

"I turned back toward the bedroom. I took one step toward the bed, held the gun straight out, and fired into the dark. I couldn't see anything until the gun went off. Then there was a white blast and I saw Jimmy's arm jerk up and heard him start to say something like, 'What the ... ' Then I fired again. And again. I don't remember how many times."

In one swift motion, June pivoted toward Helen and tossed her the gun. She caught the weapon in midair, then disappeared as June ran to her daughters' room and grabbed Jana. A minute later, Helen reappeared. She had gone to the kitchen, unlatched the wet/dry vac, and stashed the gun inside. Now she snatched up Pam and ran down the front stairway behind June.

"At the bottom of the stairs, Helen looked at me with this weird look. Then she smiled. I had no idea what she was smiling about. I was petrified that Jimmy was going to come down any second, and here was Helen *smiling*. Then out of nowhere, like an actress on cue, she screamed as loud as she could.

"I started banging on Jack and Tom's door. Helen is screaming and screaming, and I'm banging on the door. Tom opened the door because Jack was in his cast and couldn't get up. Tom was putting on his camouflage pants at the same time and said, 'What's going on?' I said, 'You gotta get upstairs. Someone came through the back door and went for Jimmy.'"

Tom disappeared into his apartment and came back with a shotgun. He ran upstairs to the apartment, then came back down screaming, 'What the fuck! What the *FUCK*!' In the meantime, Jack had called the police. Then Tom ran outside and all around the building. All he had on was his camouflage pants. It was freezing outside, with snow and ice everywhere, but he didn't notice that he was barefoot and without a shirt. Jack finally made it to the door and said he thought he heard firecrackers.

What he heard, of course, was June murdering her husband. She did not know it at the time, but in the pitch dark, without aiming at anything, she had fired four bullets directly into Jimmy Briand's forehead, killing him instantly. Three of the lead slugs passed through his brain and lodged at the back of his skull, and the fourth came to rest at its base near the spinal cord.

Now, in the corner of Tom's kitchen, June huddled on the floor with her children, rocking them back and forth trying to comfort them. Pam was in June's lap with her head against her mother's chest, and Jana was on the floor next to her. The girls were both still sleepy, but Jana was old enough to realize something was radically wrong. After a few minutes she lifted her head and looked up at her mother.

"Is Daddy dead?" she asked.

"I don't know," said June truthfully.

Just then, Tom bolted back into the apartment and yelled, "Jesus, it's bad. It's real bad!" Hearing this, Jana looked up at her mother again, now looking for an affirmative response to her question. June just pulled Jana's head to her chest and kept rocking back and forth.

Tom was crazed now. Still half naked, he ran back outside with his shotgun. June knew he was not thinking rationally — no one was — but he was about to get frostbite on his bare feet. She ran after him and stopped him on the front porch.

"I was telling him to go back, go back inside and put some clothes on, when the police came. Two cars came skidding into the driveway. The police jumped out of their cars and saw Tom with his shotgun and thought he was holding me hostage. They drew their guns and yelled at him, 'Lay down on the ground, NOW!' Put the gun down!' I yelled back, 'Don't shoot! He's a friend!'"

Rotating blue lights were everywhere, and cast an exotic cobalt blue hue over the surrealistic scene. It was one-thirty in the morning, and suddenly, legions of policemen appeared seemingly out of nowhere like army ants thrust into action. They dispersed in all directions: upstairs, downstairs, around the back, on the porch, back upstairs. One finally stopped and asked Tom exactly what happened. "I don't know," he said. "My friend's upstairs; he's been shot."

June was throwing up now. She couldn't stop. Three times. Four times. Every time she went to vomit, a policeman followed her to the bathroom, where, after retching, she washed her hands — and in the process washed away traces of gun powder that would have provided telling evidence of the murder she had just committed.

"When I stopped throwing up, I sat back down with the kids. I thought the police were upstairs fighting with Jimmy. He hated police so much and always said he'd take down five or six of them before they took him down. I was sure he'd knock them all over and come down looking for me; I just knew it."

Helen was in the living room smoking a cigarette. Two policemen were interrogating her. Over and over they asked, "How did he get in? Are you sure it was through the back door?"

"Yes," answered Helen. "It was the back door. I'm sure of it."

But the police knew it was *not* through the back door — it couldn't have been. Earlier in the evening a light snow had fallen. The back stairs were dusted with enough snow

— *undisturbed* snow with no footprints — to indicate that no one had been up or down those stairs that night. No one had come up the back stairs, shot Jimmy, and escaped by the same route. Whoever shot Jimmy came in another way, and the police were sure Helen knew it.

"Okay, everybody," said the policeman who had been talking to Helen. He was standing between the living room and the kitchen and everyone stopped to listen. "We've all got to go down to the station." He then turned to June and asked if she wanted to take anything — a purse, coat. She said she did, and the officer escorted her upstairs to her apartment.

"When I opened the door, all I was focused on was the coat rack. I wanted to get my purse and coat and get out of there. I didn't want to be around when Jimmy came flying out of the bedroom to get me. Then I saw Frank. I hadn't seen him before then, and he was standing there talking to the policemen. I thought they were telling him to go back and calm down Jimmy. But they were really telling him Jimmy was dead."

When Frank saw June, he walked over and hugged her. "He's gone," said Frank.

"What do you mean, gone?" said June.

"There's nothing we can do."

"What are you talking about?"

"Jimmy's dead."

"No, he's not," said June adamantly, refusing to believe such nonsense. Then she saw the policeman over Frank's shoulder nodding his head, confirming what Frank had just said. It was true: Jimmy Briand — invincible, omniscient, all powerful, undefeated and everlasting Jimmy Briand — was dead.

Frank lurched forward and hugged June tightly, weeping out loud, "He's gone, he's gone, he's gone."

"I thought Frank was losing his mind. I said to myself, 'Do they have any idea who they're *talking* about? This was

Jimmy, Jimmy Briand. Jimmy didn't *go* down — he took the *other* guy down. No one could stop him. And any minute, he's going to come flying out of that bedroom and kill me; I just know it. Oh God, will he be raving this time.'"

PART IV: PRISON

The tall detective in a well-worn tweed sport coat slammed his hand down on the desk. "I want the *truth*, goddamn it! *The truth!*" He thrust his weather-beaten face close to June's and held it there, only inches away, glowering at her with clenched teeth that made his over-developed jawbones quiver. He had been at this for hours now, and he was losing patience.

Having been roused from a deep sleep at two in the morning, he was in no mood for games. The ringing telephone on his nightstand had startled him that late at night, and he wondered what could be so important that it would not wait until morning. Hudson, New Hampshire, was a small, relatively peaceful suburb, and rarely had a serious newsworthy event — let alone one that would be picked up by every major news organization in the country.

Officer Billings had thrown on his tie and run a quick comb through his thinning hair. When he got word that a shooting had occurred, he advised his wife that he would not be back any time soon. "This will be an all-nighter — and then some," he had said, kissing her goodbye and shutting off the light.

Upon entering the police station, he received a hurried briefing from an officer who walked alongside the veteran detective spewing the relevant facts. One such fact was that the Attorney General of New Hampshire, Stephen Merrill (who later would become governor), had already been called at his home and told about the killing. After hearing the details, he instructed the police to charge June Briand with first-degree murder.

Having heard enough, Officer Billings waved the younger cop off, saying "Thanks, Roger, got the picture," and opened the door to the interrogation room June had been sitting in — alone — for the last hour and a half. She, Helen, Tom, Jack, and Frank had been ordered to drive to the Hudson Police Department to sort out what happened in the early morning of February 12, 1987. After announcing in Tom's apartment that everyone needed to go down to the station, the policeman in charge led the convoy of vehicles while his fellow officers followed behind the group.

June and Helen rode with Frank in his truck; Tom and Jack rode together in Tom's car. Frank's wife, Deena, had thrown on a heavy, wool overcoat over her nightgown and taken Jana and Pam into her apartment as the cars backed out of the driveway. June told them she "would be right back," fully believing the statement, and told them not to worry, to go to sleep in Aunt Deena's house and that she would see them in the morning.

After everyone got into Frank's truck, he turned the ignition but then opened the door again and got out. In the confusion, he had forgotten his wallet and ran back to his apartment to get it. While he was gone, Helen turned to June and said, "I can't even cry." June was looking at the floorboards and said nothing. Her eyes, too, were dry.

No one spoke on the ride to the police station. When they arrived, everyone was separated and ushered into different rooms. The police needed to interview everyone, and wanted to keep people isolated in order to compare stories. The first questions were of an exploratory nature: "Did Jimmy have any enemies?" "Was there anyone who might have had a grudge against him?" "Was he involved in any business dealing that might have gone sour?"

At this early stage, the police still believed that an intruder may well have entered the apartment, and that the women's story, though somewhat confused, was valid. They theorized that perhaps the shooting was gang-related, and said to June, "We know Jimmy was involved in motorcycle gangs. We know the kind of people he associated with. Don't worry, you can tell us what happened; we'll protect you."

Due to the nature of the crime — four shots to the head at close range — the police believed that it may well have been "a hit" in payback for some deal gone bad. That notion was strengthened as June held to her story, insisting that someone came in and shot Jimmy. But she did not know who or why, and could offer no further details.

After three hours of this unproductive dialogue and vague responses to specific questions, the interrogatories took on a different flavor. The likelihood of an unknown assailant magically materializing to assassinate Jimmy in the middle of the night, then disappearing without a trace, seemed more and more remote. The police began asking different types of questions, such as, "How did June and Jimmy get along?" And to June and Helen specifically, "Are you *sure* it was the back stairs?" "Are there any weapons in the apartment?" "Have you ever fired them?"

After one such series of questions, and still without results, the two policemen interrogating June left her alone and went back to Helen's room. A few minutes later, June heard one of the men yelling angrily; it was Billings. He was becoming more and more aggravated with the dearth of information coming forth. Helen was sticking to her story; June was confirming it; it was getting late and he was getting nowhere.

The police then changed tactics: They brought Helen into June's room and left them alone, saying they needed to take a break. Whether or not the police had listening devices in the rooms is not known (there is no evidence of this, but June believes it to be the case), but while they were alone together, Helen said to June, "Remember, don't tell them I know anything. Someone came up the back stairs. That's all you know. Someone came up the back stairs." June nodded in agreement.

The police did not test June's hands for traces of gun powder until after she had been to the bathroom and washed her hands — both at Tom's apartment and later at the police station. Thus, the powder test came back negative, and it seemed to put Billings in an even greater state of agitation. Now he came back to June, but his demeanor had changed markedly.

He again entered the interrogation room with Officer Redfield who, unlike Billings, was soft-spoken and seemed to have a sympathetic, fatherly way about him. If Billings portrayed the image of the tough "bad cop," Redfield was its antithesis — the "good cop" who was friendly, understanding, and who genuinely felt sorry for June and the situation in which she found herself. After all, here sat a frightened young mother who had been married to Jimmy Briand — a man well-known to the Hudson police for chronic violence and assaults of every type — including those on their own officers. Redfield could do nothing but sympathize with her. But Billings was the one in charge.

The interrogation room was unusually small, with only enough room to stuff in four wooden chairs and a small oak desk. Redfield sat down across from June again, but Billings refused to even look at her and paced back and forth, thinking. Then he turned suddenly and smacked his hand down on the desk.

"We know you did it! *Just tell us you killed him*!" He was screaming now, and utterly frustrated. June looked down at the floor and said nothing. "There weren't any *footprints* on the back stairs, June. No one went up those stairs! *You* shot your husband! Now, goddamn it, *admit it*!" He struck the desk with his fist.

Officer Redfield then took over. "June. Listen," he said softly. "We knew your husband; he was a bastard. Everyone knew that. Now, what you have to do is tell us the truth. Just tell us what happened and everything will be all right. The truth, June. We need to know the truth because what we have here doesn't add up. It doesn't fit. Do you understand?"

June looked at the policeman and nodded that she understood. It was time. Daylight was breaking through the trees outside the window, and June was starting to sag in her chair. She was exhausted. And she was scared. Never having been in trouble with the law before, she did not know her way around the legal system. Up to this time, she had not even asked to make a phone call. Now she did.

"I made a deal with the police. I said I would tell them what happened, but first I had to know that my kids were safe. I said I wanted to call my grandmother, and they agreed that I could."

Billings grabbed a phone from somewhere, plugged it in, and slammed it down on the desk. "Go ahead," he said, still refusing to sit down. He towered over June, glaring at her as if he wanted to physically grab her and rip the truth from her but was restrained by the regulations of a legal system he swore to uphold.

"Hello, Grandma?" June started. "Grandma, this is June. Sorry to call you so early."

"What's going on?" asked Mary Jackson.

"I'm at the police station. Jimmy's dead."

There was a brief pause on the end of the line. Then Mary said matter-of-factly, "You killed him, didn't you?"

"Grandma, I need your help," said June, ignoring the question. "Deena's got the kids. You've got to call her and have her bring them over, okay? Will you please do that for me? I can't leave here for a while, and they'll be awake pretty soon."

"You did it, didn't you, June?" Mary repeated placidly.

Again, June failed to respond. Even if she had tried, Billings would have cut her off. He was pacing like a caged animal while she talked, and again thrust his red, angry face close to hers and screamed, "*Where's the fucking gun?!*" At that moment, he looked to June remarkably similar to the man she had just shot.

June was taken aback by the explosive query and profanity she expected from the likes of her husband but not policemen. Maybe Jimmy was right. Maybe these really were "the enemy." This one was certainly acting like it.

"I've got to go now," said June into the phone. "Thanks, Grandma. Give my love to Grandpa." And she hung up.

Officer Redfield, the good cop, took over again. It was time — way *past* time — to read June her rights. He pulled out a dog-eared three-by-five card from his breast pocket: the Miranda warning. "Now June, we're going to have to keep you here. I'm going to read you your rights. I'll go slowly so you won't have any problem with this, okay?"

June nodded in agreement. Redfield then began slowly reading the Miranda warning line by line, advising June that she had the right to remain silent, and that anything she said could be used against her in a court of law. He stopped after each line and asked, "Do you understand that?" She did not, but she nodded in the affirmative. After completing the reading, Officer Redfield asked her another question: "Do you want an attorney?"

With this, Billings threw his head back and jammed his hands into his trouser pockets. He stalked back and forth in the tiny office, scratching the back of his head, looking up at the ceiling, then scratching the back of his head some more. He was a man in pain. It had already been hours, and now, with Redfield offering June *an attorney* of all things, the process would become hopelessly bogged down.

Redfield turned to Billings and said, "Can you get her a phonebook?"

"Jesus!" said Billings, who stormed from the room and returned a minute later, throwing the book down on the desk. Redfield pushed the book gently across the desk to June. But she did not open it. Redfield waited. June didn't move. They waited some more. Billings was in agony. June had no idea how to use the book because Jimmy didn't allow it. He had given her the two or three numbers she needed to survive in her isolated cubicle, and now she was in the big world and had no idea how to proceed.

Finally, June opened the book to the yellow pages and stopped. "I didn't know if I should look up attorney or lawyer. I didn't know which was which, or if there was any difference between the two. I didn't know what I'd say if I found one. I didn't know *anything*. It was hopeless, all so hopeless. I was totally lost.

"Just when I got the courage to start thumbing through the book, the bad cop starts yelling at me. 'We know you did it! Why don't you just *admit* it, goddamn it?! You shot him. Just say it, for Christ's sake. *Say it!*' He went on and on like that while I was trying to figure out how to use the phonebook. He kept yelling at me and talking to me while I was trying to find a lawyer. I couldn't do it. I finally closed the book and said, 'I don't need one.' I was too embarrassed to keep trying. I didn't want them to see I didn't even know how to use a telephone book."

The instant June closed the book, Billings screamed his same question: "*Where's the fucking gun?!*" This time June looked down at the floor. It was no use. She was exhausted. There was no way out of this. She looked back up. Billings was drilling into her with his ferocious eyes. She looked to Redfield. Now *he* was looking at the floor.

Finally the tears came. Whatever iron wall had been holding them back all these years, it now gave way. June covered her eyes with her hands, bent forward and laid her head on the desk and cried like she never cried before. It had been a long time, and now the tears came in torrents, as if making up for lost time. In between sobs, June tried to answer Billing's question, but she couldn't get out a word. For once, he seemed to understand, and let the woman weep without interruption.

Finally, she looked up. "It's ... it's ... it's behind the bureau in the kids' room." That was all Billings needed. He turned on his heel and bolted from the room and sped off in the direction of Central Street. (For some reason, Helen had moved the gun from the wet/dry vac just before the police arrived and had told June about the switch just before leaving for the police station, saying, "They'll never look there").

Twenty minutes later, Billings returned wearing latex gloves and holding a brown paper bag. He stood in front of June and reached into the bag. He withdrew a small caliber handgun, holding it gingerly between his thumb and forefinger. Again, he moved his face inches from June's and said unctuously, "Is this it?" Before hearing June's answer, a wry smile spread across his tired face. He had finally won, and he was proud of himself.

"Yes," was all June said. The detective seemed uninterested in her response at that point, and turned away as he put the gun back in the bag and left the room. Redfield stayed behind with June, who now was ready to make a complete confession — complete except for implicating her friend Helen. As she had promised she would, she left Helen out of the story entirely. What she did not know was, Helen had also left *herself* out — and put June squarely at the center of the crime with no complicity whatsoever for herself.

Before Redfield began to record the confession, he asked June one question: "Why did you do it?"

June's answer was simple, and as truthful a statement as she had ever made: "I couldn't take it anymore."

Two hours later, the confession was over. June explained everything the best she could, but still left out Helen's involvement. (That would come out later when June met with her court-appointed attorneys.) By now, Helen was home in bed. The police had seen no reason to hold her, and had let her go home with the others. Besides, they had their prime suspect, and would soon have the case wrapped up; minor details no longer mattered.

When Redfield finished his paper work, June turned to him and said, "What happens now?"

"You're going to be booked, then arraigned," he said.

Having never been in trouble before, June had no idea what the terms meant. And she had no time to ask Redfield, who was already on his feet leading her to the booking room, where a photographer was waiting.

"Officer Redfield left me with the photographer, who told me to stand in front of the camera. I could see he was more than a photographer because he was wearing a gun. That's when I asked, 'What is this all about?' He said, 'You're under arrest for the death of your husband — look down.' I did, and saw a sign in front of me that read First-Degree Murder."

It was now seven in the morning. After the photographs and fingerprints were taken, June sat on a small bench awaiting her fate. Almost immediately, a new policeman came into the room and took June by the arm. He walked her into another small room and told her to sit down. Five minutes later, he was back.

"Let's go," he said.

"Where are we going?" June asked.

"To another room."

The police station was small, but it seemed to have an endless number of tiny rooms off the main hallway. The policeman led June toward the new room which was in the direction of the front door. At that moment, there was a commotion near the door. June looked up. Frank was back.

And he was trying to break free of two officers fighting to restrain him. He had come for June, and he was carrying a shotgun.

"I'll kill you, you fucking bitch!" he screamed when he spotted her. One of the officers grabbed the barrel of the gun while the other one tried to hold Frank by the waist. But he was wild, and wriggled free of the officer's grasp. Just then two more policemen came from the flanks to subdue him.

"You're dead, bitch! You're fucking DEAD!" The officer holding June quickly shoved her into a nearby room and ran to help his fellow officers contain Frank. (It is not clear if Frank was ever charged for entering the police station with a loaded firearm.)

June sat in her room with her arms wrapped tightly around her. Her head drooped forward and her eyes were closed, as if trying to block out the world around her. A few minutes later, she heard someone step to the open doorway, and looked up to see the familiar face of her grandfather.

Harold Jackson looked pale and drawn and worried. He held his mesh fisherman's hat in his hands and looked into the room with watery eyes. "When can I take you home?" he asked weakly.

June had been badly shaken by Frank's furious outburst, and now, at the sight of the man who had raised her from an infant, the sobs returned. She tried to choke them back, hoping to keep from upsetting the frail man any further. "Grandpa, go home," she said sternly. "Go home. Everything will be all right." Then she broke down again.

Harold Jackson heard someone behind him. He turned to see Officer Billings emerge from a room a few feet away, and asked him the same question: "When can I take her home?"

"She's not going anywhere!" snapped Billings. "You've got to go back to the waiting room. No one's supposed to be near the prisoner."

Prisoner. Harold turned back to June. The impact of the word nearly knocked him down. He grabbed for the doorjamb to steady himself, and in so doing, dropped his hat on the floor. He bent down to retrieve it, and when he stood up, he too was crying. He looked back at his granddaughter with tears running down his face. He tried to wipe them away with the back of his hand, but it was no use.

In the twenty-four years June had known her grandfather — from the day she was born and left at his door to the day she was arrested for murder — she had never seen him cry. On top of all the other emotional chaos churning inside her, this was too much. She felt an urgent need to vomit again.

"Please. Please," said June, leaning out the doorway in the direction of Billings, who was talking to another officer in the hall. "Please. I have to use the bathroom. Could I *please* go to the bathroom — right away?"

Fortunately, Billings was accommodating. He escorted June to the bathroom where she immediately retched, but nothing came up because there was nothing in her stomach. Again she retched. And again. She stood over the toilet bowl, panting, exhausted, her stomach twisted in painful knots. Then she got hold of herself and splashed some water on her face and blew her nose. She washed her hands, but did not dare look in the mirror. When she emerged from the bathroom, her grandfather was gone.

"Okay, it's time. Let's go," said Billings as June exited the bathroom.

"Time for what?" asked June.

"Transfer time. You're going to the district courthouse for arraignment. Turn around and put your hands behind your back." June did as she was told. Billings pulled her right arm back and snapped a handcuff around her wrist. Then he cuffed the other wrist and led her down the hallway.

"Everyone was talking in whispers. There were a lot of people scurrying around, and all of a sudden, things were happening fast. I was up by the front door with policemen all around me. Then a police car pulled up and the policemen picked me up and swooped me into the car. Someone pushed my head down, and someone else said, 'Stay down. Keep your head down!' I found out later that they received death threats from people who called the station saying they were going to shoot me.

"I heard car doors shutting — lots of car doors. There were police cars everywhere — some in front of us, some behind. They boxed us in. The policeman in the front seat said again, 'Keep down!' I was by myself in the back seat, so I stretched out along the floor, but it was hard to get between the seats because my arms were locked behind me. He said, 'Stay down; this will only take a few minutes.' It seemed like forever."

As quickly as June was hustled into the car at Hudson Police Department, she was rushed into Nashua District Courthouse. "I could barely keep up. I was so tired, and they were all moving so quickly."

Up the stairs. In a door. Through another door. Suddenly, June was in a courtroom. There she was handed off to Officer Patterson, a female police officer who, at a slower pace, led June into an empty jury box. It was quarter to eight in the morning and the courthouse was mostly empty, as was the courtroom in which June now stood with her attendant.

Patterson held June up by the arm. Had it not been for her support, June would have collapsed. The officer felt the sagging weight and asked June, "Do you want to sit down?" June nodded that she did, but would not be given the respite: the judge entered the chamber. At the sight of him, June's knees buckled; Patterson caught her. She whispered to June without turning her head, "You'll be all right. This will just take a few minutes. Hang on. I've got you."

The man in black took his seat at the bench. An armed bailiff had entered just before him, as did a court reporter. The bailiff now stood to the side of the bench with his thumb hooked into his heavy leather belt, and waited for the reporter to set up her stenographic equipment. When she was ready, she gave him a slight nod, after which he said in a booming voice, "Court is now in session."

Officer Patterson again whispered under her breath, "I've got you. Just hang on." Judge Ernest Scott then began speaking very rapidly.

"Ms. Briand, you have been charged with first-degree murder in the shooting death of your husband. Do you understand?"

June did *not* understand. She did not comprehend that Jimmy was dead, nor did she have any recollection of shooting him.

Patterson whispered, "Say yes."

"Yes," June replied softly.

"Do you also understand that I cannot accept pleas from you at this time?"

Again Patterson coached June: "Say yes."

"Yes."

"Do you also understand that anything other than a not guilty plea would automatically sentence you to life in prison with no possibility of parole? Do you understand that?"

"Say yes," said Patterson.

"Yes," said June, whose entire weight was now being supported by the officer next to her, who continued to whisper, "Don't worry" and "Hold on" throughout the short proceeding.

Three new policemen took over custody from Patterson and rushed June down the courthouse hallway toward the main entrance. The hallway was dimly lit, almost dark, while outside the sun was brilliant, especially with the reflection of the white snow. When the police hit the bar on the front door and it swung open, a blinding bolt of white light exploded onto June's entourage. It intensified tenfold as photographers' cameras flashed, camcorders rolled, and television crews trained their high intensity lights on June. Reporters surged forward yelling questions, holding microphones, notepads, and tape recorders.

"Ms. Briand! Did you kill you husband?"

"Can you tell us why?"

"Where are your children?"

But there was no time for answers. Instantly, an officer shoved June's head down as she was whisked into another patrol car. "Stay down!" came the command again, and again, June wedged herself between the back and front seats, her hands still cuffed behind her.

Word of the shooting had spread quickly after the morning news broadcasts, and more death threats had come into the Hudson Police Department and the district courthouse. The earlier threats had come from members of the Norton clan, who vowed that June would "not get away with killing one of our brothers." But after the morning news shows, the threats were more generic in nature: Men unhappy about a female killing a male called saying, "We've got the bitch in our sights" and "We're gonna take her out." The threats were considered so serious that officials took unprecedented steps in protecting their now-famous prisoner.

Realizing this was not their run-of-the-mill prisoner, they took extra measures to assure nothing happened to June on the way to the Hillsborough House of Corrections in Goffstown, New Hampshire, where she was now headed. (The facility, a few miles northwest of Manchester, was also called Grasmere at the time, and later changed to New Hampshire State Prison for Women).

The state police, who now took over custody, also made sure to keep her head well below the car windows. Amidst shouting reporters and flashing lights, a convoy of four black unmarked vehicles and two white and tan state cruisers left the courthouse. Another patrol car lagged behind the convoy, ready to head off any of the media or curious public who might try to follow the fleet.

Nevertheless, the police maintained a heightened state of alert. As a precaution, after traveling for fifteen minutes, the convoy slowed to a stop. Several officers got out and switched cars. One opened June's door and transferred her to a different vehicle, again keeping her face down on the floor behind the front seat. The car was driven by a lone state trooper, who, like the officer before him, said nothing to the prisoner.

"I remember staring at the black floor mat and thinking, 'I don't know where we are or where we're going. No one is speaking. God, I'm tired, I'm so tired.' By then I'd been up for something like thirty hours and I finally started to fade off. I had just laid my head down on the floor mat and closed my eyes when the road suddenly got bumpy. We were traveling down a dirt road. That's when I got scared because I knew bad things happened down dirt roads."

The rest of the convoy peeled off and dispersed just before entering the prison grounds, leaving the state trooper alone to drive the final distance to the prison. Finally he spoke: "You can sit up now, it's okay." The break-up of the entourage seemed to relax the young man with the curly blond hair, who now became more talkative. "How are you doing?" he asked June.

"Okay," said June, slithering backwards up onto the car seat the best she could. The officer saw her struggling in the rearview mirror and stopped the car. He got out and opened the passenger door.

"You don't need the cuffs anymore," he said. "Here. Turn around, I'm taking them off." Removing a prisoner's handcuffs in this manner is against police procedure, but the trooper was not worried about police procedure — he was worried about June. He got back into the front seat and put the car in gear. He drove for a minute and spoke up again. "I don't really want to do this," he said. June did not reply.

The car kept moving, but at only ten miles per hour. The prison loomed a quarter mile ahead. Two minutes went by and the prison drew closer. There was still a hundred yards to go when the trooper said again, "I *really* don't want to do this. You have babies, June. You were trying to protect your babies."

For a moment, June had the distinct impression that the sympathetic young trooper was about the spin the car around and drive off as fast as he could in a miraculous, Herculean act that would save her from the fate that awaited her — now fifty yards and twenty seconds away. As he admitted later, "I thought about it; I really did." But reason got the best of him and he slowed to a stop with the woman he knew should be anywhere but here.

The gate opened slowly. The trooper hesitated a moment, then rolled into the prison compound. The gate clanked shut behind them as he drove the short distance to the receiving area of the old brick building. He got out of the car and opened the rear door. He knelt down and asked June, "Are you ready?" She nodded that she was. Then he patted her knee and added, "If you need to talk to me, my name is Steve Walker." With her head down, June nodded again but said nothing. Walker took June's hand and helped her to her feet. He walked her the ten yards to the door and stopped. Before she walked in, June took a quick glance at the ten-foot-high cyclone fence surrounding the property.

Three gleaming strands of circular razor wire lay perched across the fence like silver serpents, daring one and all to come close and touch. Years before, one desperate inmate at another prison had done just that. Having made it to the top of the fence, he reached to haul himself over and grabbed the virulent snake, instantly severing four fingers at the knuckles.

June looked away and stepped through the doorway into the intake room. "Everyone spoke in hushed tones. A woman named Debra escorted me to a small holding room where eight correctional officers stood in a semicircle. I don't know what the room looked like or what they looked like because I was looking down at the floor like I always did. But I knew there were eight people because I saw eight pairs of shiny black shoes on a waxed green linoleum floor.

"It was the smell of the wax that got to me. I almost threw up again. The wax made me think of Jimmy. It was that same, awful smell of floor wax that I'd smelled so often when my face was on the floor. Now it made me sick to my stomach."

Two women stepped forward. One looked over to Steve, who was standing in the doorway watching, and said, "Why isn't she handcuffed?"

"I didn't think it was necessary to bring her in here like that," he said.

The matron turned back to June. "I'm Miss Thomas," she said. "We'll get you processed as quickly as possible, then we'll get you where you need to be. Is there anything you need right at this moment?"

Still looking at the floor, June shook her head, indicating that she did not. Just then she felt a hand on her shoulder. It was Steve. She turned slightly in his direction, and he gently lifted her face to his.

"It was the first time I saw what he looked like. He was so young, maybe twenty, if that. And handsome. He was so sweet. He said again that if I needed to call him, that I could. That's when I started to cry."

Miss Thomas took hold of June's arm. The other correctional officers then stepped forward. Three moved to one side of June, two to the other side, and the rest fell into place behind her. When everyone was set, Miss Thomas said, "Okay, let's go," and the group moved out into a long hallway.

"The hall was about thirty feet long, but it seemed like a mile. Everyone was walking slowly. I must have been barely shuffling along because it took forever to get to the end.

Then we turned and Miss Thomas put me in a little four-by-four room that had a small desk but no chairs. When she walked out, two other officers walked in.

"This time I looked up. One woman looked like a bulldog. She looked mean, and she was. She was only about five feet tall, but must have weighed about a hundred and fifty pounds. Her hair was spiked up punk-like. The other woman was the complete opposite: she was a little peanut, real thin, studious-looking with thick glasses. She was real nice though, and said, 'This is the hardest part, but it's necessary. We need to do a complete search.'"

June was not prepared for what was about to happen. For one thing, she was so exhausted she could barely remain standing in the chair-less, window-less room. Unlike Officer Patterson, these officers didn't seem to notice her fatigue. Or perhaps they did not want to draw attention to it and instead, complete their work and get June "processed."

The short, stocky woman gave the first command: "Take off your clothes — all of it." June seemed not to hear. She didn't move. "I said take your clothes off *NOW!*" This time the command startled June, and she came out of her trance. But she was not quite sure what to do. The soft-spoken attendant offered help.

"Miss Briand, it's important that we ... uh, well, it's just that you have to ..." She stopped in mid-sentence. June had started unbuttoning her blouse. After a moment's hesitation, she removed it and slowly unzipped her jeans. The thin woman seemed nervous; the big woman seemed anxious, and did not take her eyes off the attractive twenty-four-year-old before her.

When June was completely naked, the heavy woman stepped close to her. "Show us your hands," she said. Again, June faltered, not knowing quite what to do. "Like this," said the woman, lifting her hands in front of her at waist level, palms down. June did the same.

"Turn them over," she said. "Spread your fingers. Shake your hair. Turn around. Shake your hair again. Lift up your foot. Not that way; bend your leg so I can see the *bottom* of your foot. Now lift the other one. Lift up your arms. Lift up your breasts." Then she paused. The woman reached in the desk drawer and withdrew a flashlight. She flicked it on, looked at the beam, and continued. The smaller woman looked away as if embarrassed — or ashamed. June's legs were quivering now — from the cold, from the fatigue, from the abject humiliation she was being subjected to. But it was not over yet.

"Turn around," said the heavy woman. June complied. "Bend over and spread your buttocks." Besides taking sexual abuse for years on end, rectums and vaginas could be used to store any number of dangerous weapons, drugs, and whatever else the demanding matron thought she would find in such a location.

This time June hesitated a little longer. Then she looked to the ceiling as if asking some unknown entity for help that had never been forthcoming in the past. Waiting only long enough to know nothing had changed, June slowly bent over, tears streaming silently down her face.

The matron took an interminably long time on this part of the examination. Then, apparently satisfied, she continued with the commands. "Squat and cough." June did as she was told, having barely enough energy to produce a cough and not nearly enough to return to a standing position. The small woman looked back to the trembling heap on the floor and helped June to her feet.

Naked, cold, and exhausted, June stood and wrapped her arms around her breasts, assuming the inspection was over. It was not. "Drop those arms! Open your mouth. Spread your mouth with your fingers." The woman shined her flashlight into June's mouth, checking for "drugs and paraphernalia." She was determined to find some, and was exceptionally thorough: "Lift your tongue. Stick it out. Fold over your ears, I want to see the back of those ears." She stepped to June's side and shined the light into her ears, in search of what would have had to be the smallest drug cache on record. Then she was done.

"All right. Take off your rings and earrings. And take off that cross. After that, you can get dressed." The woman turned away in a huff, as if disappointed she had not found contraband to make matters worse for a mother of two who had just been charged with first-degree murder.

After she dressed herself, the smaller officer handed June a towel and bar of soap. The larger woman then took command again. "Follow us," she said, and opened the door. Expecting another long hallway, June was surprised when the trio marched a total of five feet and stopped. To their left was an open metal door leading to a room with a damp concrete floor: The showers.

June undressed and again stood naked, only this time, she was alone on a cold cement floor, water pelting her back. She did not feel the water; she was numb. She'd lost track of time, of when she last slept, ate, urinated. Her system had shut down. She was operating on some unknown source of power that kept her conscious and standing, but just barely. Then the water shut off and the thin, threadbare towel was thrust back into her hands.

June dried off, then tried unsuccessfully to dry her long hair with the threadbare towel that had gone limp from the moisture. It was no use. The larger woman handed June a pair of black "scrubs" (lightweight cotton drawstring pants similar to those worn in operating rooms but providing little warmth during the cold New England winters). On the back of the pants was a tag with the number 17160 emblazoned in large type across it. Next came a red sweatshirt with the same number on the back. And finally, a pair of cheap rubber sandals (now standard footwear in most prisons because of their inability to provide adequate footing in the event of an escape attempt).

"Get dressed," came the command. "We'll show you where you need to be." Where June needed to be was on "the tier," as the prison living quarters were called. "This way," came the woman's voice again as she grabbed June's towel, tossed it in the hamper, and led June by the arm a few more feet to an open door.

The room was large, about forty feet by seventy feet. June had just glanced up to look in when she was jerked to a halt. The larger woman stopped her and now they waited. There didn't seem to be any reason for the delay, but still, they stood quiet for several minutes. Then the woman nudged June and they walked to the doorway. Like a zookeeper releasing its captive into a pen, she let go of June's arm and said, "Yours is the last on the left."

As June took a step into the room, she heard a loud *clunk* behind her. The automatic door had slammed shut, locking her into her new prison world of green walls and waxed linoleum floors.

June waited a moment, then took her first step down the long green tier. Then another. Then another. Somehow she was managing to place one foot in front of the other. But it took monumental effort to keep moving. After all that she had been through — the hours without sleep, the hearing, the journey to the prison, the degradation of the body-cavity search — she was on the verge of collapse. But if she could just keep moving, keep the stamina up for a few more minutes, she'd soon be to "the last on the left."

A row of six cells lined each side of the tier, with each cell housing two women each, for a total capacity of twenty-four inmates on this particular tier. This number would vary from time to time, with new inmates coming and old ones leaving after serving their time.

June hadn't noticed the metal cell doors with their six-by-six-inch windows — openings big enough for a guard to look through whenever he or she wanted, but too small for an inmate to climb through. (The women's prison used both male and female guards, which the inmates protested against without success. Male guards could enter cells unannounced anytime they felt like it, and often did so when a prisoner was undressing or sitting on the toilet.)

A few inmates sat watching television as June walked the length of the tier. She felt eyes on her, but had no way of knowing how many eyes there really were. The reason the guard had delayed June at the doorway was to prevent her from seeing herself on television. At the very moment they had approached the tier, the television was showing a news clip of June being led from the Hudson police station to a police car. When the heavy-set guard saw this, she jerked June to a halt, and said under her breath, "Oh shit." June, however, had her gaze fixed on the floor and had not seen the television — but her fellow inmates had, and they now did a double take as she entered the tier.

"There she is," whispered one woman to another. "She's the one on the news. She just blew her husband away."

But June was oblivious. She did not heard the inmates' low whispers or see the television, too intent was she on placing one foot in front of the other until she made it to her cell. She found it with the help of Lydia, a huge, twenty-year-old inmate whose amorphous mass overflowed the steel chair she was sitting on near June's open cell door.

"That's yours right there," she said in a friendly voice. "Your door doesn't stay closed; you'll have to use a towel."

June barely acknowledged the advice as she collapsed onto the stiff lower bunk and immediately fell into a deep, vacuous sleep. Fifteen minutes later, someone was shaking her awake.

"Get up, we've got to move you." Blinking into the bare light bulb hanging from the ceiling, June saw the dark silhouettes of two uniformed guards looking down at her. She stumbled off her bunk in a stupor, grabbed her blanket, and was marched directly across the tier to another cell housing a woman on suicide watch. Prison officials felt June, too, might try to take her own life, and decided to put the two women together so they could watch them both.

June did not ask any questions, for she was interested in only one thing: sleep. She took no notice of her cellmate and again collapsed onto her bunk, falling asleep immediately, this time not moving until her new world came to life at six o'clock the following morning.

The Hillsborough House of Corrections was really two houses. Old House was the men's facility; New House was the women's. Old House was used to temporarily house the state's most violent criminals — men classified as "pre-trial" and awaiting hearings on such crimes as murder, rape, armed robbery, arson, and drug trafficking. These men were sent to this strict lockdown facility commonly referred to as "the dungeon."

Old House was, in fact, an old house that was at one time used as a nursing home, but fell into such disrepair that it was eventually abandoned. After sitting idle for years, the dilapidated four-story building was taken over by the county, which felt the rat-infested structure would be more than adequate — and appropriate — for housing "the worst of the worst."

The county, however, also neglected the facility, and over the years the dungeon began to look like one. Rusty barbed wire encircled the building, and corroded steel bars turned windows into sorrowful grids — windows so dirty that on the brightest of days, the cells were still shrouded in shadows and remained bone-chillingly cold.

The problem with Old House — other than its residents — was its precariously close proximity to New House, the newer women's facility where June was incarcerated. The two houses were separated by a distance of only a hundred yards — but *connected* by an underground tunnel that was once used as the nursing home's morgue. With a mere three hundred feet separating caged men and women, the tunnel's morbid history was the last thing on their minds. What they were interested in was *each other*, and like moles in heat, found ways to burrow to one another for illicit, ecstatic, forbidden sexual liaisons.

Gaining access to the underground tunnel was difficult though — and often unnecessary because of the security, or lack thereof, in New House. Before it was later revamped, New House lodged both men *and* women. One section of New House was used to confine a different caliber of men: those convicted of petty crimes such as drunk driving, minor assault, and other misdemeanors, as well as those nearing parole and on work release — low security prisoners.

The other section — only a long hallway away — housed women whose crimes were rarely violent, and thus, on a similar level to the men's. For this reason, security at New House was lax. So lax, in fact, that the two doors at either end of the hallway were often held open with blocks so the guards didn't have to bother with the formality of buzzing each other in. Only during the third shift — 11 p.m. to 7 a.m. — were the doors secured. So unless there was an urgent need to be with a particular individual from Old House, plenty of sexual interaction was readily available in the newer facility.

Having sex with violent men, however, was the furthest thing from the mind of the new, special inmate who walked down the tier the afternoon of February 12, 1987. And it was not something prison officials concerned themselves with in this case. What bothered them was, June Briand was an anomaly: she was a killer in amongst the "lightweight" female convicts — bad check artists, shoplifters, drug addicts — and they had no idea how to handle her. And until her trial date was set, there was nowhere else to send her. The maximum security facilities out of state were for women who had already gone to trial and been found guilty of violent crimes. June would not have her hearing for several months, and thus would remain at the Goffstown facility for the foreseeable future.

A guard in the control booth pushed a button and the cell doors automatically buzzed open. June was startled by the buzzing three feet from her head, and awoke instantly. Her cellmate, Nancy, was already awake, and was washing her face at the sink in the back of the room. The sink and toilet were a single, unadorned stainless steel unit without a toilet seat. On each side was a small table for personal items such as hair brushes and radios, and next to that was a slightly larger table for reading and writing. Other than that and the two bunk beds, the cell was bare.

Nancy smiled when she saw June jump at the buzzing noise. "Hi," she said, remembering her own first morning in prison. "Don't be afraid, they're just unlocking our doors."

It was precisely six o'clock in the morning, and over the loudspeaker came a three-word announcement: "Chow time, ladies." Nancy told June to get out of bed quickly, that they didn't have any time to lose. It was time for breakfast, and they had to hurry because "you're on a schedule in prison." And indeed, they were.

June recalls, "All meals are twenty minutes long. If you're ready to go right at six when the announcement comes, and you're first in line, you have the whole twenty minutes to get your food and eat. If you're last, you get about twelve minutes until you hear the second announcement: 'Let's go, ladies.' That means mealtime is over.

"When I was first incarcerated, I wasn't eating much and just picked at my food. I ate so slow that I never got done in time. Some of the other women were nice, and they'd sneak out a cookie or piece of bread for me to eat later. But others take advantage of you when you're new. You learn pretty fast that you have to protect your food tray at all times. For one thing, you could get hit with it; and the bully types would take your food if you weren't watching!

"For breakfast, we usually had either frozen waffles or mush. But once a week we got a special treat and had fried eggs. The cooks would fry them for you however you liked. You start looking forward to little things like that when you can't walk into a restaurant anymore and order anything you want.

"It was amazing how everyone made such a big deal over fried eggs. Some people would pay the cook on the side with the money they earned from their jobs, and he would give them four eggs instead of two. The cooks were taking a risk and could get in trouble for that, so you had to cover the extra eggs with your toast.

"When we bussed our tray at the end of the meal, a guard stood there and counted silverware. If he ever came up short, the correctional officers would go to one end of the tier and start ripping cells apart looking for it. Then someone would throw the spoon or fork out into the hall and they'd stop searching. There was a lot of peer pressure to do right and behave."

After meals, the women were free to return to their cells or watch television at the end of the tier. The television was on virtually all day from 6 a.m. until "lockdown" at 10 p.m. Many of the women, though, stayed in their cells reading or sleeping the day away until supper, which came at the odd hour of 3 p.m. Apparently, the employees of the commissary had complained that they were not able to feed both the inmates and their own families at a reasonable supper time, so the those dining at the Hillsborough House of Corrections did so in the middle of the afternoon, whether they liked it or not.

"Usually we would come out of our cells at three o'clock and have supper. Then we'd take our showers and put on sweats or PJs and watch television. That was a fiasco. When I first got there, four women — the bad guys — controlled the TV. They were the women who were there the longest, or had been sentenced for the worst crimes. Nobody messed with them. They decided what everyone else was going to watch, and that was it. No one would argue with them. It they wanted to watch *Miami Vice*, it was *Miami Vice*. The two evening guards, Rhonda and Katie, liked *Miami Vice* too, so they'd tell everyone to shut up, that it was going to be *Miami Vice* or nothing. It was like a never-ending soap opera at New House."

For the first six months of her incarceration, June's children were allowed to visit once a week. Pam was four then, and Jana was seven, and had been placed under the protective custody of DCYF — the Division of Children and Youth Families the day after the shooting. The Hudson police had come to the Jacksons and removed the children to the DCYF. Because of their frequent run-ins with "crazy Uncle Charley," they had been there before, and now knew right where to go after June had gone to jail.

After six months of allowing the children to visit their mother in prison, the department made a decision to curtail such visits, but did not explain the reasons behind it. Instead, they made excuses, saying the children needed to concentrate on therapy and schoolwork. "I'd be so looking forward to seeing them, and then I'd get the message that there was a phone call for me. I knew what that meant: DCYF was calling to say something came up and the girls weren't coming on Sunday. I'd be looking forward to it all week. It was like my one bright spot — something I could think about that would make me happy.

"But the truth of the matter was, DCYF realized I wouldn't be getting out of prison any time soon, and finally admitted that they thought it would be best if I made a break with the kids as early as possible so there wouldn't be so much pressure on them later. It broke my heart."

DCYF wanted the children on a "new path" and subsequently sent the girls to a home with an opening for two children. The new foster parents had no idea what they were in for. "Apparently no one realized the extent of the violence and abuse that was present in our home. You can't take little kids who grew up watching their mother get beaten all the time and who got hit themselves, and expect them to be perfectly adjusted little angels."

And angels they were not. Soon after the girls arrived at their new foster home, Jana began venting her pent up rage on Pam, who at four years of age, was incapable of protecting herself from her older sister's physical and verbal attacks. As a result, she, too, was turning violent — a trait she had never displayed before the move.

Both the foster parents and DCYF authorities saw that keeping the girls together would only thwart their efforts to stabilize their lives, and decided to separate them. They also saw that it was, indeed, Jana who was instigating the trouble and who seemed extremely emotionally disturbed; they decided the best place for her would be in a group home where professional counselors were available to help such kids transition back to a normal lifestyle. It didn't work.

The counselors "could not work with" Jana, and finally sent her to a crisis care home, and then to another group home. She underwent virtually endless psychological intervention, none of which was effective, so deep were the scars Jimmy Briand had slashed into her psyche. In home after home, Jana vented her rage on whomever and whatever was nearest to her; often it was her room.

"I got reports that Jana would trash her room — rip up everything, break windows, furniture. She sounded like a carbon copy of her father. She was doing terrible. She refused to do her school work and failed in every subject. When she was eight, she threatened to jump out the window. Nothing was working."

Jana continued to drop deeper and deeper into emotional chaos. After two years of intense, managed care, she was no better than when she had arrived at DCYF, and in fact, much worse. Now she was termed "suicidal" and "depressed" by the psychologists who examined her. In one of their reports, Jana described her father as "a big, black, hairy monster, too ugly to look at, with scabs and bruises, that pops your eyes out."

Eventually, the system threw up its arms and gave up. No one knew what to do with Jana. Pam was doing fine in another foster home, but Jana was uncontrollable and still not responding to therapy. So after two years in every kind of foster home, they turned to the Nortons, who offered to take both girls.

"The family Pam was living with wanted to adopt her. She was doing very well and adjusting fine. But adoption meant she would no longer be mine. I would have to give her up forever. I'd have no input of any kind — on therapy, medical, school, *anything*. I wasn't willing to give my daughter away like that because I didn't expect to be in jail forever, so it didn't make any sense.

"Then the Nortons offered a co-guardianship for the girls, which meant they would take them and raise them while I was in prison, and there would be updates, pictures, letters. It sounded like a much better option, and it was a family the girls knew."

The letters never came. The pictures never came. The girls, themselves, never came even though that, too, was promised. The Nortons refused to bring the children to the prison because they were allied with Jimmy and not to the "outsider" whom they now openly referred to as "the killer." Such brainwashing would go on for years, and what seemed like a good idea at first, turned out to be a mistake, but one June was powerless to correct.

June did have one regular visitor though. Surprisingly, it was from a person with whom she had had only minimal contact throughout her twenty-four years: her mother. "I think I saw Mom more the first two years I was in prison than I had my entire life. At first I was happy she came, but then I realized why. Nothing had changed; she came to talk about her problems.

"Mom would come into the visiting room and ask me how I was doing, and within five minutes she'd be pouring out all her problems about her relationships, her drinking — you name it. I finally told her to stop coming, that it didn't help to hear all that. Then I had *no one* visiting.

"When the holidays came, I was very sad. I'd spend all day in bed. I missed my family, my children — even my mother then. Christmas would come, Easter, Mother's Day — they were all really down days for me. But I knew better than to ask my mother to come back to the prison. She'd just complain again. Plus, it's hard to have the outside world coming in when you're doing time."

It was also hard because June was trying to concentrate on the one thing she had always wanted in life and now had the opportunity to get: an education. A month after June had been incarcerated, she heard about a correspondence course that allowed an inmate to earn a GED (high school equivalency diploma).

"I jumped at the chance to get an education. When I took the first classes and found out I could actually *do* something — actually do a good paper or do well on a test — I was amazed. Jimmy never let me do *anything* — especially something that would make me smarter than him."

June was told that in cases like hers, getting to trial could take many months, so she buckled down and made the best of her situation. She plunged into her studies with a fervor prison officials had never seen before. She isolated herself in her cell and immersed herself in English, math, science — everything she had missed while being sexually abused by Ron and beaten bloody by Jimmy.

June earned her GED in July 1987, just five months after entering prison. She obtained excellent marks in all subjects, and mastered her exams handily, attributing her success to "feeling safe for the first time in my life." Safety was something June had never had before, and the day after she entered prison, she told her cellmate how *unsafe* she felt, even behind bars.

"Those first few days, Nancy would just look at me huddled in the corner of our room. I'd be shaking and she'd ask why. I'd say, 'Because Jimmy's going to come down here and get me. You don't know him. *Nobody* knows him. You can't stop Jimmy. He's going to come down here and kill me, I just know it.'

"I was in so much fear of Jimmy that I refused to believe he was dead. People said he was, but no one could convince me. I didn't remember anything about the night of the shooting. All I knew was that Jimmy was going to be really, really mad at me and come right through those bars and kill me. No one could tell me otherwise."

When June first arrived at Goffstown, it had taken several visits from her court-appointed attorney to persuade her to let go of the fantasy that her husband was alive. He was dead — so dead that she was about to be put away for the rest of her life unless she "snapped out of it" and cooperated with her attorney.

Stan Miller was fairly new at law. He had just turned thirty and, right out of law school, decided to focus on criminal law. He went directly to the public defender's office, and after proving his competence on several difficult cases, was now assigned to the Briand murder case. He was not a picture of power, but was astute and, as one colleague said, "held his cards close to his chest."

Six feet tall with dark, thinning hair and a short-cropped beard, Stan Miller looked more like a rabbi than a lawyer. He was Jewish, and a few years earlier had graduated near the top of his class, easily passing the bar exam on his first try. Miller was an affable, soft-spoken gentleman, but his kind, easy manner was not enough to win June over to his side.

He had, however, finally convinced June that her husband was dead and that she was in serious trouble. But getting her to talk about the case or herself or *anything* was virtually impossible. He needed help, and recruited Beverly Dumas, a criminal investigator from the public defender's office who, like him, had a cordial, friendly manner, but unlike him, was a female.

"We were hoping June would bond with Beverly," said Stan. "I was getting nowhere and could see how closed down she was. She couldn't even look me in the eye and always looked down at the floor. I wanted Beverly to befriend her and show her that we were not a threat — that we were on her side and were there to help her."

The plan worked. It took months of visiting three or four times a week, but eventually June warmed up to the friendly Dumas. It would have been hard not to. Beverly was a petite woman of mixed Asian descent, and stood barely five feet tall. With her friendly manner, one would have thought she was anything but a criminal investigator who, on a daily basis, dealt with the most violent crimes in the state.

One aspect of her job — and one at which she was particularly proficient — was interviewing those involved in the cases she was investigating. Once person she needed to interview in the Briand case was Helen Lewis. Beverly had called her the day after the shooting, saying she would like to come to her apartment and discuss what had transpired the night before. Helen seemed nervous and evasive on the phone, and said she did not want to talk to anyone until she had contacted an attorney. Beverly said she understood, and said she would contact Helen the following week. But when Beverly called back, Helen still had not retained an attorney, saying she was "trying to get through to Legal Aid" and other sundry excuses. Dumas persisted, saying she would call back again, that the interview was important and that it would not take long.

When Beverly called the apartment the following week, Helen's mother answered, saying her daughter was not at home. After a brief conversation, however, she realized the problem of the interview was not going to go away, and said she would advise Helen to cooperate. The next day, a date was set for the meeting.

Beverly Dumas's report of that meeting reveals a great deal about Helen Lewis's complicity in the crime. The following excerpt from the report shows clearly how Helen's demeanor changes dramatically when Dumas moves the conversation from generalities to specifics:

Then, at this point in the interview, I told Helen I wanted to talk about the incident. [Referring to the murder weapon], I asked her if she had ever gone out with June for a practice shot. Helen said nothing and for the first time during the interview, took out her cigarettes, got up without a word and began looking for an ashtray. After finding one, she sat back down, lit a cigarette and said, "No."

Not only had Helen taken a practice shot with June that day in the woods, she had scouted out an area in which to dump the weapon after the killing, and had, in fact, purchased the bullets from a gun shop in Nashua. At one point during the investigation, detectives thought they had solidly implicated Helen when they visited the gun shop where she had purchased the bullets. But even though the clerk remembered her buying them, he had failed to register her name in the ammunition log as required, thus denying investigators crucial evidence linking her to the crime. At that point their investigation of Helen was over; they had nothing on her, and she was never contacted again.

Back at Goffstown, Beverly continued to build a relationship with June. During their initial visits together, Beverly would tell June about herself or her children, pulling out pictures from her wallet or comparing notes with June on the early years of childrearing. When Stan's wife got pregnant, she told June about it, bringing Stan back into the fold somewhat.

Eventually, Beverly brought in pictures her son had drawn for June in kindergarten class, and June opened up more. Then Beverly came to visit with Stan's co-counsel, Janet Erving, who was also working on the case. She, too, bonded almost immediately with June, and soon it was safe to bring Stan Miller back to the prison to go to work.

The first thing Stan Miller had to determine was whether or not June Briand was "one hundred percent truthful." If she was not, or if she was being prepped by another inmate on how to lie or "tell the lawyers what they want to hear," Stan would have a problem. Before he could defend June in a murder trial, he needed to know this. And again, he was not the likely one to whom she would confide. He recruited yet more help — this time a sociologist who specialized in domestic violence cases.

Theresa Doran's job was to sort out the big question for Stan Miller: Was June a true victim of domestic violence, and was she suffering from the relatively recently recognized condition known as Battered Woman Syndrome? If she was, and the syndrome "played a role in her lethal act," the finding would have important implications in the upcoming trial.

"To start with," said Miller, "we needed June free of influences. I didn't want her reading any books or talking to anyone about the case. We wanted her story, just as it happened, without embellishment."

The meeting between Theresa Doran and June took place in May, three months after the shooting. It revealed exactly what Miller had expected: June had, indeed, been suffering from Battered Woman Syndrome, and was severely incapacitated from it. An excerpt from Doran's report read:

June Briand was unable to think through her immediate relief-seeking behavior to the potential long-term consequences of these behaviors. This type of short-sighted thought process was consistent with the constant threat she faced from her husband, as well as from a series of abusive and neglectful relationships stemming back to her childhood. She had no ability to identify resources available to her (though they were few at the time), and had no past experience with others around her being supportive or protective. Moreover, her inability to perceive goals beyond survival from day to day resulted in the escapist coping mechanism of fantasy and denial ... June Briand is currently incarcerated as a result of her choice to kill her husband in order to escape from years of brutality and her own death which she anticipated at his hands. Realistic or not, her decision was based on the only scope of information and alternatives she was capable of perceiving at the time.

Additional support for Miller's defense came from a forensic psychologist from New York, Dr. Alan Olsen, who was called into the case because of his extensive work with battered women. In his report of his interviews with June in July and August of 1987, he states as the reason for the evaluation: (1) to determine whether June was suffering from the Battered Woman Syndrome at the time of the killing; and (2) if so, to assess the relationship of the syndrome to June's homicidal act.

Dr. Olsen's report stated in part:

To begin with, there is no question that June Briand is a battered woman or that she was suffering from the Battered Woman Syndrome at the time she shot and killed James Briand ... Developmentally, June fits the classic pattern of the girl who grows up to become a severely battered woman. Like many such women, her exposure to neglect and abuse began in childhood and adolescence ... From then on, she was constantly involved in one abusive relationship after another. In each of her relationships with men, she was physically, sexually, and psychologically abused. By the time she married Jimmy at the age of seventeen, June was already a battered woman, a rather easy target for another batterer ... Based on my clinical experience with battered women and the knowledge of the research of others, the abuse Jimmy inflicted upon June was extreme; this is not an ordinary case of "wife beating."

With this type of supporting evidence, Stan Miller had what he hoped would be a strong case for a reduction of the charges from first-degree murder to "something less." He was not about to raise June's hopes by stating what "something less" might be, but one thing was for sure: he did not believe — even with the powerful support he had from the expert witnesses — that June could ever win an acquittal from a jury in a very conservative state like New Hampshire.

Miller did not need to ponder the issue long. Shortly after submitting Doran's and Olsen's reports to the state prosecutor's office, they called back with a bombshell: They were not going to rely on either report. Though it had always been customary to use the public defender's reports in the past, in this case the prosecutor wanted "an expert of our own choosing."

"It was unheard of," said Miller. "Only in cases where the defendant was using a plea of insanity did the state bring in its own examiners for evaluations. Now they wanted to expand that and petition the state supreme court to include cases of battered women; it was pure legal maneuvering by the state — and the court ruled in their favor."

Miller, however, took a countermeasure — one some might have called risky. But he was convinced of June's victimization, and felt it was imperative: He asked that the interview with the state's psychologist be videotaped, and assured them that he would not tell June about the taping.

"He didn't want me to be nervous or change my story in any way. He thought offering to have the examination taped would look better to the prosecutor; he wanted to show them we had nothing to hide, and that I was telling the same story to them as I had to Theresa Doran and Dr. Olsen."

Nearly two years passed before all the examinations were completed and numerous preliminary hearings and myriad meetings with attorneys and others had taken place. It was customary in capital and other serious cases to move slowly and thoroughly, and it was no different for June's case.

Finally a trial date was set for December 7, 1988 — almost two years after June had first entered the Hillsborough House of Corrections in Goffstown. During the interim, June had not only earned her GED, but had met weekly with Theresa Doran, with whom she established a close relationship with.

"Theresa was the first one to explain domestic violence and Battered Woman Syndrome to me. She was also the first person to explain why Jimmy was the way he was: his background, how violence in his family bred violence in him, and how he, too, was a victim just like I was."

During those first two years, June also filled her days by taking classes that helped her understand the journey she had been on and why she had ended up where she had. Domestic violence courses, Alcohol and Narcotics Anonymous courses (though she was neither an addict nor an alcoholic):

all helped her understand the interrelationship between an unloving and inadequate upbringing and the choices one makes in life.

She learned about fear, diminished motivation, powerlessness, failure expectancy, mind control, learned helplessness, and the like. Prior to taking these courses, June had no understanding whatsoever of how or why a person ended up in a dependent or co-dependent relationship.

"Theresa explained that we all have self-esteem at first. Then things happen in our lives to break it down. We take on a self-image based on the people around us — what they tell us; what they do or fail to do; how they treat us; whether they validate us or criticize us. In my case, Jimmy took advantage of a person who had never known love and who never felt very good about herself. I felt I *deserved* the treatment I got. He told me I was stupid and I believed it.

"When I took the prison courses, things changed. I heard my instructors say 'Good job' or tell me I was smart. I had never heard that before — and certainly not from Jimmy. It felt good, and I knew then that Jimmy had been wrong: I wasn't stupid, I was smart.

"Theresa explained to me that Jimmy tore other people down because he felt so lousy about *himself.* People with inferiority complexes do that — they feel better about themselves by abusing and hurting others. I never had any idea about all of this until I went to prison. In that way, prison was good for me; I may have never learned it on the outside."

Nevertheless, June was not interested on staying on the *inside*. She had learned a great deal about herself and her past, but she missed her children terribly, and with her newly-acquired insights about what had gone wrong in her life, was anxious for a new start.

At first, she had been deeply depressed and extremely guilt-ridden over what she had done. But though the remorse would not let up for years to come, when she learned that both she *and* her husband were both victims of circumstances, she began to forgive herself — and Jimmy — for what they had done to one another. With this new, healthier self-image, June thought more and more about regaining the freedom she had so violently lost. Her lead attorney, on the other hand, had great reservations about winning that freedom for her.

"The problems in this case were many," said Stan Miller. "First, using Battered Woman Syndrome as the basis of the defense was risky. The syndrome was fairly new and not widely recognized in 1988 — especially by a jury of lay persons. Second, if we pleaded not guilty and lost the case, the mandatory sentence for first-degree murder was life imprisonment without the possibility of parole. No matter how we looked at it, we were in a tough situation."

The pressure on Miller eased considerably one day during the summer of 1988, six months before the trial was set to begin. A call came into the public defender's office from the prosecutor's office. They were willing to make a deal; Miller was more than willing to hear it.

The state's three-person prosecution team was led by Laura Tarcher, a strong-willed, no-nonsense woman who had climbed the ranks to the position of lead prosecutor because of her ability to try — and win — cases. Like Stan Miller, Tarcher had opted for criminal work, and had an excellent record of success since coming to work for Attorney General Stephen Merrill.

June Briand, on the other hand, had a dismal record of failure her entire life. She was never blessed with "good luck" or "the breaks," and in fact, had such a string of bad luck that a reporter who followed her story wrote:

The Briand case was an extraordinary one. Extraordinary in that one person could have such miserable luck in her life, starting from the day she was born and given away by a promiscuous mother who preferred drinking in the seediest bar in town to parenting, to the day she was shoved into a holding cell, tossed an ill-fitting prison uniform and told, "Take care of it, you'll be wearing it for the rest of your life."

With Laura Tarcher's call, June's luck — for the first time in her doleful life — changed. The prosecution was offering a plea bargain deal worked out by Tarcher herself. Often, it was the assistant prosecutors who researched and hashed out the intricacies of such a deal, but in this case, Tarcher was the one who originated the idea and would negotiate at length with Miller. (It wouldn't be until well after the matter was resolved that June would discover that Laura Tarcher was, in fact, an advocate for victims of domestic violence. It was she who put forth the idea of a plea bargain, and she who understood better than anyone in the prosecutor's office the crime June Briand was driven to commit.)

The terms of the offer were thus: Enter a plea of guilty to *second*-degree murder in exchange for a sentence of twenty-eight years to life. The "second degree" status would automatically save June from "life without the possibility of parole," and it would allow her the possibility of leaving prison after serving twenty-eight years — when she would be fifty-two years of age.

It was a deal, but not what Miller had hoped to hear. Here was a twenty-four-year-old mother of two who, as Trooper Steve Walker had said, was trying to protect them from a madman who had driven June into such a state of mental disarray that to some experts who examined her, she was "clinically insane" at the time of the shooting. Her behavior immediately after coming to prison seemed to bear this theory out, as another reporter noted:

June Briand believed beyond a doubt that at any moment, her raging monster of a husband would burst through her prison bars and rip her to shreds. This was not a woman who should be held in prison until she was fifty-two years of age. Indeed, many of those who had studied the case closely felt June Briand was suffering from "isolated explosive disorder" — a condition most commonly characterized by a single instance of failure to resist an impulse that then leads to a violent act with tragic consequences.

Others felt June should not spend one minute behind bars for a crime that was clearly one of self-defense. But the law on such a defense was iffy at best. "Self-defense" had different interpretations in different states. In many states, including New Hampshire, a person had to be in "imminent danger of lethal bodily harm" in order to pull a trigger in self-defense. Was June is such a state? Did the knife that Jimmy so often held to June's throat have to be present at the very moment she pulled the trigger? Miller wasn't willing to leave that question up to a conservative jury with the stakes as high as they were.

Stan told Laura Tarcher he would discuss the offer with his client and get back to her. He thanked her for the option and said that like her, he preferred to work out a plea bargain rather than go to trial. It's just that this one "wasn't much of a bargain." At the moment, though, it was all Miller had.

By the summer of 1988, June had made remarkable progress and, in the words of one prison official, "was a different person from the one who walked in here shaking in her boots." Her transformation was dramatic: June had grown confident and now looked people directly in the eye, holding up her end of a conversation without fear or fawning. With the education she had received, and the ongoing therapy, she was growing both emotionally and intellectually, and wanted a new start in life — and wanted it long before she was fifty-two.

"I rejected Laura's offer the moment I heard it. Stan sort of prefaced it by saying, 'It's not the greatest ...' and then started to explain. When I heard the words 'twenty-eight years' I cut him right off. I said, 'Single digits, Stan. I want single digits.'"

Miller did not argue. He, too, felt that the offer was a poor one. But single digits? "They won't go from twenty-eight to *nine*," Miller said. But June was not interested in arguing. He left the prison after their brief meeting saying "I'll do what I can," and surprised June with a phone call two hours later.

"June, this is Stan. Good news: I've got eighteen."

"Eighteen? Eighteen won't work. Single digits, Stan. Tell them I need *single digits!*" June was adamant, and now mad. In the blink of an eye — the blinker being Laura Tarcher — ten years of June's sentence were lopped off. If that ten was so easy, thought June, how about another ten? They obviously never meant to stick with twenty-eight in the first place. They were bargaining, and they had the power to bargain further.

"June," said Stan patiently. "Listen. This is not a poker game. They've come way down. They're at eighteen. You'll be out in eighteen years; it's not terrific, but it's a helluva lot better than *never* getting out. Give it some serious thought, will you?"

"No, I won't," said June, who had done some math in preparation for these negotiations. She wanted single digits — meaning nine years of incarceration — because in nine years, her children would still be under eighteen and she could regain legal custody of them. "I could get them back, and that's all I was thinking about."

Miller told June he would try again, but that he didn't hold out much hope to improve on the offer and to please, *please* consider what they had come back with. June did not agree to consider anything, and simply replied that she'd wait to hear back.

This time, though, the phone did not ring. June waited in her cell — more anxious than she had let on to Stan — expecting another quick response. Things had been turning around for her, hadn't they? Luck, that elusive gift she had never received in the past, was finally coming her way. Where was the phone call?

"Chow time, ladies!" resounded down the tier at three o'clock that afternoon. June didn't respond. She lay on her bunk, deep in thought.

"Let's go, June. Dinner," said a friend passing by June's open door.

"Not hungry, Margie. Thanks," said June.

With a minute gone and only nineteen to go, Margie didn't have time to coax June to dinner. She said, "Suit yourself, honey" and hurried to keep her place in line.

June had been eating well, and had put on a healthy amount of weight during her two-and-a-half-year stint. This day, though, she had no appetite. The same feelings of anxiety and doom she had felt with Jimmy now crept back into her mind, thwarting any hope of eating more than the morsel of cookie Margie smuggled out of the dining hall for her.

By lights out, June was emotionally exhausted. Stan Miller had not phoned back, even if it was just to say that her counter offer had been rejected. What did the delay mean? What did the no phone call mean? Was the news so bad that Miller was putting off as long as possible telling June? If the news had been good, certainly he would have called, wouldn't he?

June dropped off into a fitful, dreamless sleep. The next morning she was jerked awake by the dreaded "Chow time, ladies!" blasting over the loudspeaker. She turned over and pulled her blanket over her head. She wasn't hungry, and she didn't want to talk to anyone.

Before going to bed the night before, June had done the math again: Forty-two. With the prosecution's latest offer, she would be forty-two when she got out of prison. *Forty-two*. She could not get the number out of her head. And upon waking, she promised herself that she would not accept the deal under any circumstances. When her attorney called, she would tell him to prepare for trial on first-degree murder charges.

But Miller did not call. The chow time call came again at three o'clock, and again June stayed in her cell. Four o'clock came. Four-thirty. Five. Something was wrong, and Miller was not telling June what it was. Another day had gone by with no call. The picture now looked bleak.

At five-thirty, the loudspeaker crackled again. "Briand. Visitors. Come to the visiting room." *Visitors*. What did *that* mean? She had expected a call from her attorney, Stan Miller. Who were the *visitors*? June pulled on her sweatshirt and walked slowly to the visitor's room, which was partitioned off from the rest of the building by a bulletproof glass wall. When June turned into the holding area and waited for the buzzer to let her through to the room, she spotted Stan Miller. With him were co-counsel, Janet Erving, and Beverly Dumas. All three were doing what June used to do: looking at the floor.

"It was a depressing sight. They all had their heads down and they had on poker faces. No one was smiling. I had to wait ten seconds for the buzzer to let me through and I watched them the whole time; it was a long ten seconds.

"No one would look at me. I figured that meant one of two things: either they had lost the plea completely, and I was going to face life in prison, or maybe, just maybe, they had good news and they didn't want to show it through the window. But with the three of them there together, I figured they needed moral support for one another, so the news couldn't be good."

But June was wrong. When she was buzzed through to the visiting room, the three heads turned upward and everyone was beaming. Smiles broke out across their faces and they lurched forward to hug June.

"Good news, June," began Stan. "They've agreed to reduce the sentence to fifteen years."

June's face fell. Single digits. Where were the single digits? What was everyone smiling about?

Stan continued. "It's better than it sounds," he said. "Or at least it *could* be. Fifteen is just a cap, it's the most you'll get, and during the sentencing hearing, we can appeal for less. If the judge goes along with our argument, and sees things our way, he could reduce the sentence from fifteen years to whatever he wants — even *no* time. That's unlikely, but technically, it *could* happen.

"Plus," added Janet quickly, "you'll be eligible for sentence review hearings every two years. If you're doing well and can make a strong case that you've been rehabilitated in the court's eyes, you may well be out in less than fifteen years — maybe even your single digit."

Janet stopped to let her words sink in. June looked around for a chair; Beverly produced one and slid it under June as she sat down to ponder what she had just heard. Beverly and Stan pulled up chairs as well, and they surrounded June to go over the new offer.

"What they were saying to me was this: There are pros and cons of accepting the plea bargain. The pros were that I would not be spending the rest of my life in prison; that I would be in for no longer than fifteen years no matter what; and that I could possibly be out sooner. It was even possible — but not very likely — that I'd be sentenced to just the thirty-four months I'd already served and that would be it.

"The cons for accepting the deal were that we didn't know what the judge would do, and most likely he'd sentence me to the full fifteen years. If we decided not to accept the plea bargain and instead go to trial in December — and win — I'd be free and would spend *no* more time in prison. I'd be giving up that possibility if we agreed to the plea bargain. The other con was that if we went to trial and lost, well, life in prison with no parole ... I'd never forgive myself for not taking their offer."

June's attorneys earnestly wanted her to accept the reduced sentence plea bargain. They knew it was the best the prosecution would do, and were actually surprised when the counter-offer had come in so favorably. But they were bound by ethics to leave the ultimate decision up to June. "We could not take that responsibility," said Miller. "June was intelligent and mentally competent by then. She would have to make the toughest decision of her life, and she — not us — would have to be the one to live with it."

June asked Stan one more time how he felt about taking her case to a jury. He said that with this being conservative New Hampshire, and the state's expert witnesses swearing she had no justification in killing her husband, June would have little chance of winning. June listened intently, looked around the table at Stan, Janet, and Beverly, and said, "I agree. We won't win. Take the fifteen."

Everyone exhaled. Beverly hugged June tightly and said, "It was the right decision, June. We couldn't advise you on this one, but we were praying you'd say what you said. We're going to do everything we possibly can for you."

"Thanks, Beverly," said June. "I know you will."

The defense team changed gears. Now, instead of preparing for a trial, they needed to prepare for the sentence hearing, which would be heard in front of a judge rather than a jury. This was a much different situation: less risky, a known quantity of fifteen years to deal with, and the possibility of reducing that sentence further if the judge were to be sympathetic to Battered Woman's Syndrome.

In some cases, having a hearing before a single, supposedly-impartial individual can be an advantage —

unless that individual's impartiality has somehow been compromised. A lawyer not related to the case later said, "If you're standing trial for rape before a judge whose wife or daughter has been raped, you can bet the term 'equal justice' will be tossed out the window like a bucket of dirty water."

Likewise, if a judge has something to prove, or has a personal reason or prejudice influencing his decision, the chances of changing his or her mind, even with a brilliant argument, are virtually nil. Such was thought to be the case in the matter of *The State v. June Briand*.

"Judge Scott — the judge I stood before when I was first arrested — had recently moved out of the district court and was now in superior court. We had a feeling this might work against me; that since I was his first female homicide case, he might want to make an example of me. We wouldn't know until the hearing if that was true."

In October of 1988, with less than three months remaining until the December hearing, Stan Miller started, in earnest, prepping June. He knew the holidays were coming, and that things would get bogged down, so he wanted to get the bulk of the preparation done early. The first thing he did was advise June about what to expect the day of the hearing.

"He told me the Nortons would be there: Randolph, Leslie — probably the whole thirty or forty of them. He also said the public would be there. I had a taste of what that was like when I was first brought into Nashua District Court. I didn't want to go through it again, but I didn't have much choice."

Miller took the hearing as seriously as he had the trial. He saw it as an opportunity to greatly reduce — perhaps with a miracle, even dismiss — June's sentence. And he wanted his client ready. "Stan would role play with me. He'd pretend he was the prosecutor and slam his hand down on the table and grimace and yell at me. He said I had to expect the worst and wanted me prepared. He was toughening me for the real thing."

Regardless of how much preparation Miller put June through, on the morning of the hearing, June was hunched over her toilet bowl vomiting. She had not slept well the entire week, and the night before had afforded her no rest at all. With nerves frayed and her stomach in knots, she had barely been able to scratch out the prepared statement she wished to read before the court. Now, an hour before she was to be transported to superior court, she was shaking, vomiting, crying, and generally in no condition to do anything.

June was holding onto the sides of the bowl with her head hanging low when she heard over the loudspeaker: "Briand. Report to the intake area." It was time to go. June's heart fluttered wildly in her chest. She stood up, blew her nose, picked up her one-page, hand-written statement, and put on her coat. Several of her prison friends had heard the announcement and came over to wish her well. She hugged them all, and ran to the door through which she had come almost three years earlier, this time hoping to go the opposite direction and never come back. It was an unlikely wish, but one she carried in her racing heart all the way to the superior court building.

June was led into the courtroom with a phalanx of city and state police surrounding her. Though everyone in the courtroom had passed through a metal detector, June felt anything but safe knowing the violence-prone Nortons would be sitting directly in front of her, very much aware that this was the woman who killed one of their own. And when she testified, she would be facing the courtroom and see not only the Nortons, but reporters, photographers, and members of the general public who came simply to gawk at the woman they had heard so much about in the news. June was flanked at the table by Stan Miller, investigator Beverly

Dumas, co-counsel Janet Erving, another co-counsel, Joe Escher, a paralegal and law student. She had just sat down when there was a commotion in the rear of the courtroom by the doors. Everyone turned to see three tall men in full dress white uniforms — replete with medals and ribbons — walking down the center aisle.

Leading the group was Lieutenant Dillard, a high-ranking guard at Goffstown who, like the other two officers, had become friendly with June and admired her for the strength and courage she had displayed under the difficult circumstances in which she found herself.

Dillard was a big man, standing six-foot-six and weighing three-hundred pounds, and was known in Goffstown as a tough disciplinarian who would allow no departure from the prison rules and regulations. For example, if he happened to see an inmate watching television with her feet up on the chair in front of her, he was quick to yell across the tier, "Keep your feet on the floor where they belong!" But when June made the same mistake, Dillard's demeanor would change markedly. He liked her, and saw how good she was for other inmates and how she could get others up when they were down. And he knew the circumstances under which she had come to Goffstown. "June," he would say softly. "Your feet? The chair? Sorry, but you know the rules."

Next to Dillard was Sergeant Chapman, and next to him was Captain Ellsworth, both of whom had also grown attached to June during the course of her incarceration, and believed she had been given a "bad shake" and should have the minimum possible sentence for her crime. They came to the hearing to testify to the character of June Briand, and do what they could to help her win her freedom.

No sooner had the three officers taken their seat than another officer, dressed in a standard blue uniform, strode in the door and down the aisle, taking a seat next to the other three. He was Sergeant Mosher, the K-9 unit leader, who had often brought his German shepherd into the visiting room when June was visiting with Pam and Jana before their break off. He had seen her with her children, and seen how much of a loving mother she was. Mosher, like the others, was there to say that June did not belong in prison, that she was not a "hardened criminal," had never been in trouble before, and showed no signs of doing harm to anyone. They would take the stand and argue for the minimum possible sentence for June Briand.

June mustered the strength to give the men a little wave and then suddenly turned back to the counsel table and leaned over to say something to Stan. He quickly motioned to the bailiff: June needed to vomit again. The bailiff led her to the restroom and stood guard outside while June retched in a stall, and prayed to God, "Let me get through this day."

"All rise," said the bailiff when June was seated back at the counsel table. Everyone stood and Judge Scott entered the chamber; court was in session. One of the prosecutors was on his feet immediately. He made a motion, then called his first witness, the state psychologist who had interviewed and videotaped June, Dr. Richard Hailey.

When the prosecutor finished questioning him, Stan Miller moved toward the witness stand to clarify the ambiguities Hailey had left before the court. Though he was paid fifteen hundred dollars to give his expert testimony, Hailey's answer to almost every question posed by Miller was the same: "There is no way to *conclusively* say that being battered was reason enough for Ms. Briand to kill her husband."

Getting nowhere with the intransigent witness, Miller took another tack, and started asking simple questions with obvious, simple answers that no fair-minded person could dispute. He asked, "Isn't it true that under the circumstances, June Briand might well have felt that her life was in danger, especially since she had been told numerous times by her husband that if she ever tried to leave him, he would kill her?" Answer: "There is no way to *conclusively* say that that would be the case."

After fifteen minutes of useless testimony, Miller finally threw up his hands and had no further questions. He returned to the counsel table to await the state's next witness. To everyone's surprise, there wasn't any. The prosecution had called one expert witness — Dr. Hailey — and turned the floor over to Miller.

The defense lawyer was taken aback by the swiftness of the turnover, but he knew who he wanted for his first set of witnesses: the officers in white. Miller stood up and called, one by one, the officers who, in succession, took the stand and testified that June was a "model prisoner" who should spend as little time as possible behind bars. Mosher made a passionate plea for a short sentence, and earlier, Dillard had gone so far as to put up his own house up as security for June's bail (which was denied due to the nature of the crime).

The prosecution then threw a curve no one expected: they had another witness; not an expert witness, but a *character* witness. Jimmy's stepmother, Leslie Norton, was called to the stand. June still had her back to the gallery and only when she returned from the bathroom had she seen out of the corner of her eye the Norton clan, which, as predicted, had come in force.

They were not happy about the three officers in dress whites who had walked down the aisle. They knew the men were there to support June, and with the medals and ribbons across their chests, they worried that the men would sway the judge to June's side. Leslie Norton knew her testimony would be crucial to the prosecution.

Upon hearing her name called, Leslie rose and walked to the witness stand, faced the court clerk, and raised her right hand. June looked directly at her mother-in-law, but

Leslie refused to meet her gaze. Instead, she concentrated on the oath, and swore to tell "the truth, the whole truth, and nothing but the truth, so help me God." Then she sat down and proceeded to tell lie after lie about how wonderful, kind, and gentle her docile son had always been.

"He had never, never as long as I knew him — and I knew my own child — ever struck his wife. He wasn't abusive, and he didn't have the drinking problem everyone says he had. Oh, sure, he had a beer now and then with his friends, but he was not a drunk. And he was always kind and considerate to June. She's making up all this business about abuse and hitting. Jimmy never hit her. She's making it up because she wants to get out of prison."

June's stomach suddenly stopped churning. For the first time since the proceedings began, she stopped crying. Now she felt a surge of anger well up inside of her. The hearing had been bad enough with the hired psychologist saying exactly what the prosecution wanted him to say; but June was not about to let Jimmy's family whitewash the savage beast she had put up with for six miserable years. She wouldn't let Leslie Norton twist the truth and sway the court into punishing her further than she had already been punished at the hands of Jimmy Briand.

When Leslie Norton was through perjuring herself, Stan Miller rose to his full height and said, "The defense calls June Briand to the stand." He gave June a reassuring pat on the shoulder and pointed to the witness stand. June clutched her hand-written message in one hand and her handkerchief in the other. She was not nervous anymore — she was mad.

Again, the prosecution did the unexpected: they did not question June at all. They were going to allow her to make a statement, and would let it stand on its own merits. It was as if even they didn't believe a word Leslie Norton had said, but still, they had a murder on their hands, and they were not about to shirk their responsibility to prosecute someone who had taken another person's life.

June placed her paper on the edge of the witness box in front her. She looked at it for a moment, then pulled it back to her lap. She wasn't going to read her prepared statement after all; she was too incensed by what she had just heard.

Turning directly to Leslie, June started: "I just listened to you describe someone up here, but I don't know who you were talking about. Your description of Jimmy was *wrong* and you know it! I lived in fear every day with your son. He beat me, he beat his children. I don't know who you were describing, but it wasn't Jimmy ..."

June continued on, ignoring her statement and expertly addressing each point Leslie had made. She countered with the facts — facts no one could have made up or exaggerated. And by the looks on faces of those sitting at the prosecutor's table, they believed her. And their actions — or *inactions* — confirmed it: They made no objections and did not interrupt as June described the horror of living with the man she finally shot. Her story was then corroborated by Theresa Doran, who followed her on the stand. Then by Dr. Olsen, who turned and looked directly at the state's psychologist and said, "Beyond any doubt whatsoever — *any doubt* — I can categorically, *conclusively* say that June Briand's actions the evening of February 12, 1987, stemmed directly from the Battered Woman Syndrome from which she suffered due to the physical, sexual, and verbal abuse she received from James Briand."

To conclude the proceedings, Miller called June's sister, Diane, who had flown in from California for the hearing. She took the stand and described June's loveless childhood, and the alcoholism and insanity that characterized it. By the time she was through, and with the testimony of Doran and Olsen and June, Stan Miller and his team felt better. Everyone had made a compelling case for leniency. Leslie Norton had made a fool of herself, and at one point, the judge, who appeared to be totally unimpressed with her over-dramatic, unctuous description of her "innocent child," told her to move the testimony along, and that if there was nothing new to add, end it altogether. She did.

Now all eyes turned to him. Judge Scott had said little during the hearing. He heard testimony from both sides, and to the reporters and lawyers who were present, it seemed likely, based on the testimony, that Scott would reduce June's fifteen-year minimum sentence to something less — perhaps even discard it altogether.

He began his statement optimistically, saying he recognized June to be "a classic battered wife." Then he totally disregarded that fact and announced that he was going along with the prosecution's recommendation that "Ms. Briand will remain incarcerated in the Hillsborough House of Corrections for a minimum of fifteen years. Court adjourned."

In the late morning, inmates watching television on the end of the tier kept one eye on the screen and one on the Intake door. They knew that at any time, June would come walking through the door. Her sentencing hearing would be over, her fate sealed. Would she be smiling or crying? That was the question.

She was crying. She did not want to talk to anybody, and walked quickly to her cell, closed the door behind her, and threw herself onto her bunk. It had been a morning filled with anticipation and hope. And then, like a storm cloud passing in front of a glorious sun, June's world went dark. She was sentenced to a minimum of fifteen years in prison. She had already spent three behind bars, walls, and razor wire. Now another twelve loomed in front of her, and it made her sick.

June lay curled up on her bunk for over an hour when she heard the door open. Anna Rosen entered the room; she was counselor at the men's prison in Concord, and also in charge of the women's facility in Goffstown, where she came twice a week to "do urines" (urine tests routinely done to screen inmates for drugs and alcohol). June, however, had been exempt from such tests during her first two and a half years because she was still on "pre-trial" status and had not yet been "state sentenced" (sentenced to a year or more). Now she was.

But Anna had not come to take urine. Rather, she came to give moral support to a woman she knew would be feeling very badly right about then. June had met her once before, a few months prior when she was throwing garbage in the dumpster behind the prison. One of the guards who knew and liked June had told her to do it, and while she was outside, Anna noticed the security door open and came to investigate.

"Aren't you June Briand?" said Anna, who saw the woman accused of first-degree murder working in an unsecured area with only an eight-foot chain-link gate standing between her and the woods.

"Yes," said June.

"What are you doing out here?"

"Throwing out the garbage like I was told."

"Told to by who?"

"By Johnny."

"Well, go on inside. I'll have a talk with Johnny. This is not going to continue any longer."

Now Anna was to play more of a mother than a prison official. She looked at June curled up on her bunk and said, "Hi. It's me, Anna. Remember?"

June turned over and saw the woman who had once reprimanded her. "Hello," she said, not yet sure of the woman's motives.

"How about a hug?" said Anna. The words went straight to June's heart. This was the darkest, loneliest time of her life, and the one thing she needed more than anything else was love — love that in all her twenty-six and a half unfortunate years had never been forthcoming.

June got up from her bunk with her handkerchief in her hand, stepped into Anna's warm embrace, and broke down again. She let loose with tears she didn't think she had left. Crying all morning and all during the morning's proceedings, June was surprised at the copious amount of saline solution still left in her tear ducts.

She put her head on Anna's shoulder and wept shamelessly. She needed to cry. Her life had been a mess from day one, and now, on this day, it sank even further into the depths of despair and loneliness and depression and hopelessness.

"*What more could go wrong?* I asked myself. I would never take my kids to a toy store again. I'd never help them with their homework again. I'd be almost forty when I got out of there, and who knew where my kids would be by then? They'd be grown up and gone away for all I knew.

"Then Anna held me out at arm's length and asked me something. She said, 'I need to know one thing from you. Are you going to run on me?' Like everyone, it had crossed my mind — especially out by the dumpster. She knew that area was not secured, and that's where someone would try an escape if they were going to. But I hadn't thought about it long. Now Anna's asking me for real: 'Are you going to run on me?' I said, 'No.' Then she said, 'Are you sure?' I said I was sure — and I was.

"She said the next step would be classification. That's something that happens once you're state sentenced. She said, 'When they classify you, don't worry about it. Everything will work out all right.' I didn't know exactly what that meant, but I knew there were different classifications for different prisoners. They went from C-1 to C-5, with C-5 being the worst. It's given to high-risk inmates who are then sent out of state to maximum security facilities. If you get a C-5, you can say goodbye to your family and friends. And they're a lot tougher on you in those places; you don't want a C-5."

Later that day, a guard came to June's room and told her it was time to go to the men's prison in Concord where the "state sentenced" were officially booked into the system. Newly-sentenced individuals are photographed, fingerprinted, and classified, then transported to their respective facilities for incarceration of up to life imprisonment. June had heard about this processing procedure from others who had gone through it. "Pray they don't give you a C-5," a friend had said. "Waters got a C-5 and they shipped her out to a snake pit in Georgia. She wrote me a letter saying she'd rather be in a concentration camp. You don't want a C-5, girl; not under *any* circumstances."

Walking through a men's prison is not something anyone relishes — least of all an attractive young female with flowing, brown hair to her waist and a slim — and very female — figure. "Everyone's looking at you and whistling, catcalling. Even the guards get into it. They don't do anything to stop the inmates from harassing you; the vulgarity was unbelievable.

"When I got through with the photos and fingerprints, I was moved to the receiving area; that's where they classify you. A Mr. Martin was the classification officer, and he asked me a series of questions: 'Have you ever used drugs? Have you ever run away from home? Do you drink? Have you ever been suicidal?' I answered yes to all of them. He filled out the form and said, 'Okay, Ms. Briand, your classification is C-5. We're shipping you to West Virginia Federal Penitentiary.'

"I just stood there looking at him. It was like someone punched me in the stomach — and I knew what *that* felt like. I couldn't believe it was so quick and so easy for Mr. Martin; he didn't even have to think about it. I was a C-5 and that was that. I had never had any violations in prison or had any disciplinary problems or *anything* that would justify the C-5. I'm sure it was because of the crime I committed even though that was not supposed to be the determining factor.

"All the way back to Goffstown, all I could think about was that Anna had lied to me. *How could she?!* She said, 'Everything will work out all right.' What I thought was the worst day of my life — getting the fifteen-year sentence — got even *worse.*"

This time June entered the tier but did not make it to her cell. Her friends knew where she had been, and they could see by her tear-streaked face and hunched shoulders that she had not done well in Concord. They gathered around her to hug her and hold her, knowing that in twenty-four hours, she would be gone.

The next morning, June missed breakfast. She stayed in bed, not wishing to join the line, not wishing to do anything but turn off the pain that again racked her stomach. Eating was out of the question, just as it had been the last year with Jimmy. She would be leaving her friends and a place — as bad as it was — that she called home.

West Virginia Federal Penitentiary was one of the worst places she could be sent to. She had heard about most of the maximum security prisons for women, and West Virginia was one to avoid at all costs. But with the misfortune June Briand had always had in her life, it made perfect sense that she should end up precisely where she did not want to be.

After breakfast, June's cellmate, Nancy, returned carrying a letter. "Here," she said. "This just came for you." June turned over on her bunk and took the letter. She opened it and saw that it was her classification paper from the state of New Hampshire which read: *Classification overridden by Warden Conners. New classification: C-3.*

"It's my classification," June said. "They changed it!"

"*Anna* changed it," said Nancy. "I knew she would. You're not going anywhere. Welcome home, June!"

June sat up so fast she hit her head on the top bunk. Anna had said, "Everything will work out all right," and she saw to it that it did. She had called Mr. Martin from her office at the other end of the men's prison, and asked him what June's classification was. When he told her C-5, she "reamed him out," according to her assistant, and told him she was going directly to the warden to get June reclassified.

"When Anna came to see June later that day," said Nancy later, "she told her there was no reason for the C-5 classification. June had proven that she was no flight risk and no danger to anyone; I mean, after all, hers was a domestic abuse case — not an armed robbery killing or murder for hire."

Though Anna was the head of the women's prison at Goffstown, she was not there full time, and therefore, was not considered to be warden (known in Goffstown as superintendent). So she had gone to the men's warden in Concord, whom she knew well, and gotten June's classification overturned. A few months later, however, she was transferred to Goffstown permanently.

By then, the prison had been rebuilt and was no longer the Hillsborough House of Corrections, and no longer under county control. It was now called New Hampshire State Prison for Women, run by the state of New Hampshire; hence, Anna's transfer from the men's state facility to the new women's. And with the new name and new superintendent came new rules.

"Anna was tough. She was loving and warm and understanding, but she had a tough side to her. Working in a prison, how could you *not* be? No one — and I mean *no one* — made the mistake of crossing her twice."

Anna Rosen was a thirty-five-year-old, strong-willed Jewish woman who was five-foot-four and hefty, about one hundred and forty pounds. Her short, black hair framed a confident, intelligent face that was neither hard nor soft. Rather, it was powerful. "People wanted to be like Anna.

I know I did. And they wanted to be around her. She had something about her that made people want to do well. For instance, she'd say, 'Go wash that wall,' and I'd go over and scrub the wall as hard as I could. When I was done, she'd come over and say, 'Great job.' I loved hearing that. It gave me confidence.

"Anna was like my mother, sister, mentor, friend all rolled into one. She was a key influence and one that I know caused me to pull out of my depression and feel better about myself and my situation and make the best of prison. She said if I listened to her and did this, that, and the other thing, I would do well. And I did.

"But she didn't have much tolerance for sloppiness or laziness. Sometimes she'd plant a seed by saying, 'What's the matter, aren't you feeling well today? I asked you to do such and such, and it's still not done.' It would be a hint rather than a criticism. She had a way of motivating people."

Anna Rosen had a way of irritating people, too. And frustrating them and making them angry. When the prison fell into state hands and she first took over the job of superintendent, Anna "laid down the law." Prior to her taking over, women were allowed to wear personal articles of clothing in the evening, such as sweats and pajamas. They were allowed to keep personal hygiene articles in the rooms, even stay in their rooms all day if they felt like it. All this changed with Anna.

"It was a free for all when I first came to prison. The security was lax and there was no one in command. To a large extent, people did what they wanted. If they didn't want to go for meals, they didn't have to. They didn't even have to make their beds. When Anna came, everyone had to show up for meals, report for exercise at exercise time, work at assigned jobs. She took away our personal clothing, and required everyone to wear uniforms and name tags as a security measure.

"The name tags had to be clipped to the front of your shirt at all times, and if they weren't, you were written up. If guards weren't around, people would take them off; but everyone knew to keep their name tag in their back pocket. You didn't want a write-up because that meant you had to do extra work, or you got isolation in your room, or no television. With the few privileges you had, you wanted to *keep* them."

Now that it was clear that June would remain incarcerated rather than be freed with the sentence of "time served" as she had hoped, she plunged into life behind bars. The first thing she needed to do was work. Inquiring into openings, she found that a job was available in the laundry. Though it was the night shift — from 9 p.m. to 7 a.m. — she took the job, and immediately found it to be an eye-opening experience. She learned that even with Anna Rosen at the helm, an inordinate amount of illegal activities were going on in the prison. The laundry, it turns out, was a popular vehicle for transporting messages, money, and drugs.

"We did both the women's laundry and the men's laundry from Old House. When the guys needed to communicate with a woman in New House, they'd send the message down in their dirty clothes with instructions on what woman was supposed to get it. The clothes came down in laundry carts, and each cart held fifty mesh bags of clothes. A message might be: 'Find Smith's bag and bring it to A-10.' Or it might be money for a drug payoff or sex. Whatever it was, whoever got the message knew what to do."

June held her late-night laundry job for six months, then transferred to a new position in the prison kitchen. What illegal activities she had seen in the laundry paled in comparison to those she was to observe in the kitchen, where she would hold her job for the next two years.

"This time I worked the 4 a.m. to 2 p.m. shift. At first, my job was prepping. I'd peel hundreds of potatoes, chop lettuce, prepare soups. Like the laundry, our kitchen took care of the men in Old House, too. There were three hundred of them, plus us women, so you can imagine the food we went through.

"Later, I learned to cook and then serve. Serving was the best job because you could talk to people and have some interaction with them. It was the servers that also did the drug dealing. For example, they'd put money or drugs under a particular seat for someone, then tell them which seat to look under. And servers were the ones who passed the news of an upcoming raid by the guards. Someone might say, 'Get the stuff out of your room; there's going to be a raid tonight,' and that person would clean out whatever it was they were holding."

Working in the kitchen had another distinct advantage which made those jobs the most prized in the prison: it gave women access to *men*. After the prison went from county to state control, the men doing time for petty crimes in the other part of the building were moved, and the facility became exclusively a women's prison. Thus, the only men in the area were the hardened criminals of Old House who were lusting for women in New House. And that lust was just as intense the other way around.

Separating the forlorn lovers was the old underground tunnel and former nursing home morgue, which ran the hundred yards from the men's facility directly to a locked door in the far corner of the kitchen. Whoever had access to that door had access to immeasurable power. And the ones who had the access were the cooks.

"We had three cooks — David, Louis, and Grant. They were originally guards, and were transitioning to full-time cooks. Being a cook was a more desirable and higher-paying job. And it had benefits — especially access to the tunnel."

Because of its proximity to the kitchen, foodstuffs and other supplies were stored in the cool rooms located on each side of the long, dark tunnel, which was constructed of cinder blocks and reinforced concrete. The floor was made of cement that had been poured directly over the dirt and boulders when the nursing home was constructed. When a cook needed something, he sent a worker into the tunnel to retrieve it. Because the tunnel was originally used as a morgue, the cold storage rooms with their foot-thick wooden doors were formerly used to house dead bodies.

Even the stainless steel gurneys that once carried the deceased were put to use. Now they carried fresh vegetables, meat, and canned goods to the kitchen. Deep wells on each end of the gurneys — once used to collect body fluids oozing from the dead — became convenient compartments for keeping fruits and vegetables from falling off the gurneys as they bumped along the rough cement floor.

Naked light bulbs hung every fifty feet from a single wire that ran the length of the tunnel. "It was scary down there. As soon as you left a lighted area, you were in the pitch dark until you got to the next light. It was damp and smelled bad because no air ever got down there."

As the gurneys carried supplies back and forth over the bumpy floor, it became more of an obstacle course around which the driver had to maneuver skillfully. But even if she was good at negotiating the terrain, an inmate might well bump into something — or someone — she wasn't expecting.

It was well-known that the cooks were "on the take." Twenty dollars was the standard charge to gain access to the tunnel for a lovelorn inmate whose "boyfriend" had sent instructions to meet her there. The cooks would act as lookout for anyone "using" the tunnel, and vice versa: when the cooks wanted to use it for their own sexual liaisons, they would have an inmate watch the door for them.

"The cooks had girlfriends. They were all married, but they had inmate girlfriends that they would buy clothes and gifts for. They'd even pay for their lawyers to help get them out of prison. They'd use the tunnel, too. They thought they were in love — and the women went for it.

"Once when I was going to one of the storage rooms for canned peaches, I walked in on Adrienne giving Louis oral sex. Another time I went for supplies and saw a naked guy from Old House on top of a woman from my tier. The cooks would leave the door open for the women, and they would meet the men for sex. The thing is, these weren't the nicest guys in the world. They were men from *Old House* — and those were the violent ones: rapists, robbers, arsonists. But the women didn't care; they wanted love. Or money. The guys would pay them like prostitutes.

"Sometimes, men from Old House would intentionally stage a fake fight in order to get sent to the 'down time' rooms located at the far end of the tunnel. They'd pay the women at New House who would, in turn, pay off the cooks who would leave the door unlocked for them so they could go down and have sex. It was amazing what went on it that tunnel."

The women of New House did not have to enter the tunnel to know what was going on in that subterranean world. They could hear everything that went on there through the heating grates in the prison floor. And it was not all sex and good times. Out-of-control inmates from Old House were often sent to damp, unlit isolation cells and would sometimes be there for weeks on end. "By the end of their stint, they'd be screaming and yelling to get out of there — 'howls from hell' we called it. It was awful. Sometimes you'd hear people fighting and screaming at each other; other times you'd hear women crying or moaning. It was hard to listen to but you couldn't help it."

The underground free-for-all would not last. For one thing, Anna Rosen was now in charge. And for another, one of the cooks would cause the demise of the furtive tunnel liaisons. "Grant was my favorite. He was head cook. He was a short, round little guy. Real nice, soft-spoken. But he shouldn't have been working in a prison; he was too sensitive for it.

"Grant fell in love with Rachelle; she was a crack addict and prostitute. She was a pretty girl, tall, about five-eight, with dark, shoulder-length hair. And funny. She could really make you laugh when you needed it. Grant fell head over heels for her. But she had lots of problems. Her wrists were all scarred up from lots of suicide attempts. And she was a controller — especially with Grant. He was shy and she was bossy. They'd fight and he'd get so upset he'd cry. Then she'd play him along to get what she wanted out of him.

"Their affair went on about six months until one day Grant's wife called the prison. She saw collect calls on their phone bill and then everything came out; it was a big scandal. That's when Anna shut down the tunnel. And that was bad because it caused more tension in the prison. She didn't have any choice, but when it was open, there were less fights, less drug abuse. It was an outlet for people; they needed it. Then it was shut down and the guards started watching everyone much more carefully. That's when the problems started."

Shortly after the closing, a group of women on the tier were watching television one evening after dinner. June had just gotten up to get a drink of water, and was walking across the tier when suddenly she heard a loud thud. "It sounded like someone punched a wall. I turned and saw Rachelle's arm up against the inside of her door window; it was all bloody, and she was dragging it down along the glass smearing blood as she went. She had slit her arm open with a razor.

"Another time a woman was put in lockdown. She was considered a suicide risk and was supposed to be constantly monitored because the welfare authorities had just come and had her sign papers giving up her kids. She went crazy and was crying and carrying on.

"Hank, the guard, was standing by her door. She had already been in there for two days and was quiet, so everything seemed all right. He thought it would be okay to take some other prisoners outside for yard time, and was only gone a few minutes. But when he came back, he started screaming, 'Help! Help! Someone get in here and help me!' The woman was hanging by a sheet from the water sprinkler in the ceiling. She had climbed up on the sink, tied the sheet around her neck, and jumped off. Hank grabbed her legs and tried to take the pressure off her neck, but it was no use. He gave her mouth-to-mouth but she was already brain dead."

Other pressures affected the women too — not just from the tunnel closing, but from the sheer day-to-day drudgery of living within the confines of prison walls. Like the men, frustration among women grew to the point where something had to explode. Too often, it was an inmate's head.

"There were microphones and speakers throughout the prison and in all the rooms; they let the guards monitor what was going on at all times. But many times they weren't listening. One time in the pool room, two girls went at each other with pool cues. They started fighting about something and then both of them stood back and took full swings with the heavy ends of the cues. "Both sticks landed at the same time and they split each other's heads open. One girl had a deep gash over one eye; you could see her skull poking through. The other one had a cut on the side of her head; her hair was all wet and matted down, and there was blood everywhere. I've never seen anything like it.

"Everyone grabbed towels as fast as they could to clean up the blood. If the guards found out there was a fight, everyone would be punished, and we'd be monitored that much tighter. We knew they'd be coming soon, and they did. One of them saw some blood we missed and said, 'What's that?' Someone said, 'Oh, it's just juice; I'll clean it up,' and grabbed a mop and bucket and went to work. The two who were fighting were barely conscious. By the time the guard showed up, we had dragged them off to the showers to clean them up.

"Another close call came when a girl named Ginny got mad at Erin for snitching on her. Ginny had taken a carton of milk from the dining hall. You're not supposed to take food out of the hall, and Erin saw her do it. She hated Ginny, so she told a guard about it. They came to Ginny's cell and wrote her up.

"The next day, Ginny saw Erin standing by herself near her room. She went right up behind her, and said, 'Why did you tell on me?' Erin didn't have time to answer. Ginny was a lot bigger than Erin, and grabbed her by the back of her hair and slammed her face right into the wall as hard as she could. It knocked Erin out cold, and her nose was bleeding all over the floor. I saw the whole thing and ran over and put Erin in her bunk like she was sick. When the guard came by, I know he saw the blood on the floor, but he was a friend of mine and didn't say anything."

June was not without her own enemies. Many of the women were jealous of how well she was doing, and saw that she was highly intelligent — much more so than the average inmate, many of whom were bordering on illiterate. In prison, the way to get to someone is to get them in trouble. Though they were not the brightest of individuals, prisoners could be crafty when they wanted to be.

"I went directly to Anna with the knife. Someone had planted it in my locker. It was a straight piece of steel called a shank, and someone — I had a good idea who — put it there with the intention of telling a guard. Fortunately, I found it first and brought it right to Anna.

"I wasn't worried about fingerprints, and held it out in front of me and walked into her office and said, 'Funny how these things end up in my locker.' Anna looked over and saw the blade. She gave a little laugh and said, 'Sure is, isn't it? Just watch your back, June. Watch your back.'"

June heard about another position that had just opened up — a professional job that would influence her greatly in the months to come. A handsome young dentist named Dr. Greg Presley came to the prison three times a week to treat the inmates. He did not bring along a dental assistant, preferring to train an interested inmate in dental assisting and hygiene. Since his last assistant had been released from prison, he needed an new one, and June applied for the job.

"Since my other job was not full-time, I could fit in a second one. Greg was such a nice guy. And so good looking! I loved being around him. He was the bright spot of my week. He was funny and easy to be with, and he taught me so much. He was patient and really cared about me; I felt lucky to have landed the job with him.

"We became good friends right away — so good that I nicknamed him Elvis; he liked that, and he liked me. He'd bring me roses on my birthday, and he'd sneak in food, which was against the rules but he didn't care. He'd bring me ice cream in Styrofoam containers, and once he brought me a special treat: shrimp. He snuck in six huge shrimp with cocktail sauce in one of the Styrofoam containers and said, 'Eat. I'm going to the nurses' station.' Then he closed the door and left. I couldn't believe it. Shrimp! I devoured them! We never had food like that in prison, and it had been years since I had anything like it.

"When Greg came back a minute later, I was just sitting there. He said, 'What did you do with the shrimp?' I told him I ate them. He said, 'What do you mean? You couldn't have, I've only been gone sixty seconds.' He didn't believe me, but we learned to eat fast in prison, and the shrimp was such a fabulous treat, I didn't want anybody to catch me and take them away. He started looking in the cabinets and all around the room; he just couldn't believe I finished them off so fast."

Dr. Presley's influence on June was twofold: One, she liked the professional type of work she was learning, and soon started thinking about what it would be like to have such a job "on the outside." Two, for the first time since she had been incarcerated, she was being exposed to — and enjoying immensely — those things that were only available on the outside: roses, delicious food, wonderfully kind men. She began to long for a different life.

By then, June had been in jail for nearly five years, and the thought of another ten was weighing heavily on her. The first years spent learning about herself and Jimmy had helped her through the grieving process — grieving for her children, her husband, herself. She had always felt deep remorse for having taken a life, and no matter what those around her would say — that her husband "deserved it," that he "had it coming," that it was "self-defense" — she never felt they were right.

Now, after years behind bars on a charge that so many felt was unjustified and which resulted in a sentence thought by many to be unduly extreme, June began to feel differently. She did not agree with the opinion that she was in any way justified in committing her crime, but with the help of extensive therapy, she did understand why it had happened and that, at the time, it was an act she was incapable of preventing.

On a Friday evening in mid-1991, after four years of incarceration, June had seen all too vividly that indeed, she was not the only woman who was driven to kill. There were other women who had been the victim of monstrous men who sought to pulverize their women into trembling, subservient slaves. It was not until that Friday night, while sitting with her fellow inmates in the New Hampshire State Prison for Women, that June Briand saw she was, in many ways, a political prisoner — an unfortunate, now-forgotten prisoner of a legal system that required expensive expert defense witnesses and powerful attorneys in order to win.

June saw that after being punished for years by a ruthless beast of a husband, she was now being punished further by an equally merciless system, a system incapable of judging her act of self-defense as justified because it had no understanding of the true nature of domestic violence. Neither had June until seven o'clock that Friday evening, when the lights went out.

PART V: THE HEARING

Julia Roberts was not smiling. Her broad, toothy grin was conspicuously absent, and her eyes were filled with terror. The movie, *Sleeping With The Enemy*, was showing in the darkened recreation room at the Goffstown prison. Some inmates had selected it, not knowing what the story was about or that one of their own — June Briand — had led an almost identical life to the abused woman played by Julia Roberts.

The two women's stories paralleled each other in eerie, uncanny ways. As the movie progressed, June watched with amazement at just how similar Roberts' husband was to her own Jimmy. One scene showed how obsessed the man was about orderliness when he led his wife by the hand into the pristine bathroom she worked diligently to keep clean. Nothing seemed to be out of place, and the room looked perfect for the cover of a home decorating magazine. But she had made a mistake.

Walking her into the bathroom, Roberts' husband stopped and pointed out her grave infraction: the two hand towels on the towel rack were not perfectly even at the bottom. One hung an inch or so below the other, and it was not the first time he had called her attention to it.

"I'm sorry," Roberts' said meekly, looking like a scolded child. "It won't happen again." Her husband was understanding and accepted his wife's apology, saying he really did expect more from her, and had every confidence that she would do better in the future. She agreed to try harder.

"Jimmy. It was the first thing that came to my mind: that's Jimmy! It was the *exact* behavior I had seen in him. Another scene was even spookier. Julia Roberts opens the cupboard doors and everything is perfectly in order: same sized cans together, hot cereals together, cold cereals together, all labels are facing out. Jimmy. She was living with Jimmy! I got goose bumps."

June was uncomfortable watching a carbon copy of her husband on the screen, and visibly flinched when he punched Julia Roberts in the face, knocking her to the ground, after which he leaned down and said he was sorry that he "had to do that." But June was riveted by the story and could not take her eyes off the screen — especially when Roberts accomplished something June could not: leaving.

In the story, Roberts had planned her escape well, and waited for the perfect moment to execute it. But what June always feared would happen if she left Jimmy did, in fact, happen to Roberts: her spurned husband tracked her down. It was at this stage of the movie that June became edgy. She never wanted to come face to face with Jimmy after leaving him, and when Roberts is confronted by her husband, she barely saves herself by shooting him to death.

"At that moment, everyone in the room had the same reaction: they cheered. Even the guards cheered. The women on either side of me put their arms around my shoulders. I was shook up by the film. After we turned the lights back on, we started talking about it. I had no idea there were other men so identical to Jimmy, so controlling and obsessed with orderliness.

"I knew there was a lot of domestic violence around, but until I saw that movie, I hadn't realized the men were so similar. When I lightened up a bit, I said, 'They must all go to the same school.' Everyone laughed, and they agreed."

The movie had affected everyone. They all knew what June had gone through, and they sympathized with her. The film just made more graphic the conditions under which

June was forced to do what Roberts had done. June was not interested in debating the merits or mistakes of the past, or whether or not she should have been able to see the options — few that they were — that were available at the time. She was now looking to the future, with the ardent hope that it would be brighter than the past twenty-nine years had been.

Renee, one of the women who had watched the movie with June, was deeply affected by it as well. She took the movie to heart, and dropped by June's room the following day to talk about it and June's situation.

"You shouldn't be here, June," said Renee. "You did what you had to do, just like Julia. You know that. I know that. *Everybody* knows that. But there's politics involved, and you've got to get involved in them. That's what will get you out of here. People need to know your story; they need to know what happened to you. You never had a trial, so you never had a chance to defend yourself.

"Your attorney may have done the right thing, taking a plea bargain. No one wanted to take the risk of you going to prison for life. But the truth is, you shouldn't have gone to prison for *one day*! Look at Julia Roberts. If she didn't kill her husband, he would have killed her. The movie made it so clear. There's got to be a way for *you* to make that clear. You've got to get out of here. There's no way you should be in prison with the rest of us."

June listened quietly. There was a time when she would have argued Renee's points, an earlier time when she felt the guilt, the fear, the sin, the deep remorse for what she had done. But though she still felt these things, they were not as virulent as they once were primarily because she had learned so much from the counselors and teachers she had worked with over the years.

One such teacher was Margaret Simmons in the Vocational Department at Goffstown. She was a softer, more gentle woman than Anna, and relied heavily on spirituality and the belief that there is something outside of us, a higher power that we can tap into and from which we can reap great benefits. Other than the radical version June had learned from her grandmother, spirituality was something she knew little about.

Through Margaret, June learned to find peace in adversity rather than fear or anger. "She taught me that *trying* was the important thing in life, not necessarily winning every time or getting the A grade. But if you keep at it, you'll eventually succeed.

"I took a sixteen-week office class from Margaret; that's when we became close. She taught me that I had power over myself; that I shouldn't worry about other people — what they say or do. Concentrate on myself, stick to it, never give up, and above all, *believe* — in myself and in the Higher Power.

"I always believed in God, but I never really *thought* about my belief much. He was just sort of there. You prayed when you needed something, and that was it. Margaret showed me that we are not alone, that things will work out the way they're supposed to. Don't be crushed by every little failure or if you don't meet your expectations. Do the best you can. If the result isn't what you expected, maybe it wasn't meant to be; try something else. I felt so much better after learning all this; it took off a lot of pressure."

Renee's words resounded in June's head: "People need to know your story." The statement rang true. But how? How, from behind thick prison walls — without a famous actress, production company, and millions of dollars — does one tell her story? The beginning of an answer came three days later.

Alicia, a quiet, unassuming, woman doing time for fraud and bad checks, had become friendly with June. She was much older than the others, perhaps fifty, though she would never reveal her true age. She was an extremely intelligent woman who was never without a book in her hand. Like Renee, she, too, had seen the Roberts movie, and it jogged her memory about an article on domestic violence she had recently read in a feminist publication, the *Sojourner*.

Admitting to being "a pack rat," Alicia had kept the paper — and by the looks of her comically cluttered room, everything else she had ever come into contact with. When she came by to visit June, she had the paper in her hand and suggested that June might be interested in the article since it tied in so closely with the movie they had just seen. "Who knows," Alicia said, "maybe it will help you somehow."

"By prison standards, Alicia was an old maid. Most of the inmates were in their late teens and early twenties. Having someone fifty there was like having a mother around, and that's just what Alicia was to me. She sat down with her thick glasses on and opened the paper to the article.

"Before I even looked at it, it dawned on me that it was the second time in three days that someone had brought up the idea of doing something about my situation. First Renee saying, 'People need to know your story,' then Alicia saying, 'Maybe it will help you somehow.' Help you. It was like they had already determined that I could do something more than sit in prison for fifteen years; before that, I hadn't given it much thought. After I read the *Sojourner* story, though, I started thinking about the possibility of getting out early, and became intrigued with the idea."

The *Sojourner* article told of a conference on domestic violence that had been held in Quincy, Massachusetts. At the conference were judges, lawyers, legislators, and others concerned about the growing problem of domestic abuse and the laws — some very outdated laws — relating to it. June read the article with great interest, and for the first time saw that a real cross section of people were discussing the topic; it was becoming an issue of interest to more than just women.

The fact that the judicial and legislative elite cared enough about this issue to hold a conference on it impressed June as it had Alicia. After all, these were the very same people who had taken June's children away and sentenced her to fifteen years to life.

Now it was time for action. She could accept her fate and languish in prison, or she could fight back intelligently and methodically. She had truth and newfound courage on her side, and with her developing self-confidence, decided to fight for what was right — and win. As Renee advised her to do, June "took the bull by the horns" and began to wrangle with the system.

The person who noticed June's burgeoning self-confidence most was Anna Rosen. She was not an openly effusive woman and kept her emotions closely controlled, and was careful not to play favorites or show more interest in one inmate over the others. But she had always kept an eye on June.

"Almost from the first, we detected potential in June," said one of Anna's assistants. "She was frail and scared when she first entered Goffstown, but then, most first-timers are. But she was different. When she got acclimated and settled in, she saw opportunities the others didn't. And she *listened*. She was a good learner with a sense of responsibility."

Anna made the most of June's ability to self-actualize and move ahead. "She helped me stay motivated, and not let the system get me down. If Anna caught me pouting or feeling sorry for myself, she'd call me on it. She was the motivating factor behind everything I did. 'People have choices,' she said. 'It's all about choices. *You* choose the path you take, nobody else.' Anna taught me that *I* was the one who had control over my life, not the prison. It was the most important lesson of all."

As the head of the institution, Anna could not suggest, as Renee had, that June "take the bull by the horns." After all, it was *her* bull, her system, and one in which she believed. But she also believed in June. She had personally trained her to take on challenges, and now used reverse psychology on her student.

"She reminded me about the sentence review hearings Stan Miller had mentioned earlier (during which a prisoner could request a reduction in her sentence), and said I would be eligible for mine in a few months. Then she nonchalantly tossed in the fact that there wasn't much chance of my getting the sentence reduced. She said it would be a 'long shot' if I were released before the minimum fifteen years were up; she said that on purpose."

Anna was a clever woman and knew June would rise to the bait. She knew "long shot" would be the stimulus, and she was right. "I'll look into it anyway," said June after Anna cautioned her about the unlikelihood of succeeding at the hearing. But when she investigated it further, June found she had a seemingly insurmountable obstacle in front of her. It looked like Anna was right.

June called Stan Miller to ask him about it, and to see if it were true that he would not able to represent her during her hearing. When she called him, he confirmed what she had heard, saying he had bad news for her: "Sorry, June," he said. "There's a new law that was recently passed that says, in essence, that prisoners no longer have the right to a public defender in sentence review hearings. You'll have to find your own attorney; I can't help you on this one." It was an ominous start to June's bid for freedom. But she was undaunted and knew exactly what to do.

June sat on the edge of her bunk and wrote a letter to the editor of the *Sojourner*, commending her on the article on the domestic violence. She asked that it be forwarded to the judge who had attended the conference and was interviewed for the article, and said that there needed to be more judges like her. (She was not only a female, but also an advocate for battered women.) June wanted to thank her for her concern and advocacy for those who had been victims of abusive relationships.

Unfortunately, the judge to whom June corresponded would not be the judge sitting on the bench at the sentence review hearing. That would be Judge Scott, again — the Hillsborough County Superior Court judge who had originally put June behind bars. June was told by various corrections officials who knew Scott's record that he was not likely to reduce her sentence. But as one said, "You've got nothing to lose and everything to gain, so you might as well go for it."

In the last line of her letter to the editor, June mentioned that she was going for a sentence reduction, but that the public defender was no longer able to help her. She needed an attorney, but could not afford one. Did they have any ideas?

They did, indeed. Not only did the *Sojourner* editor send June's letter to the judge — who wrote back to June thanking her and promising to keep working on domestic abuse — they sent a copy of the letter to a hundred attorneys known to be sympathetic to the cause.

At first, nothing happened. A week went by. Then another. Then a month. Then a bright, young feminist attorney named Bridget Moretti wrote June a letter saying she had received a copy of her letter and was interested in the case. She said she would like to meet with June to discuss it, and that June could call her collect anytime.

"I didn't want to call her collect. I felt funny about that. I didn't know her, and here I'd be asking her to pay for my phone call. I decided to write instead, and I told her that I was reluctant to call. She wrote back saying it would be fine, to go ahead and call her, so I did.

"She was very sweet on the phone. We talked for only a few minutes, and set a date for her to come visit me the next week. When I got off the phone, I was ecstatic. I was smiling from ear to ear. Everyone said I looked so good because they had never seen me smiling like that.

"Bridget and I liked each other immediately. She was young and pretty and Italian: dark hair and eyes, red fingernails manicured beautifully. I hadn't seen anyone that pretty in years. She had set an appointment to see me just to get started, to get some background information. She said it would be a short visit, but it lasted for hours — most of the day, actually.

"Bridget was encouraging. She was experienced in domestic abuse cases, and said I definitely had a chance, that it was possible I could get a reduced sentence, and if that didn't work, I could even go for a pardon. If everything I told her was true and could be documented by the psychologists and others, I had a case for a reduced sentence. But *making* the case, she said, would take a lot of work."

At the time of the meeting, there were still three months left before the hearing. Bridget heard then that Judge Scott would be hearing the case, and told June that although she had a strong case for sentence reduction based on Battered Woman's Syndrome, it would most likely not be granted by the likes of Ernest Scott. She knew him, and knew him to be a stickler when it came to changing sentences — especially the ones *he* handed down.

"From the start, Bridget was thinking pardon. She knew we were more likely to get a fair hearing with several people involved, and for a pardon, the hearing is done before the governor and his five-member executive council. I didn't like that idea though, because Stephen Merrill was now the governor, and he was the former attorney general who had prosecuted me in the first place! That didn't sound too promising. Neither did facing Judge Scott. I started getting depressed again.

Bridget Moretti pulled June out of her gloom by reminding her that the although the governor would have the power to veto the executive council's decision, he probably wouldn't. He would listen to them, and if they could be convinced of June's victimization, he might very well go along with them. The case would be strengthened further if it could be shown that June had received extensive counseling and was thoroughly rehabilitated.

June had no other alternatives. It was either a sentence reduction or, failing that, executive clemency. If those both failed, June would remain in prison for at least fifteen years — and possibly more if her prison record was not impeccable or it was determined that she was not fully rehabilitated. "It was entirely possible, then, that I could one day replace fifty-something Alicia as the old maid of the prison. It was a prospect I preferred not to think about."

Bridget Moretti did not think about it either; she was too busy during the next six three not only preparing for the hearing, but more important, building support for June's appeal. Wherever she went, she brought up the June Briand case. At social functions (which she made a point of attending regularly), interacting with other attorneys, in court and out — everywhere Bridget went, she broached the subject of domestic violence and June's incarceration.

To broaden awareness of the case, Bridget got a story into one of the local papers. It explained June's situation and her bid for a reduction in sentence. Bridget was "planting seeds" and "putting feelers out" to the community to test support. The response she received was overwhelmingly in favor of mercy for the June.

One woman who read the story, Heidi Guhrer, was immediately taken with the cause. She was an older German woman with strong views and the ability to voice them. She had been an advocate for battered women for some time, and now became interested in June's plight. She wrote her in prison.

"I saw the story and decided to contact June," said Heidi. "I wrote her asking if anyone was coming to visit her, and she wrote back saying no, she had no visitors at all, except for her mother who came to see her about once a year. Other than that, there was no one.

"I went to see her and we got along very well right away. She was soft-spoken and very warm. I felt it was tragic what had happened to her, and offered to come visit often if she wanted me to. She said she did, and we became good friends."

Heidi became more than a friend, she became an advocate — and a vocal one. She was active in the New Hampshire chapter of NOW (National Organization for Women), and regularly went to the seacoast meetings. After visiting several times with June, Heidi became convinced that June needed to be out of prison — for her own sake and for the sake of other battered women, whom June expressed an interest in helping.

Heidi brought up the issue of June Briand's "political imprisonment" at the following month's NOW meeting. Yes, June had committed a serious crime, so the term "political" was a loaded one. Nevertheless, records across the country proved that women with similar circumstances to June's — but with the resources to wage vigorous and expensive defenses — rarely spent one day in prison, and usually went from bail to trial to acquittal. June's incarceration, then, did have distinct political implications, both because of her inability to defend herself adequately, and the system's inability to comprehend the true nature of her crime. She needed help, and it was NOW that would wholeheartedly offer it.

Trish Morgan was the president of the local chapter of NOW, and it was easy to see why. She was an articulate, intelligent woman who cared deeply about women and the inequalities they often suffered in certain male-dominated environments. Equal employment issues; equal rights; non-violence; sexual harassment. Trish was up and vocal on the contemporary women's issues, and was immediately interested in the June Briand story as related by Heidi Guhrer.

"Trish has tremendous energy," said another member of the NOW. "She's a fighter, but a nonviolent one. She uses her head and her heart to convince people, to make them see the truth. She's relentless, and that's just what June needed — a strong advocate that could make her case visible."

Trish Morgan, however, was too late. She did not become involved until just before the sentence review hearing, and by then, there was little she could do to build support throughout the community. And that was what was needed: local support with plenty of press coverage showing how unjust June's incarceration was and why she should be given mercy. Not that any of this would have had the desired effect on Judge Scott — it probably wouldn't.

Long shot or not, it was a shot, and one that had to be tried with or without support. Neither June nor Bridget Moretti felt the hearing would be successful, but they knew the next step might be — the pardon. Trish felt the same way, as did Heidi and the rest of the NOW organization. They'd wait for the sentence review hearing, and if that failed, they would forgo the next two-year wait for another hearing and start a grassroots drive to put the issue before the executive council. That was what Bridget had wanted in the first place, and NOW concurred that it was the right course of action to take.

Moretti was an excellent attorney, and smart enough to know that massive preparation for the sentence review hearing was not needed. For one thing, she knew Scott to be an intransigent judge. It was highly unlikely that he would set aside the sentence he had imposed, even with the greatest of arguments by a room full of venerable lawyers.

Second, it was too soon. Letting someone out of prison after serving only five years of a fifteen-years-to-life sentence would be a political bombshell Scott would never drop. "He'll keep her in," said those familiar with the case. And he did.

The hearing was over almost before it began. Bridget had filed with the State of New Hampshire a Motion to Suspend Balance of Minimum Sentence, which concluded: "WHEREFORE, Ms. Briand respectfully requests that this Court: 1) schedule a hearing on this motion; 2) after a hearing, suspend the remainder of her sentence to make her eligible for parole; and 3) grant any other relief that this Court deems is fair and just."

Only the first item was granted. "Like we expected, Jimmy's stepmother took the stand again, and said the same things she had before. She said I killed her son and I served only five years. How could they let me out? How could they even consider reducing my sentence? I took the stand saying how much I'd developed and grown in prison — the courses I'd taken, the jobs. None of it mattered. The judge was very civil, just like he was during the original sentencing. He said I should be proud of myself for doing so well in prison and for educating myself and being a leader for others. He even said I'd do well in society. My heart jumped a little then. Society? Why was he mentioning that? Was he going to reduce my sentence after all?

"Then he added, '*But* it does not discount the fact that you took a human life and must be in prison.' My heart sank back down. He ended the proceeding in less than an hour and said he'd take the case under advisement. Two days later, I got a letter from the court saying our plea was denied. I wasn't crushed; we all expected it."

Immediately after the hearing, Bridget Moretti turned her attention to executive clemency. Pardons are rarely granted, and they are even more rare in conservative states like New Hampshire with conservative chief executives like Governor Merrill. But if there was enough support to make it look politically incorrect to keep an abused woman behind bars, then perhaps there was a chance.

Plus, Merrill, on this issue, was not all that conservative. He had shown an awareness of, and interest in, the issue of domestic violence, and had even set up a commission to study the problem. There was a faint but distinct ray of hope here, and thus the wheels of progress began to roll. But here, too, they would encounter an unexpected mountain up which they could not climb.

The first thing Trish and her co-workers did was sit down for a brainstorming session with all those interested in working for June's freedom. They were going to take this slow, she advised, and do one thing at a time — methodically, thoroughly, and completely. "This is not something that can be rushed," she said. "This is a campaign like any other campaign. We need support. We need strategy. And we need commitment to what is right, and *this is right*! We can leave no stone unturned. June Briand was a victim, is still a victim, and we are going to get this woman out of prison."

With Trish leading the way, the troops went into action. At the brainstorming meeting, NOW members held legal pads and made a list of steps that needed to be taken: First, gain support. How? From whom? The group scratched down "churches; temples; coalitions; politicians; media; civic leaders; family, friends, and acquaintances" — including those in the Goffstown prison, from inmates to counselors to correctional officers and even the guards. Leaving "no stone unturned" became a plowing party with workhorses in every part of the field. And a fertile field it was.

People everywhere joined the cause. A command post was set up by volunteers who started calling anyone and everyone who might be able to lend support. They explained June's situation and offered to come to offices and homes to explain the reasons for the clemency request. They said they urgently needed letters — either from those who personally knew June and could attest to her character, or from those who understood her situation and believed that she was indeed a victim of circumstances and an intolerant, myopic system — a victim who had been punished enough and would be of much greater value to society outside of prison than in.

And the letters came. Support came from those who knew June and those who wanted to. The media, too, was beginning to pay attention, and the members of NOW were growing optimistic. They knew that little pressure could be brought to bear on the executive council and governor without the media, and now they were showing interest in the cause.

By definition, the executives had to be sensitive to the community's sentiments, and if through the media, the community saw the Briand case a "travesty of justice," the executives would have to respond. The more pressure from the media, the better the odds the executives would see things in their true light. This is all June asked for, but it would not be forthcoming.

The wheels of progress had just begun to roll when the mountain appeared and everything came to an abrupt halt. The media had another matter that would occupy its time — and front pages — for well over a year. "Pam Smart ended June's bid for freedom," said one of the NOW members. "Just as things were beginning to take off, just as support was building for June, Pam Smart hit the front pages. She was the woman accused of having her teenage lover kill her husband. It was a sensational type of story that the media loves. All attention turned to the Pam Smart case, and of all places for it to happen, it was in New Hampshire. She even ended up in Goffstown with June."

Bridgett Moretti called a halt to everything. Being the savvy lawyer she was, and, like NOW, very conscious of the need for strong public support in June's clemency bid, she decided to wait for the Pam Smart hoopla to die down. Her reasons were twofold. First, she did not want June to get "lost in the media." Everywhere in the news, reporters were following the Smart case. And it was everything the public wanted: sex, murder, an underage lover. It was a soap opera, and one which June and her supporters could not compete against. Nor would they try. "Beside getting June out of prison," said the NOW supporter, "our purpose was to increase awareness of domestic violence."

Second, Moretti did not want June "mixed up" with Pam Smart. Smart was neither a battered woman nor a victim of circumstances. "She was a sick, calculating woman out for her own pleasure," said one reporter. "And she would stop at nothing to get it." The court would have no trouble proving her guilt, and Bridget knew the bad press and concurrent community sentiment against women perpetrators would likely spill over to June if she were to share headlines with Smart; it would taint June's case. And so they had to wait.

Bridget, however, did not foresee that the media circus would continue for as long as it did. "By the time the Pam Smart media frenzy ended, over a year had gone by," said Moretti. "When we got back into action, it was only a few months before June would be allowed to go for another sentence review hearing. You always take that option first because a pardon is the last resort. Since she was so close, it made sense to try it again."

The infamous June Briand bad luck came to disrupt progress once again. And again, it came at the most inopportune possible time. In early 1994, four weeks before the hearing was to take place, Bridget Moretti phoned June. The call came midday, and it hit June like a tank.

"June," said Bridget over the phone. "I've got something to tell you, and you're not going to like it. But I haven't any choice: I've got to leave the case. I've been asked to work for the state and it would be a conflict of interest if I continued to represent you."

The Department of Children and Youth Family Services had offered Bridget an excellent position which she could not turn down. She enjoyed working with women and children, and had proved her competency in that field. She would take the job, but not before contacting a colleague, Ralph Anderson, who, like her, also had experience in the field of domestic violence. Anderson agreed to take June's case.

But before handing the case over, Bridget went to one last meeting in support of June's cause. It would be a critically important move, and one that would leave June in a far stronger political position when the hearing came around. Bridget attended a meeting of the New Hampshire Coalition Against Domestic Violence. It was a strong, well-respected organization with political clout, and one that June had written earlier asking for support. When it did not come, June was devastated. And Bridget was incredulous.

"When I wrote them, I made it clear that I wasn't asking them to condone what I had done. I had done wrong, and I was aware of it and still felt deep remorse. If there was any way I could undo what I had done, I would; but of course, there wasn't. I said that the closest I could come would be to help other women who were going through what I went through, and I couldn't do that behind bars.

"They didn't see it my way. This was a coalition for helping battered women, mind you, and they had no doubt about my victimization. But they couldn't see their way through to supporting just *me*. They told me to 'get a group together,' whatever that meant. They said join up with others and *then* they could support me. But just me alone? Not interested.

"I was furious! I told Bridget about their response, and wrote a letter for her to read at their next meeting. Maybe if they knew what really happened to me, they would change their minds."

Bridget took June's letter to the meeting at which the head of the coalition, Jeri O'Leary, was present. She was the one who had written to June suggesting that she form a group. When Bridget was called on to speak, she stood to talk to the members, but she turned in O'Leary's direction.

The letter was as much a catharsis for June as it was a revelation for the group. In it, June's fury, despair, and hopelessness came through clearly. It said, in part:

This is not about a *group* of identical people, it's about *one* person and what she went through. It took me so long to finally reach out for help. How dare you say I'm not important enough as one woman! I need your support — just me!

Members looked sheepishly at each other and began slouching down in their chairs. Bridget continued, only this time she related the things June had lived through, and it was painful to hear.

Bloodied faces, twisted arms, bruised ribs became a way of life. The taste of blood became as common as drinking milk. I became a meek little mouse who was living in a lion's den with only one thing to strive for — to survive. Scared all the time, I was jumping at shadows but with no place else to go ...

With my pregnancy I hoped there would be a change in Jimmy's behavior. Two kids, two cars, the American Dream would be mine! Jimmy had been calm during most of my pregnancy, but then, one night when I was six or seven months pregnant, it all crashed down. Jimmy attacked my oldest daughter, Jana. I tried to protect her but he shoved me out of the way and I fell to the floor. When I crawled over to her and tried to pull her away, he turned and kicked me in the stomach. I shrieked — not in pain but in terror that he would kill the unborn child that was still in me. He slapped me, punched me, and kicked me. I tried as hard as I could to protect my unborn baby. I covered her with my hands and arms not knowing if she was damaged or not. But I knew it had to be as terrifying for her as it was for us. Then Jimmy stopped hitting us and started screaming. He subjected us to hours of screaming, terror, and threats of death if I ever got in his way again when he was disciplining Jana. He said he'd kill me if I ever ran away …

Standing up straight became something I had to practice, like a child, until I could do it without wincing from the ribs that felt like they were pushing to get out of my skin.

I now sit in prison, much like the one I lived in with Jimmy. I cry for the father of my children whose inner self was so tortured that he became the destructive force that he was. I cry for my children whose lives have been devastated by the losses they have endured and the memories they will hold forever. I also cry for the society that will not recognize domestic violence for the epidemic that it is; and for a judicial system that does not comprehend the workings of a mind that has been terrorized and believes that death is an inevitable end.

June was not the only one who cried. By the time Bridget finished, she was crying. She looked up and saw that everyone else was weeping too. After they dabbed their eyes and pulled themselves together, a member of the group stood up and made a motion to support June, saying, "The coalition has a duty; here is a cause that cries out for advocacy. She's right; we need to support her. This does not have to incorporate all the battered women of the world; it should be a movement to help a woman who desperately needs assistance and has come forward to ask for it." Jeri O'Leary stood up and seconded the motion.

It was Bridget Moretti's last direct effort to help June before turning the case over to Ralph Anderson. And it was a vitally important one. With an organization like the New Hampshire Coalition Against Domestic Violence on her side, June's motion to suspend the balance of her sentence would carry weight.

Before leaving, Bridget put in place everything June would need to make a strong case for that sentence reduction, and failing that, a pardon. She had always believed June's case might go as far as the governor's office, and had for months been garnering support for that eventuality. She had contacted politicians and personally called executive council members, explaining that if June failed in her upcoming sentence review hearing, she would immediately proceed with a request for a pardon hearing. She implored them to support June if that came to pass.

Bridget's efforts would become useful in the very near future, for as valiantly as Ralph Anderson argued his case, Judge Scott again denied June a reduced sentence. It made absolutely no difference to Scott that during the two years that had passed since his first refusal, June had grown even more, being labeled not only a "model prisoner," but "a leader among her peers," "a great help to prison officials," "educated and eloquent," "a mature, loving, and well-respected individual," and, as one prison guard would later write, "someone who had no business being here."

"We had more hope this time, but we knew who we were dealing with. And Ralph was new to the case. He didn't have much time to prepare, and he hadn't built up much momentum. I could see going in that our chances were still slim, but it made sense that we should go for it."

What made *no* sense to anyone — on either the state's side or June's side — was Judge Scott's position on the case, the true nature of which he finally revealed at the end of the hearing. When character and expert witnesses for both sides concluded their testimony, and June again made a plea for freedom, citing her excellent work and educational record in prison, the judge, as before, with utmost civility, commended her for the progress she had made "rehabilitating" herself. Though it was arguable that "rehabilitation" was ever the issue, June nodded her acceptance of the compliment.

Then the judge's demeanor changed drastically. A frown formed above the bridge of his nose as he took a deep breath and looked directly at June and said what he should have said four years earlier, saving attorneys for both sides hundreds of hours of preparation time, and June years of anxious, futile hoping: "Ms. Briand, I have no intention of *ever* reducing your sentence. The motion to suspend the balance of your minimum sentence is denied!" And he got up and walked out of the courtroom.

Rather than being crushed, June was elated. She had all but given up hope on Scott anyway, knowing he was and would always be a "lost cause" who could not see past his own small-minded thinking and his obvious ignorance — or prejudices — regarding domestic abuse. No argument in the world was going to change this man's mind, so the sooner June knew it, the better.

The delay of four years in discovering Scott's intransigence would be to June's benefit. The team of supporters that had amassed behind her had grown measurably, and would now go "full bore into pardon mode." The moment Scott made his announcement, he opened the gates for a stampede neither he nor anyone else could have imagined. There would be no turning back now. It was going to be "all or nothing," and "nothing was definitely *not* an option."

Unlike sentence review hearings, pardon hearings are not automatic, and granting them is solely at the discretion of the executive council. Convincing council members that such a hearing was warranted would be the first obstacle — and a formidable one. Pardon hearings are extremely rare, and are considered only in the most compelling cases. Such cases must be founded on solid evidence detailing why an individual should be considered for clemency, and how they have rehabilitated enough to return and be of service to society. That all comes *before* the actual hearing in hopes that it be granted. And it is what June's supporters would need to work on in preparation for making the request.

June, on the other hand, had been unwittingly preparing for the pardon hearing since she entered prison — most diligently during the two years just preceding it. Pam Smart had been of great service to June, as had Judge Scott. The delays they caused allowed June to broaden herself in many ways — ways that would be particularly impressive to council members and the governor during the pardon hearing, should it be granted.

During the prior five years, June had been on "minimum security status" and had "great accomplishments" according to prison official Jan Lamore. "June had time to examine the emotional damage in her life and work on healing it. At first, she was so frail-looking that she looked like a twig that might break at any moment, but over the years she blossomed from a scared little girl into a mature woman.

"She got things started and inspired others. For example, she saw potential in one class project — producing a prison newsletter — and developed it beautifully. She founded and became editor of the prison's first newspaper — it was remarkable! Later, she organized the first prison Summer Olympics. Then she asked for permission to paint a large children's mural on the visiting room wall. It was a major undertaking and had beautifully drawn pictures of balloons, animals, clowns, hillsides. The room was a dingy pale green and she wanted to liven it up for the children who came to visit their mothers. June thought about things like that; she was the only one who did."

Expanding on the artistic talents she developed in prison, June took a quilting class and became expert at designing and sewing intricate quilting patterns. She became a leader here too, and organized the AIDS quilt project so other inmates could get involved.

To broaden her life skills — and with an eye for developing marketable skills for when she got out of prison — June added to what she had learned in Margaret Simmons' office class by taking computer classes. She learned all the important software applications, and became so proficient in them that she eventually taught her own computer classes.

Following that, she decided to add to her GED education and took additional independent study classes in algebra, sociology, advanced math, and English. Again, she took a leadership role and formed her own prison classes, teaching writing, art, and humanities to inmates. She started a "Child Within" group and a "Long Termers" group to help those with long sentences cope better with their life behind bars. She was so effective at leading these groups that inmates started coming to her for individual counseling.

"These are accomplishments you just don't see in a convicted felon," said Lamore. "To achieve what she did while incarcerated. Well ... *I've* never seen it before, and the other prison personnel are just as impressed. June Briand was one of a kind. And the longer she was behind bars, the more we saw it was the wrong place for her."

The one who noticed June's accomplishments most was, as always, Anna Rosen. She saw the leadership June was providing the other inmates, and the thorough understanding she now had of domestic violence — its roots, its consequences, and the options that were now available to battered women.

"I saw what she was doing to help inmates," said Anna, "so I approached her one day and asked her if she would like to speak to others *outside* the prison — tell them her story and teach them what she had learned about domestic abuse. It would be educational for them and therapeutic for her. She didn't like the idea, but I worked on her. Still, she didn't want to go. Eventually I said she didn't have a choice, she *had* to go."

June was taken aback when Anna insisted she come with her to speak at the local college's Criminal Justice and Law Enforcement class. "She knew I was ready, but *I* didn't. I was petrified of getting up in front of a class of college kids and speaking. I didn't mind teaching classes to the women in prison, but going *outside* — that was another matter.

"Anna eased me into the speaking. She'd start off the lecture by talking about the Department of Corrections and how a prison is run. Then she'd introduce me and have me talk. I'd say a few words and then stop and look at her for help. She'd rescue me and talk again, then throw it back to me.

"It went like that the first five or six times. Then I got more comfortable speaking in front of people. After we'd gone about ten times, I had it down. We got to the point where she would just drop me off and come back and get me! I was like a *normal* person — for an hour anyway.

"But I'd dread the drive back to the prison. We'd be driving along and I'd see people walking and holding hands; people driving nice cars; stores with pretty clothes in the windows. How I hated going back on the tier! I wanted to educate myself like the students I was speaking to. I wanted what they had — what other normal, happy people had."

So she went to work on that too. June wanted a college education, and she was going to get it. "A college education?" one of the guards said later. "No one ever got a college education in Goffstown before. Never. But that didn't stop June."

June inquired about correspondence courses from Castle College in Windham, New Hampshire, which offered an Associate Degree for classes taken via mail and computer. She jumped at the chance to get it. There was one problem, however: the degree would cost money — way more money than June had, and more than she could possibly earn through her prison jobs. The college tuition was three thousand dollars for a year-long curriculum. June had a net worth of two hundred and forty dollars, "not including my upcoming paycheck of twenty-five dollars." She was crushed when the fee schedule flashed across her computer screen. But not so crushed that she would give up.

She inquired further, and discovered that Pell grants were available for student aid. She applied for it and received it, and in the fall of 1994, began her courses. Her lifelong dream of getting an education was coming true and she was thrilled. Her elation, however, would soon be dampened.

Though she excelled in all her classes, and was thoroughly enjoying them, she sensed something was different in the prison. "It was midway through the school year when I had this feeling. I couldn't quite get a handle on it, but the environment felt different. Eventually I saw what it was: I had alienated the other inmates."

June was now alone at her classroom computer terminal for hours each day, while most of her friends continued in their old routines: watching television, reading *People* magazine, eating junk food, sleeping the day away. A resentment was forming amongst them, and it was so insidious that June did not realize it until Valentine's Day, when she discovered a "June Briand Boycott."

"I noticed a coolness towards me that wasn't there before. I was breaking away from the rest of the group; I was at a turning point; I was on another path, and in prison, it was much like it was living with Jimmy: anyone who is getting educated and getting ahead is a threat — to the other inmates, to the guards, to *everyone.* I even saw it in Anna.

"I was getting well-known for speaking, so people would call and invite me to speak for their organization or class. But if it wasn't something Anna had arranged, she wouldn't give her permission. There was no reason in the world for her not to, but she saw me growing to her level and she didn't like it.

"I read somewhere that when the student reaches the mentor's level, watch out. And that was the case with us. Anna was very competitive, and when she saw I was becoming as educated as she was, she tried to hold me down. It was a control issue, but then, that was her business — controlling people. I was surprised and hurt by it, but I knew human nature so well by then that I understood it."

At the beginning of the summer the following year, 1995, June applied for her second year at Castle College to complete the remaining courses required for her degree. This time it would not be so easy. Like everything else in her life, an unexpected roadblock threatened to derail her aspirations: the law changed and there would be no more Pell grants allowed for inmates.

"When I heard that, I didn't know what to do. I was halfway through with my degree, and loving every minute of it. I knew we would eventually go for a pardon, and I needed an education for when I got out of prison. I had to finish that degree.

"I called Trish Morgan and Heidi Guhrer, my advocates, and told them about my problem. They pooled their money and gave me several hundred dollars towards the tuition. But I still needed about a thousand dollars, and the cutoff date was September 15. The only way I knew to make a lot of money fast was to sew quilts and sell them in the prison goods store. I had sold one before, so I knew it was possible."

Though it was possible, it was unlikely June could sell enough quilts to fund her college courses. But selling was only one problem; *making* was another. She had been ostracized by her fellow inmates, whose help she could no longer rely on. If she was going to make quilts, every stitch would have to be sewn by her.

"My fingers were raw by the middle of summer. Every spare moment I sat on my bunk sewing. I was sewing and selling, sewing and selling. Other than the fact that nobody liked me anymore, everything was going well. And by September 1, I had almost enough money. I just needed one more quilt to sell — but I didn't *have* one! I stayed up all night one night, then worked all day the next day and the next. Finally I finished it, but who knew if it would sell in time? I had five days left when I turned it into the store. I can't believe — after all the hearings and everything else I'd been through — how nervous I was about that quilt. But the day before the registration deadline, the store called and said I had the money. Trish and Heidi were so happy for me. I knew then that things were turning my way — or at least they seemed to be."

June went on to complete her studies with Castle College. Unable to attend graduation ceremonies, she received her Associate Degree in the mail. That was fine with her, for at that moment, June Briand became the first woman in the history of the state of New Hampshire to earn a college degree while incarcerated. It was a stunning achievement, and one that would be most impressive when June went before the executive council to request a pardon hearing.

"After that I set my sights much higher places — like over the walls and out of that place. Earning my degree made me want to get out of there for good, and it made me want to go for the pardon more than ever. The pardon was my last hope: I had to win."

Adding to June's sense of urgency was her desire to be with her daughters. She had not heard from either of them ever since the DCYF had stopped the visits seven years earlier. The Nortons had taken custody of Pam, and Jana was still moving about from one crisis center to another, still unable to cope with life. At one point, she had written a note later found by the supervisor of her home. In it she said that she "wanted to die" because "kids are making fun of me," and then went on to attempt suicide several times.

Pam, however, had been faring better. She had always been more resilient than Jana, and over the years had coped fairly well — even in a loud, violent home that was frothing with hatred for her mother, whom the Nortons openly called "a monster" and a "cold-blooded killer" and "the bitch that killed your father." Pam seemed to know instinctively that the animosity was not so much a genuine sentiment towards her mother as it was the Nortons' general state of mind.

The mother-hating indoctrination worked for a while. But as Pam grew into puberty, she grew beyond the Nortons' ability to "parent" (though in their case the verb seems ludicrous; they had demonstrated that they knew nothing whatsoever about healthy childrearing, with Jimmy being a prime example).

When she turned fourteen, Pam suddenly had a desire to see her mother, and "out of the blue," contacted June one day during the summer of 1996. "I had just received my college degree at the end of June and was very happy. Then I got a message saying Pam was calling on the telephone. Pam? Pam who? I couldn't believe it would be *my* Pam.

"I ran to take the call and sure enough, it was Pammy. She said she wanted to get out of the Nortons' house, that she wasn't happy there. Because I still had co-guardianship, the welfare department required her to ask my permission to leave. I told her to come to the prison and we could talk.

"The whole prison was watching when Pam came. They knew I hadn't seen my daughter since she was a little girl, and they wanted to see what happened. So did I. When she walked in, I could see the Nortons hadn't done a very good job: She was dressed way too sexy. She had on a little, short top with her belly all exposed, tight flared jeans, makeup. She was only fourteen; she looked twenty.

"The first thing she said was, 'Why didn't you write?' I was shocked. I wrote her all the time. And I sent Christmas presents and birthday presents. The Nortons hadn't given her any of them. I told her I could prove I sent them, and called over a friend of mine who had helped me wrap presents for the girls and knew I had written them letters. Pam listened to her, then she looked at me. She hesitated for a moment like she was trying to believe it, then she reached over and we hugged. It was very emotional. We were both crying. I was very, very happy to see her."

June told Pam that she would help her find a place to stay. Cynthia White, one of the women working at the local chapter of NOW, had said to June that "if you ever needed anything, you know you can always call me." Now June took her up on her offer. And indeed, she would help. Cynthia was a single woman, and had an extra bedroom she could give to Pam. The only condition was that Pam would have to go to school (which she was inclined *not* to do), come in by curfew, and generally obey her rules. Pam promised to cooperate, but within a week was in court for breaking every rule Cynthia had set.

"When you have lived in a home with no rules and a bunch of people screaming obscenities and hitting each other, you're not inclined to mind a new parent. Cynthia had to go to court because of some trouble Pam had gotten in immediately after moving in with her. But she agreed to buckle down and do better — and she did.

"She started improving her grades in school, and Cynthia had her visit me twice a week. That was a little difficult though. Since it was a rule, the visits were strained. And it didn't help that she had been living with a family that hated me. Plus, I was dealing with a teenager now. I could tell she wanted to be somewhere else a lot of the time, and it turned out it was with her boyfriend."

Cynthia told June that she had grounded Pam because she went into her boyfriend's house without the parents being home. She told Pam she couldn't do that, and found out that she had. When Pam visited June the next time, June asked her about it.

"Cynthia told me about you and Eric," said June. "You know you weren't supposed to be in the house alone. Why did you do that?"

"We weren't really in there alone."

"What is that supposed to mean?" asked June.

"I mean, I was in there just to change my bathing suit."

"Oh, I see. So you're saying that you were in the house naked, right?"

"No, I was just changing my suit."

"Well, you must have been naked if you were changing your suit."

"Not really."

"Yes, really," said June. "You're trying to con me and you can't. I can tell a con — I know them personally."

The prison visits would not last long. A month later, Cynthia was fed up with Pam, and the Nortons had asked for her back anyway. She left, and she stopped visiting her mother.

During the two years June had been completing her college degree and various other accomplishments, great progress was being made on the campaign to bring her case before the governor and his executive council. By mid-summer of 1996, it was time to move ahead with the pardon request. June hoped that if she was successful in winning her freedom, she could reunite with her daughter in a healthier setting, somehow bridge the gap of years that had passed, and re-establish relations.

There were no more sentence review hearings to worry about, and, thankfully, no more delays; the last delay occurred in the fall of 1995, and was the one thing that kept the pardon effort from moving forward. But in hindsight, it was another blessing, for it allowed June to complete her college degree and take that outstanding achievement with her into the pardon hearing.

The delay had come about that fall when June suddenly and unexpectedly lost Ralph Anderson as her attorney. As had happened with Bridget Moretti before him, Anderson was offered a position with the federal government, and had to withdraw from June's case. It was then late in 1995, and, thanks to the women of NOW, the movement to pardon June was mushrooming. Since the failed sentence reduction bid, they had mobilized and gained strength. Volunteers from other chapters of the organization, as well as the public at large in New Hampshire, Maine, Vermont, and Massachusetts got behind the movement.

There was only one gaping hole: no attorney. By this time though, nothing worried June. She had been through every possible adversity, delay, and disappointment, and she was still standing. She did not have an attorney. Fine. She would get one. And she did.

"I didn't panic, I just called Bridget and asked if she knew any attorneys that could help me. I called Ralph too. They both gave me names of attorneys — about twenty-five in all — who were likely advocates and might take the case pro bono. I sent them all letters, and this time got a quick response from Pat Moss, a woman and staunch feminist who practiced in Portsmouth, New Hampshire. She took over where Ralph left off, and by the following August of 1996, the pardon petition was completed and we were ready to request a hearing."

Enough support had been garnered by June's supporters through their mailings, phone calls, and petition drives to make a strong case before the governor and his executive council to grant June a full and fair pardon hearing. There had to be strong, convincing evidence that such a hearing should be held, and Pat Moss put together such evidence, and presented it to the council on October 23, 1996 at the Fidelity Investments building in Merrimack, New Hampshire, where the monthly meeting was held.

"This was almost more important than the hearing itself, which came a month later. If they hadn't granted us that hearing at the October meeting, we would have been sunk. But they listened to what Pat and the others had to say, and granted our request."

Twenty people came to the council meeting in Merrimack to support June's request for a hearing. They included Heidi and Trish, many of the volunteers, several NOW members, and numerous others who were sympathetic to the cause. All wore lapel cards with purple ribbons and a picture of June and the words **PARDON JUNE**. Trish said, "My hands were shaking when I went in there. It was an incredible feeling of relief when he granted the hearing."

June was not present at the meeting. Her case was item number twenty-six on the day's docket, and when the council went down their list of sundry community issues and came to June, they skipped over her and continued on to complete their regular business. When they finished, they returned to item number twenty-six.

Pat Moss then read her request for a hearing. Earlier, the council had been given enough information about the case to make a decision, and after discussing the matter briefly, the five members of the council retired to a private room to take a vote. With them were the governor and the attorney general of the state of New Hampshire. It did not take long. The governor came forth and indicated the result: 5-0 in favor of granting a hearing. The councilors had unanimously decided that a hearing was in order, but it was the governor, more than anyone else, who had deep reservations about making such a move.

As he said later, he "agonized" over granting the hearing, knowing full well that it would be the first step toward letting a convicted killer go free. But he decided that though he had the power to veto anything his executive council decided, he would not block their vote on this matter.

"I've actually changed my mind twice on this Briand matter in the last twenty-four hours," he said. "I've talked to the prior chair of my commission on domestic violence, and the current chair ... and [we've decided that] we ought to consider domestic violence and spousal abuse in such matters as pardons."

The tide had turned. June was on her way. The next hurdle would be to present an compelling case that could not lose. They had come too far to allow any further defeats. A defeat now would be unconscionable. Too much work had been done; the cause was too great. Indeed, it was about more than June Briand now — it was about women everywhere who were suffering, unseen and unheard, in their own private hells. June had to win — for herself and for them — and Pat Moss would stop at nothing until she did.

The first thing Moss did was hire a brilliant law student named Vera Lansky to help with the Pardon Petition. It would be a major undertaking, requiring hundreds of hours of work reviewing thousands of pages of documents, records, etc., then more time preparing the final document with all its attachments, appendices, and other ancillary materials.

"This has to be a powerful and well-organized piece of writing," Moss had said. "It has to highlight June Briand's background; the abuse she suffered from her husband,

James; and it must have full documentation by expert witnesses explaining the result of that abuse and hence, her state of mind at the time of the crime. It must show how impressive her rehabilitation had been, and include letters of support from those who knew her and witnessed her dramatic transformation."

Moss emphasized that there had to be *reasons* for the governor to let a convicted killer out of prison before her allotted time was up, and those reasons had to be brilliantly elucidated in the materials brought to the council. "June has to prove to the council that she was not just a battered woman who is now rehabilitated," said Moss. "She has to show she is shining now, and that she would make a major contribution to society if she were given executive clemency."

To accomplish this herculean task, and produce a first-rate, convincing, and legally sound petition, Pat Moss and Vera Lansky amassed a wealth of material that had not been considered when June was originally sentenced for her crime. At that time, she did not stand trial, so was unable to present what Moss and Lansky compiled for the pardon hearing: witness statements, Jimmy's police record, June's hospitalization records, letters and recommendations of those who knew June to be a rehabilitated and educated woman of character, and letters from friends, inmates, prison staff, and people who had heard June speak on domestic violence.

Perhaps the most telling statement of all was a profile personally written by June detailing the tragic and brutal life she lived with her husband. (Parts of that profile were later omitted, with attorney Moss stating, "the specifics of his sexual abuse are too horrific to detail.")

All this was given to the governor and five council members who held June's fate in their hands and hearts. There would be ample time for them to read and digest the materials before the official pardon hearing, which was to be held one month later at 2 p.m. on Wednesday, November 20, 1996, at the Merrimack County Superior Court. It would be a month of anxiety and anticipation for June and her supporters, but no one would have time to get mired in emotion. Too much needed to be done, and once again, the wheels of the Briand pardon machine churned forward, this time building so much momentum that nothing could stop them.

"It was remarkable what had happened," said Ben Humphrey, a reporter who knew the case well. "Here was a woman who began the pardon process from her jail cell in Goffstown, writing letters to newspapers and attorneys in a last, desperate bid for freedom. What she got in response was a virtual tsunami of support from people who understood her plight and understood Battered Woman's Syndrome; they pulled out all the stops to win that freedom for her."

Humphrey had not exaggerated. Activists circulated petitions, put out mass mailings, contacted the media, even set up a website to inform people of the issues involved in the case. They won for June the support of numerous agencies, clergy, elected officials, even the mayor of Portsmouth, New Hampshire, who would later send her letter of support. Volunteers telephoned politicians and council members asking for support.

But the successful outcome of that hearing was anything but assured. "Don't presume this hearing will lead to approval of her pardon request," said the governor. "I can tell you that the councilors haven't made up their minds on this case — nor have I." June and her lawyers knew the governor meant what he said; and kept in mind that it was Merrill himself who had prosecuted June for murder ten years earlier.

The November 20, 1996, hearing was to be a public one. "We're not going to try her in the press," said Ann Wilson, one of the councilors. "This is going to be a public hearing where Ms. Briand is going to be given an opportunity to tell her story completely and plea for forgiveness and freedom." And among those listening would be the angry Norton clan.

Prior to the start of the hearing, the governor met separately with both sides — the Nortons and June's supporters. "Ostensibly, he wanted to comfort the family," said Moss. "But he also wanted the Nortons to know that he would not tolerate outbursts of any kind, and that they would be removed from the courtroom and possibly arrested if they failed to heed the warning."

Because of the numerous death threats June had received from them and others over the years, security at Merrimack County Superior Court was extremely tight that day. The state took the death threats seriously, and had both uniformed and plainclothes policemen surround June when she arrived from prison. As they had done for her initial hearing in 1987, the police moved June along quickly, and this time, surreptitiously brought her into the building through a secret underground tunnel system.

Upon entering the darkened tunnel, June felt anxious. She knew about tunnels, and remembered the moans and wailing that had come from beneath the Goffstown prison floor. Underground tunnels, dirt roads, isolated places — they were never good things. Stepping into the tunnel seemed like a bad omen again, one she could do without — especially at a time like this.

But June had no time to ruminate. From the moment she emerged from the unmarked police vehicle and entered the building, her entourage zipped through the dimly-lit tunnels at nearly a full run. At this point, and after ten years of incarceration, the authorities didn't want any foul ups.

Edgy, plainclothes police kept turning their heads to the side and speaking into small, black microphones attached to their coat collars. June was too nervous to discern what they were saying, and kept moving through the murky bowels of the building until suddenly, the group popped up into a brightly-lit courtroom.

Cameras flashed and television lights blazed, blinding June as she was quickly hustled into the jammed courtroom. Reporters, journalists, news anchors, police, supporters, opponents, witnesses, public — everyone was there. Even the vice president of the national headquarters of NOW flew in from Washington, DC, for the hearing, and was sitting in the front row.

Squinting at the flashing cameras, June looked around in confusion and saw Pat Moss and Vera Lansky motioning her to move to the large oak conference table, where she sat down in a straight-backed wooden chair. Next to her sat an armed policeman; in front, a phalanx of squatting, kneeling photographers aimed lens-tipped barrels of every size and description at her head and clicked away with abandon. June showed little emotion, but her lips were tight and her face a pasty white.

The hearing was slated to last two hours; it would go on for over six, during which time witnesses from both sides would testify in support of their claim that either June should be released early, or conversely, she should serve out her entire fifteen-year term. Not unexpectedly, the Norton contingent came out "with guns blazing. They were there for war," said a reporter who was present. "And they did everything they could to win it — including fabricate nonexistent incidents, and deny those most damaging to their case."

As during the original sentencing hearing some seven years earlier, the Nortons were intent on one thing and one thing only: "Punish the bitch that took our son away." They would take the stand and plead — with every dirty tactic they could dredge up — to keep June Briand behind bars.

"It was amazing. Jimmy's parents hated him until the day he died. Then, all of a sudden, he's an archangel." And it became the Nortons' goal, their mission, to continue the punishment one of their own had failed to complete. And they had a helper.

Before they testified, some of the most damaging statements had already come in a letter to Governor Merrill from Dorothy Parker, a senior assistant attorney general. The letter said, in part, "The criminal Justice Bureau of the Attorney General's Office feels strongly that a pardon should not be granted." She felt that because of evidence of abuse, the state had already shown June compassion. "Instead of seeking a minimum of twenty-two to thirty-five years, the state took the unusual step of recommending a minimum of fifteen years ... The sentence imposed in this case recognizes the sanctity of human life and the importance of deterring others from resorting to the taking of life, even in extreme cases."

Jimmy's father, Randolph, also wrote a letter to the governor. It said, in part, "She will go on with her life, but my son will still be dead. The thought of her being released before her time is up makes my blood run cold. Releasing her now would make a mockery of my son's death."

As it happened, the only mockery came from the Nortons' own mouths. A reporter wrote: "The hate and loathing that spewed forth from these people was hard to believe, and hard to listen to — but not at all convincing to the council members who sat wondering how so many members of one family could breed such contempt for another human being."

When Jimmy's cousin, Phyllis, took the stand, she said, "We can't get on with our lives knowing that a murderer might be let out of prison. She sentenced my cousin to that grave forever. June pulled the trigger four times at Jimmy's head and she's only served ten years. We're not the criminal, she is. Jimmy is not the criminal, she is."

Phyllis was followed by Jimmy's stepmother, Leslie Norton, who took the witness stand but did not have the courage to look over at June as she sat next to her attorney, taking in stride venomous Norton testimony that was about to self-destruct. Said Leslie, "Every time a sentence review comes up, she [June] comes up with all these new little goodies to spread out there. And I'm sure there are a lot of people who read these comments about our son and think: 'The bastard got what he deserved.'" Just as she had done in sentencing hearing, Leslie Norton testified that her son was a perfect gentlemen, a rowdy-but-kind chap who never laid a hand on his wife. "Never. Never," said Norton, when she took the witness stand. "There is no evidence whatsoever. We have asked the state of New Hampshire for years to show us evidence of abuse. There is none. You've all been *fooled* by June! How can her supporters support her without any facts? All they have is her word and that's the word of a murderer."

At that point, Pat Moss asked the council members to please turn to the document entitled Master List, whereupon Leslie Norton's testimony fell utterly to pieces. The thick document was a seventy-five-page report containing June's medical records, dating back twelve long, tortuous years to 1984. In it was chronicled injury after injury for the years she spent bent over with arms wrapped around herself trying to protect herself from her husband's blows: "Unexplained shoulder pain; lower back pain; unexplained cessation of menstrual periods; facial swelling and bruises on the right side; multiple contusions about the head and face; collarbone injury; rib injury; acute cervical pain; radiculopathy down right arm; chronic headaches; chronic depression; unexplained nervousness ..." and on and on.

Pat Moss then followed with a devastating witness. He was Milt Grenwald, a neighbor of the Briands when they lived on Central Street. He had called Moss's office after reading an excerpt of an interview with June that was ran in *Double Time*, a prison newspaper. The article was subsequently picked up and reprinted in his local paper, whereupon his conscience got the best of him.

Grenwald had called the bar association and asked who was handling the Briand case. They gave him Moss's phone number, after which she asked him to come to the hearing. When he took the stand, he destroyed any remaining credibility the Nortons may have been clinging to in regard to Jimmy Briand's innocence.

"I'm the neighbor who saw Jimmy hang the baby out the window," said Grenwald.

"And why didn't you come forward before?" asked Moss.

"Because my wife is related to the Nortons, and they told us not to talk."

Pat Moss then gave her own knockout blow to Leslie Norton by reminding the governor and council members of Jimmy's long police record sent earlier, including statements by officers who had been both verbally threatened and physically assaulted by Briand. She handily refuted Norton's denial of her stepson's violent nature by referring the council to the Appendix to the Pardon Petition — another voluminous document that contained one hundred-eighteen pages of testimony from expert after expert stating that June had gone through, as one wrote, "a hell no one could imagine."

Psychologists, sociologists, professors, doctors — they all made statements or wrote letters that were included in the appendix and which summarily demolished Leslie Norton's claim that June had "fooled" anybody. Letters also came from former inmates; correctional personnel; a nun at Castle College who characterized June as a "straight A student, except for one B+;" people who had heard her speak; and seacoast residents who wrote, "We welcome June into our community when she is released."

The mayor of Portsmouth, New Hampshire, Eileen Foley, wrote, "Obviously she had been a battered woman. A great many people have come to her aid." Other supporters included clergy such as Rabbi David Mark, who said, "her value to society is much greater outside prison than in." Reverend Robert Stiefel, rector of Christ Episcopal Church, said, "Our society has yet to accept the seriousness of abuse from spouse to spouse. The woman has suffered greatly and a pardon is morally right."

Witness after witness — including those who attended June's numerous other hearings — took the stand in her defense, all of them ardently believing that the time had come for her to return as a useful member of society. But the Nortons, though they were knocked down, were not out cold yet, and they retaliated in the most scurrilous possible way.

The first shocker came when they offered up June's estranged daughter, Jana, now eighteen, who testified that she hoped her mother would remain behind bars, that she feared for her life and believed her mother had killed her father "in cold blood." Though she was not directly raised by the hatemongers Pam had been influenced by, she visited at the Norton home often enough to absorb the deeply-entrenched loathing they had for June. "If she's released," said Jana, with her mother sitting less than twenty feet away, "I'll be waiting for the day she kills me — or hires someone to do it."

"The accusation," wrote one reporter, "came out like a dagger, thrown recklessly across the packed Merrimack County courtroom and cutting deep into the gut of June Briand."

But it was quickly countered by more credible witnesses, Theresa Doran, the sociologist and domestic violence expert who had worked extensively with June: "The children were raised and surrounded by people who were clearly hostile to their mother, who portrayed her as a calculating, cold-blooded murderer ... When that's the type of message you get over and over for years, that becomes your reality. For kids to survive, it's crucial for them to fit in with the family that's nurturing them...[so they] learned hate for their own mother."

Failing here, the Nortons tried again. This time they produced Jana's mother, Cheryl — Jimmy's ex-girlfriend who had given her away at eighteen months of age. Like Leslie, she testified that Jimmy was not a violent man in the least, and that all the stories June and the psychologists had told were "made up." When Moss questioned her about the abuse she suffered at the hands of Jimmy Briand — such as the time "she got mouthy" and was "knocked out cold" by him — she denied it ever happened.

"So is it your testimony that James Briand never physically assaulted you?" asked Moss.

"That's correct."

"And you had no problems whatsoever with him, no reason to fear him?"

"That's correct."

Then Moss sifted through the papers on her table and produced the one she was looking for. She lifted up a yellow document and said, "Then can you tell the governor and councilors why you took out this restraining order on him?"

Cheryl looked around the courtroom nervously. Her eyes darted to the attorney and then to the Norton contingent; then back to the attorney. She could not answer the question — couldn't even form the beginning of a response.

"I have nothing further with this witness," said Moss, and Cheryl shakily stepped from the stand.

The governor had sat patiently listening to the profusion of propaganda touting the merits of James Briand and the misdeeds of June Briand. Finally, he stopped the barrage; he had heard enough of the one-sided testimony from the Norton clan. By then, to everyone in the courtroom — except the Nortons — their attempt to color their dead comrade as a fallen hero rather than the sadistic brute he was, was becoming ludicrous —if not patently absurd. Governor

Merrill decided it was time to do some questioning of his own.

He turned and began to grill the Norton family. He said to Leslie that if Jimmy was not the type of man to strike his wife, why did Jack Spiller say in his initial statement to police that he saw Jimmy smack her in the mouth? And if domestic violence wasn't the reason for June's actions, what was? Why would she choose to shoot her husband? It was then that the Nortons began to falter, babbling nonsense to the councilors and themselves. With no supporting evidence whatsoever, one of the clansmen said that perhaps June had caught her husband cheating on her. Another suggested she might have had a new lover and wanted her husband out of the way. Neither the councilors nor the governor lent any credence to their feeble responses.

It was now seven-thirty in the evening. The two-hour hearing had stretched to over five. But no one was falling asleep. Rather than diminishing, the tension in the room increased as the hours went by. Like Romans watching gladiators battle lions, everyone in the jammed courtroom was watching a woman fight for her life.

Witnesses heard, arguments over, it was time to hear from June herself. But before making her statement, her sister, Diane, requested the floor. Again she had flown out from California to comfort and support her sister, and wanted to make clear to those assembled what they had endured while growing up.

"You must remember that we were raised by our fanatical grandparents; that alcohol and drug abuse and constant emotional battering were what we knew. It is nothing short of a miracle that any of us survived.

"People ask, 'Why didn't she leave her husband?' It's an easy question to ask, but a difficult one to answer. When she says, 'Because my husband threatened to kill me if I did,' that's what she means. June believed him. She considered coming out to California once, and called to ask me about it. She was so frightened even *thinking* about the idea, that even though Jimmy was across the street working, she was whispering on the phone; I could barely hear her.

"No one can say about her failing to leave, 'Oh, that doesn't make sense,' because opinions are judgments made by those who were not in her situation. You can't say what you would do unless you were June; just be glad you weren't."

One of the council members, Charles Slater, took exception with what Diane had said. Among the five council members, he was considered the most skeptical—the one needing the most convincing that June was, in fact, a woman who was so incapacitated that she could do nothing about her situation. But instead of directing his query to Diane, he focused on June and said, "You mean to tell me you couldn't pick up a phone and call for help?"

June met the challenge head-on. She had been through a great deal in her life, and this bit of aggression was nothing she couldn't handle with poise and intelligence. "There were no 800 numbers back then, Mr. Slater," said June directly and without equivocation. "No domestic abuse hotline. There was a grand total of three women's shelters in the entire state at that time. Domestic abuse was not well-recognized ten years ago. Plus, as Diane said, I was certain my husband would come find me if I tried to leave. And I assure you — he *would* have."

When the pardon hearing was first granted, Pat Moss told June that just because the first hurdle had been reached, a pardon "is not a sure thing by any means." Now those words resounded in June's head, and she began to talk "a blue streak." The councilors had said at the beginning of the hearing that they did not want any "psycho-babble" or additional information on domestic violence—they had all that. And June had no intention of giving them either one. But she did need to make her case.

"She was not timid at all," said one supporter who was present. "In fact, there was a point there when her attorney got a little nervous." Charles Slater had interrupted her again when she started talking about the Nortons and how they had raised her daughter. He tried to wave her onto another topic, saying, "Miss Briand, we know how you feel about the family."

"No, you don't!" June shot back instantly. "You have the notion that I hate the family, but the truth is, I do not hate them — I feel sorry for them having lost a son. I'm a mother too, and can imagine what that must have been like. The only problem I have with them is the way they parented my children."

Slater sat back in his chair. June continued with her final comments, and they were impressive: "When I first came to prison, I didn't talk, I didn't look at people, I didn't have any skills, people or otherwise. I was a very tired young woman who had been in one bad relationship after another .... Now I'm somebody who has a really good sense of herself and someone who has a lot of self-esteem; someone who's had a lot of therapy and a lot of education and who's been able to come so full circle that I'm actually able to help others where before I couldn't even help myself."

June spoke with eloquence and sincerity. And she spoke with love — the love she had always longed from her husband; the love she tried so hard to give him. Now the executives had a golden opportunity to let this once-broken woman spread well-being to a world of lonely, hurting women who needed it as much as she did. Would they take the opportunity? Or would they do as Judge Scott had done, and remain bound to an antiquated judicial system that was slave to its own ignorance?

Everyone — even the Nortons — listened intently as June finished her comments. She turned directly to Jimmy's family and said, "I know you won't believe me, but I truly am sorry." Then back to the councilors: "I have to find out where I'll fit in and where others will allow me to fit it. I have a murder charge and that is something that I will drag with me forever; it will always haunt me. I come here not to ask you to condone what I did or ask for forgiveness; I come here to ask for mercy."

There was a hush in the courtroom now. No one moved; no one spoke. It was as if June's words slowly seeped into everyone, percolating deep down into their souls — and they knew she spoke the truth. A moment went by, then another. Then a woman in the back row began to weep. Several others dabbed their eyes, choking back tears. And the Nortons sat like stones, not knowing what to do, but certain they had failed.

When June was through speaking, she sat back in her chair, composed and self-assured — not assured that she had won over the governor and his council, but assured that she, and all those who supported her, had done all they could. Nothing more *could* be done; her fate was up to six people who now had to judge what they had heard and read. They had to make a decision, and if the past was any indicator, there was no certainty that it would be the right one. But still, June was content.

The Nortons, however, were not. As the hearing broke up and the crowd began to file out of the courtroom, a disturbance could be heard in the hallway just inside the front door. June and her lawyers were still at the table and not aware of it, but the sheriff in the hall was: the Nortons were beating each other up again. Reminiscent of June's wedding day at the Canadian Club, when the Nortons got together, they attacked each other.

In this case, the altercation was between two cousins who were so violent and so volatile, they had already taken out restraining orders on *each other*. Neither had seen the other for several months, and they now they took this opportunity to totally disregard the serious proceedings that had just transpired, and regress back to their old hatred of one another, screaming obscenities at each other across the crowded hallway. Before it could come to blows, the sheriff moved in and grabbed one of the cousins and marched him out the door. He told the other to wait right where he was, that he would return and direct him out another exit.

Deciding there were too many law enforcement officers in the vicinity to argue, Skip Norton complied, and waiting in agitation to be escorted from the building. But after being ushered out, he stood by the front door, and this time, verbally attacked June's supporters as they left the building.

Skip screeched at the first woman, a NOW member, "How can you support that lying bitch?!" Not getting a response, he ran frantically to another woman and thrust his face in hers and said, "Remember my face! You'll be seeing it again!" But these were strong, confident women. Such childish displays of braggadocio and belligerence did not faze them at all.

After ten long years, nothing had changed with the Nortons. They had not grown; they had not forgiven; they had not *improved*. They held just as much animosity toward June as they ever had, and would be happy with nothing less than further punishment for a woman who proved she needed no more. *Revenge* was their operative motive, and they had not the intellectual capacity to rise above it. Everyone else present that day prayed that the governor and his council did.

But no one would know the council's decision that day. They decided not to take a vote at the end of the hearing, and instead, would "take the matter under advisement" (careful consideration). The original plan, it was understood, would be that if the council did not decide at the Wednesday hearing, they would announce their decision by that Friday, three days later. But Friday came and went, and still there was no word from anyone at the governor's office.

The press, in the meantime, had contacted the council members to see which way they were leaning. One member, Richard Conway, said, "I'm not leaning either way right now. I'll continue to review the testimony before making a decision, so don't count me a yes or a no." This was not encouraging news.

Another member, the tough-to-convince Charles Slater, said he had "not ruled out the pardon," but was "reserving judgment" until he could review additional evidence the following week. Ann Wilson said she was "leaning toward a pardon," but that she, too, needed more time. Councilor Thomas Pickering said, "It's clear to all sides — except Jimmy Briand's family —that there's been a remarkable change in June Briand in the past ten years, and that June has worked hard to improve herself ... This proves people do change, and she obviously has."

Lawrence Schwartz, another council member, said that after reviewing Jimmy Briand's police record, he was convinced that the Norton family had not "come to grips" with his violent side. "He clearly was not what he was portrayed to be by his stepmother," said Schwartz. "I think that other information that's come forward certainly points to a different side of the story; it certainly doesn't help the Norton family case."

Though June's "remarkable change" may have been obvious to Pickering and the others, and the Nortons' testimony had been absurdly weak, there would be no quick resolution to the matter of *The State v. June Briand.* On Friday afternoon, when it was clear that the word would not be coming back from the governor's office, the press contacted June in Goffstown and asked her how she felt about the hearing — particularly her daughter's painful attack.

"I wasn't expecting her to say that. But I knew she'd say something that would grab the council's attention. And what would be the most sensational, inflammatory thing she could say?"

Another reporter had asked council member Pickering the same question. The reporter wrote: "Jana Briand's remarks didn't cut it with the five-member council. [Thomas Pickering said] 'It's clear to me that no one feels June is a danger to anyone — not to her daughter, not to her family and not to anyone else. I would be surprised in any of them [on the council] gave any credence to it at all.'"

In her prison interview, June said that although her daughter's testimony "was heartbreaking," it was comforting to see the council's skepticism: "I think they could see that this girl was being raised in a family that held me up as a liar … I think they saw through that … they know what the court records say."

Another reporter had stopped Pat Moss on her way out of the courthouse, and asked her how she felt about the six-hour hearing. She said simply, "We believe that the truth will prevail and support June Briand's story of what happened back then."

He also caught up with Stephanie Rydell, an outreach coordinator for A Safe Place, a seacoast shelter for battered women, who said, "She is totally rehabilitated by all aspects, and she needs to be out in the public telling women that they have choices, they don't have to resort to violence or allow themselves to be victimized."

Local television station, Channel 9, opened a call-in voting line, asking *Should June Briand be pardoned, Yes or No?* Most were sympathetic to June's plight, and the result of the poll was overwhelmingly in favor of a pardon. But to a conservative, often stodgy New England populace, there were those who felt she should serve out her time.

The vote that mattered, however, did not come on Friday or Monday or Tuesday or Wednesday. Now a week had passed, and Pat Moss was getting nervous. Is it a good sign when a jury stays out for an unexpectedly long time? One lawyer will say yes, the other no. In this case, Moss quit speculating and the following week called the governor's office directly to ask about the delay. "He's not here," said his secretary. "He's in Grand Rapids, Michigan, at a Republican governors' convention. He won't be back until next week."

Next week? Michigan? No one had said that Merrill would — of all things — leave the state immediately after the hearing! Perhaps he took the opportunity to reflect further on the case and wanted the councilors to do the same. It had been a terribly difficult decision just allowing the hearing in the first place; making the *ultimate* decision would prove to be even tougher. Neither he nor the councilors wanted to make a mistake they would have to live with.

The news that there would be a longer delay was not all bad. Though June and her supporters were anxious to hear the council's determination, the fact that the delay had come from the governor's absence rather than indecision was a welcome relief. "It's not as though they were deadlocked or sitting on the fence," said one supporter. "So we were thankful for that. Still, everyone was on pins and needles the whole time."

Almost two weeks later, the agonizing wait finally came to an end. By then, Pat Moss was calling the governor's office on a daily basis, trying to get some indication of what was going to happen and when. June and Pat had become close during the long preparation for the trial, and now considered each other personal friends. Pat cared deeply about winning a pardon for June, and had taken on no additional cases during the months leading up to the hearing. She worked days, nights, and weekends on nothing but the pardon.

Reams of paper — literally thousands of pages of material — had been reviewed, written, sent, received. Motions, evidence, statements, histories filled over a dozen legal file boxes. Moss "wanted this one" and worked nonstop with her assistants to free her friend and "bring a spotlight to bear on the issue of domestic violence" which, according to the surgeon general, "has become an epidemic in our country."

Winning this case was important; determining if she *had* was torture. Finally, the torment ended late on the night of December 3, 1996. Pat Moss was at home trying unsuccessfully to focus her on attention on other things, but thinking only about June and the pardon. The phone rang much later than usual — it was the governor. He was back from Michigan and said a decision had been reached. His terse message was: "Get on the agenda for tomorrow, and be on standby." He was going to announce his decision at a public meeting rather than in a private session with June and her attorneys. The issue had been heard publicly, and he wanted the decision to be public as well.

It is not clear why the case was put on a "standby" status, but late in the morning the next day, Moss received another call from the governor's office: "Be here at 2 p.m." This time the meeting would be held in the executive council chamber of the Statehouse in Concord, New Hampshire. It was all Moss had to hear. The waiting was over; June's fate would be known in a few hours.

Pat called the prison to give June the news. "I hadn't been sleeping or eating all that well. After so many hearings and so many years, I thought I was over being nervous, but I wasn't. At least I didn't throw up. But I was definitely anxious. Our bids had been rejected so many times before that I didn't want to assume anything. Plus, what could I do now? The decision was made, and whatever it was, I had to live with it. But I was praying."

Having no appetite at all, June declined lunch that day. And it was a good thing: The van transporting her to the Statehouse came earlier than expected. Two state troopers escorted June into the unmarked van, and with a detachment of security police and two Concord policemen following in another vehicle, the caravan headed toward the majestic building with the gold-leaf dome.

June dressed for the occasion. She wore a grey skirt, white collared shirt, and black wool cardigan sweater. Her dark hair was short now, about chin-length, and parted in the middle and tucked behind each ear. It was normally a thirty-minute drive to the Statehouse, but there was a problem: they were too early. Over the police radio, the officers were told to detour and take June to the Department of Corrections building; apparently, the governor was not ready.

It was a smart move. The press had already begun to congregate at the Statehouse, and would not expect the detour; nor would anyone else who might pose a threat to June's security — and there were many. Death threats came in again, only this time there were more, and the state responded with the tightest security ever. But that was not the immediate concern; holding June safely away from the building was.

"For some reason, we had to wait, so they drove me to the office of the Commissioner of Corrections which was in a different building not far from the Statehouse. When I walked in, there was Anna Rosen. She had recently been promoted to Assistant Commissioner of Corrections, and they brought me to wait in her office. I guess they thought I needed the moral support.

"Anna was very happy to see me, but if she knew what decision had been made, she didn't show any signs of it. We talked for a little while, then she called the governor's office. They were ready. They told her to bring me over, and we all got in the van and drove to the Statehouse. About that time, I was starting to shake again. Anna said not to worry, but how could you not?"

As they had done two weeks earlier at the Merrimack County Superior Court, the officers drove the van to a rear entrance of the Statehouse and hustled June into a door on the lower floor. There they were met by six more security agents who knew the building well and took the entourage on another high-speed, circuitous route. Again, they spoke in hushed tones into lapel microphones, and again, they were running through hallways, around corners, and down corridors until they emerged into a deserted hall lined with offices.

A security agent opened one of the heavy oak office doors. Waiting inside was Vera Lansky, the law student who had put together the Pardon Petition. June nearly broke down when she saw her, but somehow maintained her composure. Anna took her by the arm and walked her to one of several chairs in the office. Again, they would wait.

"By then, I was exhausted. I was tired from not sleeping, but it was more the emotional drain of the morning. I talked to Vera and Anna for a few minutes, then bent over and rested my head on my arms and closed my eyes. I could hear people coming and going in and out of the office, and talking in whispers. But I didn't pay much attention; I just wanted to rest.

"I don't know how many minutes had gone by when I felt a presence next to me. I opened my eyes slightly and saw a man's leg out of the corner of my eye. He was standing right next to me. I sat up and turned around; it was the governor."

Stephen Merrill had personally walked over to see June before the public forum began. He felt it would be best to inform her of his decision before the meeting so she would not be surprised. He sat down in the chair next to her. She looked directly into his eyes. This was the man who had sent her to prison ten long years before. He was the man the

Hudson police had called in the early morning of February 12, 1987, asking what June was to be charged with. After hearing the brief details of the crime that night, he had said, "Charge her with first-degree murder."

Now, ten minutes before the public meeting was to begin, Merrill took June's hand. "I was the hardest to convince," he said, holding June's hand in his. "But you did it. We're going to change your sentence."

June was momentarily stunned. She heard the governor's words, but they did not register in her head. She had waited so long for this moment, and so many times before it was not forthcoming. Finally, June Briand had won. She had lost many battles en route to victory, but finally she had won the war.

When she recovered her senses, June's response to the governor was straight from the heart. She looked at the man who had prosecuted her, incarcerated her, and was now about to free her. She paused for a moment, then said, "Can I hug you?" Rather than answer, Merrill opened his arms and gave June a long, warm embrace. It was over. And now they were now going to tell the world about it.

The governor's office had attempted to contact the Norton family earlier that morning to tell them of the hastily called meeting, but failed to reach them. Consequently, the family would first learn of the pardon on the evening news later that night. But June's supporters were there and they were exuberant. When the meeting was brought to order, they instantly fell silent, eager to hear what the governor had to say.

"This whole verdict is one of the most difficult, if not the most difficult, decisions we've ever made in public life," said Merrill, referring to himself and the executive council. And indeed, for Merrill, it was. He said later that he had spent a sleepless night debating whether he and the council were making the right decision. Like the vote back in October granting the November 20 hearing, Merrill again had the power to veto the council's unanimous 5-0 vote to pardon June. And he struggled with that power all night long. Finally, he came to a personal peace about it, and knew his council had made the right decision.

"The first question for us to decide," he continued, "is, based upon a finding of the provocation of spousal abuse, how much time should a remarkably rehabilitated prisoner such as June Briand serve in order to satisfy both the law and justice under the circumstances?"

The governor continued to speak, and as he did, it became clearer and clearer to those in attendance, that he was laying the foundation for, and justifying as thoroughly as possible, the verdict he would momentarily announce. This was a story that had grown far beyond the Merrimack County border. It had become such a *cause célèbre* that it caught the attention of the entire nation, as Peter Jennings of ABC News would verify later that evening. The governor knew the country was watching, and, thus, chose his words carefully.

He went on: "We [the executive council] unanimously agree that June Briand presently bears little resemblance to the tormented perpetrator of the terrible act in question ... June Briand was raised in a chaotic and disruptive environment ... She suffered both physical and psychological trauma that affected her ability to deal in a mature manner with the circumstances of her life ... There is sufficient evidence of physical and emotional abuse to constitute a finding of what is commonly known as Battered Woman's Syndrome ... Through expert testimony, we know of her personality transformation and her outstanding achievements ... She has a persuasive record of service on the issue of battered women's syndrome ... Her rehabilitation is impressive."

Merrill concluded by saying, "Clemency is justified in those extraordinary cases ... where circumstances make executive intervention appropriate. This is such a case." And he granted the pardon.

Earlier, before he made his statement or spoke with June privately, Pat Moss had met with the executive council who informed her of their decision just as the governor had done with June. They also told her in that closed meeting that after the governor spoke, June would be allowed to make a short statement. When he finished, he turned the floor over to June.

"I would like to thank the executive council for taking the care that you did to investigate those things that I brought to you ... and I'd like to let you know that I will move forward now and I will do those things that I promised to help other battered women not end up in my position.

"I'm the result of what happens when you don't know how to get help ... I would tell other battered women that it doesn't have to end like this, and there are numerous alternatives and they need to take advantage of them. Violence is not the answer ... Let it be someone who watches this and says, 'My God, don't let this happen to me.' I can only give people my story and hope for the best."

EPILOGUE

June left the Statehouse the same way she had come in — running. If the security guards were worried about threats to her safety *before* the decision was announced, they were even more concerned afterwards, and redoubled their efforts to keep her from becoming a target. They again eluded the press and whisked June into a patrol car and back to Goffstown where she was met with hugs, kisses, tears, and cheers. The cheers were for her triumph; the tears were for the farewell that would soon be coming.

The press, however, did catch up with the executive council members and others as they left the Statehouse, many of whom explained the reasons for their actions. Thomas Pickering said, "After ... receipt of a lot of information on both sides, it became evident that the person we're dealing with today is not the person who committed the crime back in 1987."

Charles Slater, a skeptic from the start, took it upon himself to research police and medical records that corroborated June's story, and was finally satisfied that June was definitely an abused woman who was driven to act as she had. He said, "I hope Jimmy Briand's family will seek help to cope with their anger."

Pat Moss reiterated that, and also hoped that the Nortons could move on with their lives. "I hope that they can move forward in their grieving process, maybe address the hatred they have for June and realize it's not helpful in dealing with the girls. June wants to get on with her life too. She knows that there is now a light at the end of the tunnel. She would like to have her story be essentially a lesson for women in similar situations. What she did was wrong and there are now alternatives to violence. Those alternatives include divorce, restraining orders, and battered women's shelters."

Jeri O'Leary from the New Hampshire Coalition Against Domestic Violence said, "The message this sends to others in violent relationships is that we're beginning to understand how much terror and torture exist in American families and we're trying to do something about it."

Trish Morgan from NOW said, "It gives women some hope that domestic violence is being understood and recognized more and more...It took a long time to get to the point where people are willing to accept the fact that Battered Woman's Syndrome is something real and worth learning about."

But none of these statements got through to the Nortons; nor did the wealth of evidence or the hopes and admonitions of those who asked them to forgive and forget. They would have none of it, and commented publicly later that evening when the press contacted them at their home.

Leslie Norton dismissed out of hand everything that had transpired the past weeks: all the experts; all the character witnesses; all the professionals and intellectuals surrounding the case; even the governor himself. And she totally disregarded all the years June had spent in prison. "All the governor could go on is her rehabilitation. Never mind that a crime has been committed. Never mind that a life has been taken." And then, almost justifying the way she had raised her son, she said, "No wonder people take the law into their own hands."

The terms of the pardon called for June to leave the Goffstown prison in the next few weeks and move to a halfway house in Concord, New Hampshire. The pardon did not automatically expunge June's crime; it was a "conditional pardon" that took into consideration the fact that a violent crime had been committed for which punishment was deserved. But the Pardon Petition also stated "further incarceration is unproductive given the substantial contribution June Briand can offer society if released from prison."

It is standard for inmates who are paroled after a lengthy sentence to spend time in a halfway house so they can gradually be "re-integrated into society." In June's case, the step seemed hardly appropriate — she was not a hardened criminal and posed no threat to anyone. But she had taken a life, and so, was treated the same as any other felon.

After the pardon was announced, television producers from talk-shows across the country called Pat Moss, inviting June to appear on their shows and tell her heartbreaking story. But what they failed to realize was that she would be incarcerated for yet another year. She could not leave the area, let alone the state. But this time she would be housed in a minimum security setting. Her home would be the North End House on State Street in Concord, New Hampshire, located on the grounds of the New Hampshire State Prison for Men, but *outside* the twenty-foot walls and well beyond the gleaming strands of razor wire that lay atop them.

On April 18, 1997, June, with her few possessions, was transferred to the North End House. It is an unremarkable two-story red brick building that sits a few yards back from the main public road. Inmates living in this transitional housing are required to find jobs like anyone else, take periodical drug tests, and adhere to a strictly-enforced curfew. Visiting hours are also regulated, and before someone is put on the list of regular visitors, his or her background must be thoroughly checked and approved by the head of the halfway house.(Such was the case with the author who began his two-year interview process here.)

"When I first came to the house, people would laugh at me because I was always feeling in my back pocket for my ID badge like we had to wear at Goffstown. I forgot you didn't need one in Concord. I was amazed at the amount of freedom I had. It was wonderful."

June lived in a dorm-like setting, with six bunks to a room. Everyone in the house was at different stages of release, and all were happy to be on their way back to a normal life — especially June. An attorney who had been following her case offered June a job at a nearby law firm. With her advanced computer skills, she mastered the position easily and before long, was running the office by herself.

"I liked the job and thought about going to law school. But now I think I might try to find a management position in the food industry. God knows, I have plenty of experience working in that prison kitchen! And I was always good with people when I was in prison, so management might be an avenue to explore."

To get back and forth to her law job, June bought a second-hand bicycle. It came with saddle bags and a basket on the handle bars, which her friends at the halfway house used to laugh at that. "But when I took off on the bike to go to the store, everyone gave me a list of goodies they wanted me to bring back, especially those who were still restricted to the premises. It was a good thing I had the storage capacity!"

June would spend a year at the halfway house, during which time she not only had to secure work, but had to find approved housing into which she would move upon her release on April 18, 1998. In February of that year, she found an affordable two-bedroom apartment, also on State Street about two miles from the prison. Her original advocate, Heidi Guhrer, said she would give June her Volkswagen Jetta when she was released from the halfway house. And so June had her living and transportation needs taken care of, a good job, and a new life of freedom to look forward to. But she was scared.

"When April 18 came and I got the car and apartment, it was not what I expected. I felt happy, of course, but I was now on parole — and would be for the rest of my life. Parole officers could drop unannounced whenever they wanted. They could search the apartment for drugs or weapons, look in the refrigerator to see if I had any wine or beer — those things weren't allowed. But that wasn't what bothered me. It was *losing* everything I'd worked for that had me scared.

"I remember driving down the road in Heidi's car one day the week after I moved into my apartment. It was soooo wonderful! It was a nice spring day; the sun was out; I had the windows down and the radio playing. It was like heaven. I was like a normal person. Then I got real scared. I was at a stoplight and it was like a wave suddenly washed over me and I thought, 'What if I lose this? What if I do something wrong, or I'm in the wrong place at the wrong time and I get in trouble?' I still get those little panic attacks, but they pass.

"I also have flashbacks sometimes. Like when I first pulled into the gas station to fill up with gas. I was pumping the gas and got a whiff of the vapors: *JIMMY!* His overalls always smelled of grease and gasoline. Those smells are so vivid. I get goose bumps now whenever I fill up with gasoline.

"Then a friend took me out to dinner and ordered fish. He offered me some, but as soon as I got it in my mouth, I gagged. I couldn't help thinking about the fish guts in the sink. Sometimes I can even taste blood in my mouth. But I know this will all pass. At least I hope so. But if it doesn't, I can live with it. I learned to live with a lot before, and somehow I survived."

June discovered life back in society was more of an adjustment than she had ever imagined. "In prison they prepare you for getting a job, but not for getting back into life. I spent a year in the halfway house so I was still very much in the system and it was pretty confusing for me when I got out. I was not prepared to be on my own, financially or socially, and fell down a lot but luckily it came out okay. And it was something of a culture shock. I was overwhelmed by things. For example, prices were four times higher than when I entered prison. I had no idea, really, how to live. I was never prepared for living on my own."

Then June's luck suddenly changed. She had left the law practice to pursue the career in management she had been thinking about, and met the manager of a fast food restaurant who understood her situation and, though she was a felon, agreed to hire her. It was there, in early 1999, that she met a wonderful, kind, and loving man unlike any she had ever known. He became June's true love — the love she had always wanted but which had eluded her for her entire life. After a short courtship, they married, and shortly thereafter, she had a child with him. Along with the new man came an extra bonus: an eight-year-old stepson, and with that, she finally had the family she so longed for, and a chance to truly start over and live the life that until then, she could only dream of.

Four and a half years after her release from the halfway house, on October 16, 2002, June was invited to speak at a meeting of the Seacoast National Organization for Women at the Women's City Club in Portsmouth, New Hampshire. She told them how she remembered well her supporters and the posters members of NOW carried in front of the Concord courthouse as they fought for her freedom. Slogans included *Free June!* and *June has been punished enough!* "This is like a second coming-out party for me," she said. "I wanted for so long to be an advocate for other women, and these are my first steps, coming here and speaking today. I am so very lucky that help found me, and now I am ready to help back."

June told the group that deciding to share her story in this book was not an easy decision. She did not want to relive the horrors she had endured but felt that the story definitely had to be told. "I wanted to tell it all, not for sympathy, but to be able to say what was never said. I hope that my story reaches women in time for them to realize that help is out there. I want to spread awareness for other victims of domestic abuse. To come from being a person with no power to *this*

— being a person with a voice — is very empowering. I hope I can do some good. And I thank you all for everything you did for me. I'll never forget you."

AUTHOR'S NOTE

This book may have never come to be had I not glimpsed a rather sensational headline in the *Portsmouth Herald* one day in early December of 1996, which read: KILLER MAY BE HEADING FOR PORTSMOUTH. Intrigued, I read further to learn that the "killer" was, in fact, a young woman who had been convicted of murdering her abusive husband, and I was immediately suspicious about the headline, which seemed to suggested a hardened criminal was about to enter the peaceful, upper middle-class seaside town of Portsmouth, New Hampshire. It turns out that she had no intention of heading for Portsmouth, nor could she even had she wanted to, since she was still incarcerated at the time of the article.

Having recently written a parenting book that was just published that same year by Warner Books, I was interested in June Briand's story, assuming, correctly, that her upbringing was anything but normal and would be in extreme contrast to the typical family lives of those I had just written about. For the parenting book, I had researched and interviewed highly successful parents across the country who had raised well-adjusted, happy children in loving homes full of encouragement, laughter and support. June's story was the exact opposite: she had been raised under the most adverse possible conditions with absolutely no support or encouragement in what she later told me was a house "totally void of love." Her promiscuous mother, who had no interest whatsoever in raising a child, had dropped June off at birth at her own mother's house, turning the parenting duties over to June's grandmother, who was equally disinterested, but having no apparent choice, begrudgingly agreed to take the infant in. And so, the beginning of a miserable life of neglect began, where June sought but never received the love any child needs to survive, and was, thus, groomed to accept someone—anyone—who showed her even the slightest glimmer of affection.

Reading down the article, I realized that this woman's life story might be a fascinating revelation of how a dysfunctional family works in direct contrast to the successful family. The article mentioned a Portsmouth attorney, Pat Moss, who had taken the case, and I called her office, explaining I was a writer interested in June's case and intent on finding out if there was an important story here worthy of a book, and would June be amenable to the project. She said she did not know, but that I could write June at her prison address and see how she felt about the idea, which I did. In my letter I explained that I had seen the headline in the newspaper and had a sense that it was overblown and that she was no doubt the victim of severe abuse. I wrote that I sympathized with what she must have gone through to get to this stage of her life, and I was very interested in hearing her story. After several weeks, I received a response. June said she might be interested but with the holidays coming up, she wanted to wait, and would get back to me. Several more weeks went by and I thought she had a change of mind just when another letter arrived suggesting I contact her attorney again and set up a meeting at the North End House on State Street in Concord, New Hampshire, where she had been since April of 1997. The meeting took place the following month.

After identifying myself and turning over my identification to the prison official at the entrance office, I walked into a large room that housed several armed guards, police and inmates in various settings. I was immediately greeted by an attractive, young, dark-haired woman who strode up to me and extended her hand confidently, saying with a warm smile, "Hello, I'm June." I immediately sensed an aura of peace and intelligence in this woman (she was, in fact, the first woman in the state of New Hampshire to receive a college degree from behind bars), and followed her to a table where two other older women had placed themselves on either side of June, in an almost a protective, motherly posture. Their job, I quickly understood, was to determine just who I was, was I trustworthy, what my motivation was. After all, here was a man, a man they didn't know and had no reason to trust, and at this point, had every reason, indeed, obligation, to be wary of. The two women were her attorneys, and neither were smiling, though June seemed very much at ease. They also needed to ascertain whether or not June would want to work with me. And vice versa to an extent: I made it clear right from the start that I did not know if we had a book here, that I would have to hear the basic details of June's case and her life to determine if we had enough material of value to the public that would be worthy of the effort. I explained the process of publishing, and how a book proposal had to be developed; the book had to be accepted by an agent; and then a publisher had to be interested enough to, in fact, publish it. Quite a journey, and a long one, I explained. But if she was game to put forth the effort, so was I. And then we would see what happened, but no guarantees.

The attorneys had scheduled an hour for the meeting. When the sixty minutes were up, I began to gather my notes to leave, thanking them for their time, but they said no, we could continue for a little while longer. And I could see why: they saw clearly that June and I liked each other; we were getting along, and there seemed to be a certain chemistry or synergy between us that was palpable. After I did leave, June must have confirmed this to her lawyers because I received a call the next day from Pat Moss saying exactly that, that June felt she would like to work with me and we should go ahead with the project.

The first step, then, was gathering all the legal files at Moss's office, and there were plenty: over a dozen legal file boxes filled with all the material related to the June's case over the many years she had struggled to have her case heard before the executive council. The next step was beginning the interview process with June in Concord, which began the next month at a picnic table on the extended grounds of the New Hampshire State Prison where the minimum security North End House was located—a process that continued over the next two years.

Writing this book was an exhaustive and emotionally taxing project during which I personally shed many tears and had difficulty writing certain passages. It was painful to relate her decline from a vibrant young mother full of hope into an emaciated, fearful individual who was falling deeper and deeper into the state of learned helplessness, which then turned to hopelessness and such a distorted view of reality that she could see no way out of her dire situation. Had a novelist been presented with the facts of a story like June's, he or she would have certainly passed on the notion of writing a book that basically no one would believe, or which they would say was hyperbole and so outrageous that it would be too incredible to be taken seriously, even as fiction. The more I interviewed June, the more horrible, lurid and insane her tale became, but it was *not* fiction and therefore was very difficult to deal with from my perspective. Nevertheless, it was a story that we both agreed had to be told. And tell it I will, as I intend to travel throughout the country speaking at domestic violence agencies, police academies (police officers deal with this problem on a daily basis), and colleges for professors who today teach classes on Family Violence, Domestic Abuse, Sexuality, Women's Studies, Psychology, Social Work and the like, and who use books like this in their course work.

That was not the case back in 1996, the year the National Domestic Violence Hotline had just been implemented and

Battered Woman Syndrome was not yet well recognized. Now, as noted in the Preface, this issue is front and center and the spotlight is starting to shine on perpetrators everywhere—from the entertainment industry to the White House. This book is intended to augment that interest and, as Trish Morgan in the Epilogue said, "give women some hope that domestic violence is being understood and recognized more and more…"

As noted in the back of the book, there are now resources that were not available during June's ordeal, for both victims and perpetrators of domestic violence: safe houses, hotlines, advocacy groups. In addition to the National Coalition Against Domestic Violence, which is available in every state, there are now online anger management courses and batterer intervention programs such as those offered by Open Path, a psychotherapy collective designed to work with and reduce recidivism of those involved with domestic violence.

As the years passed since this book's first edition was first released, I lost contact with June who said she was going to move out of New Hampshire with her husband and two sons to live a quiet and peaceful life out of the spotlight. When I had asked if she would be interested in doing any radio interviews about the book and her life, she declined, saying it was time to move on and put that chapter behind her, leaving the publicity to me. So now I wish her well, wherever she is, and value the friendship we developed and the work we did together, and hope she has finally found the peace that eluded her for so long.

RESOURCES

1.

National Domestic Violence Hotline
1-800-799-7233 (or TTY 1 800 787-3224)
http://www.thehotline.org
24/7/365 Phone Support and Live Chat
services for getting real-time one-on-one
support. All calls and chats confidential.

2.

National Coalition Against Domestic Violence (NCADV)
www.ncadv.org
Advocates for major societal changes to eliminate
violence and have zero tolerance for domestic violence.

3.

American Bar Association Commission
on Domestic & Sexual Violence
https://www.americanbar.org
To insure access to justice for survivors of domestic
violence, sexual harassment and stalking.

4.

Futures Without Violence
https://www.futureswithoutviolence.org
To end violence against women, children and
families at home and around the world.

5.

Safe Horizon
https://www.safehorizon.org
For a society free of family and community violence

6.
MVP Strategies (Mentors in Violence Prevention)
http://www.mvpstrat.com
To change social, cultural and institutional
norms that support abusive behavior

7.
Open Path
https://mentalhealth.openpathcollective.org
Anger management and batterer intervention programs

For More News About Robert Davidson
Signup For Our Newsletter:

http://wbp.bz/newsletter

Word-of-mouth is critical to an author's long-term success. If you appreciated this book please leave a review on the Amazon sales page:

http://wbp.bz/tbila

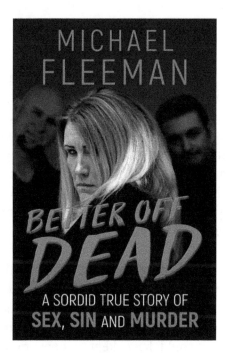

An hour before sunset, Shaun Ware swung his white work truck right off Goodrick Drive into the Summit Industrial Park, a complex of metal buildings with tall garage doors. It was Sunday, Aug. 17, 2014, a warm summer evening in the high desert. Shadows enveloped the Tehachapi Pass, the mighty turbines in the windmill farm standing still in the light western breeze. Traffic roared by on Highway 58, cars and trucks shuttling between Bakersfield and the Mojave Desert. Every half hour, a long freight train from Burlington Northern Santa Fe Railway would rumble behind the complex.

Arriving for his overnight shift, Shaun pulled his truck up to a space with "BNSF" stenciled on the concrete parking block and immediately felt something was wrong. The metal door to the work area was closed. The day-shift responder, Robert Limon, would have kept it open to ventilate the stuffy garage during the 89-degree afternoon. Robert would have told him if he were out on a service or call or making a food run.

Shaun raised the door with a remote opener. Robert's BNSF utility truck was parked next to his personal car, a silver Honda. Shaun walked into the garage along the right side of the truck. He nearly stepped on broken glass that appeared to have come from one of the fluorescent fixtures hanging from the 18-foot ceiling.

To his right, the door to the small office was wide open. That was wrong, too. The office door always stayed closed. The office appeared to have been ransacked. File drawers had been yanked open and papers strewn across the floor. A BNSF-issued Toshiba laptop was missing.

Shaun walked around the front of the work truck, which pointed toward the kitchenette against the back wall. The door of the small refrigerator was flung open. So was the door to the bathroom.

That's when he saw him.

Robert Limon was on the floor, his back slumped against the driver's side tire of the truck.

Shaun kneeled.

"Rob, what happened?" Shaun said. "Wake up, buddy."

Robert had a vacant look on his face, one eye closed, the other half opened. Blood had pooled beneath him. He didn't respond.

Panic gripped Shaun. He called 911 on his cell phone. He told the operator that he had found his coworker on the ground around a lot of blood and that he wasn't moving.

The operator asked if Shaun was willing to try CPR. He said yes. Following the operator's instructions, Shaun pulled Robert down flat on his back. He put his face close to Robert's. There was no breath. The operator asked Shaun to push his hands against Robert's chest to begin compressions.

One push and blood oozed out of Robert's mouth.

The operator told Shaun to get out of the building, now. He did, in a daze. The cell phone still to his ear with the 911 operator on the line, he wandered out to the asphalt parking area.

A man approached—somebody who worked in a neighboring unit—and asked Shaun what was going on.

"I think Rob's dead," Shaun told him.

Then it hit him. Shaun dropped to his knees and his body convulsed. He felt tears coming.

How long he was like this, he couldn't remember. The next thing he knew, he heard cars approaching. Sirens. Lights. He looked up and saw a woman in a sheriff's uniform.

Shaun pointed to the garage and said, "He has two kids."

Find Out More:
http://wbp.bz/bod

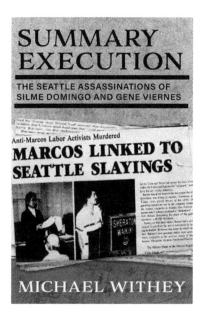

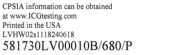